# Assessing Learning in
# Higher Education

# Assessing Learning in Higher Education

Paul Bartholomew, John Branch
and Claus Nygaard

THE LEARNING IN HIGHER EDUCATION SERIES

LIBRI
PUBLISHING

First published in 2016 by Libri Publishing

ISBN 978-1-909818-81-1

Cover design by Helen Taylor

Design by Carnegie Publishing

Printed in the UK by Short Run Press Ltd

Libri Publishing
Brunel House
Volunteer Way
Faringdon
Oxfordshire
SN7 7YR

Tel: +44 (0)845 873 3837

www.libripublishing.co.uk

# Contents

# Foreword

It is a privilege to write a foreword to 'Assessing Learning in Higher Education' edited by Paul Bartholomew, John Branch and Claus Nygaard. This is a great volume, not least in the many ways illustrated in detail and depth about how best we can actually go about designing and using assessment well.

Assessment is probably the most time-consuming part of the work of staff in universities and colleges. Assessment is by far the hardest thing we try to do. More important: our assessment is the most important thing for students – it takes all the energy they can give it, and it determines their future lives and careers.

There is now a vast literature on the scholarship of assessment, feedback, learning and teaching. Assessment, however, continues to lag far behind the known scholarship, not least with the continued prevalence of hand-written exams, even though we live in a digital age and rarely use a pen to share our thinking or expertise with others. Just about everyone realises that we need to change how we go about assessment, not least to link it much better to formative feedback. Moreover, we now know the power of helping students to deepen their learning by getting them to co-create assessment criteria with us, and make informed judgements on their own and each other's work using these criteria, enabling them to know how our minds work when we assess their work. Peer assessment, well facilitated, can bring students far more feedback than we ourselves could provide, and broaden their thinking by exposing them to the very different views that they will encounter in the wider world of employment and team work.

Despite the will to rethink and improve assessment and feedback, hard-pressed academics so often say "this is all very well, but don't give me all this theory – show me exactly what I can do – or at least give me some detailed examples of how other people have gone about changing assessment which I can use as a starting place". This book is the answer to their pleas. I have never seen so many useful examples of things that can be done, unpacked, analysed and evaluated by students as well as assessors themselves. Many of the chapters describe instances of contributors swimming against the tide, and the uphill battles (to mix metaphors) on their journeys towards better assessment and feedback.

Students entering higher education have often little idea about how exactly assessment will work. It is often very different from anything they have previously encountered. Sometimes, a good memory and the ability to write quickly were what they needed to succeed before they embarked on higher education. Sometimes, all they needed to do was to succeed in reproducing under assessment conditions what was taught. They may seldom have had the opportunity to develop skills relating to the autonomous learning which will serve them well at university, and it is important to give them opportunities to develop these skills together, and gain feedback from each other in this process.

Today's students are often very skilled in interacting and collaborating online using social media, and for many, at least some of their studying and learning will be done online. We need to be changing assessment and feedback processes so that they embrace online collaboration and discussion between students as well as between them and ourselves. Admittedly, as some points we need to be able to measure individual achievement, and do this in ways that are valid, transparent, authentic – and above all fair. We therefore need to use assessment and feedback processes to ensure that students are well-prepared for this individual assessment. What better practice could there be than the processes of peer-assessment and self-assessment, on the journey towards demonstrating what they can achieve individually? This volume abounds with illustrations of how this can be achieved.

The editors have done a great job. The respective chapters are complete in themselves, with references after each chapter, but with very useful links to ideas in other chapters, integrating the whole book very effectively. Chapter 1 already contains an in-depth guide to what is achieved by the remaining chapters, but I have taken the liberty in this foreword of providing the following summary highlighting just a few of the points that I, as an outsider to the book, gleaned from the respective chapters.

Chapter 1 'An introduction to Assessment' by Paul Bartholomew, John Branch & Claus Nygaard starts with the Donald Rumsfeld famous bit about 'known knowns and unknown unknowns' – a fitting lead in to confronting the latter when it comes to assessment. 'Into the unknown' student learning is invisible – almost ethereal in nature – and consequently assessment is rather like jumping into the unknown'. This anthology is the product of *Learning in Higher Education* (LiHE) Annual symposium, based on the 2015 one on assessment on the Greek island Aegina. John Branch describes a formative apprenticeship in assessment getting French business programmes validated by the Open University in the UK. Paul Bartholomew moved into the broad field of assessment from experiencing a postgraduate certificate in radiographic image interpretation where a 5-hour exam had a pass mark of 95%! Claus Nygaard describes how his academic progress was turned round late in his school experience by a good teacher who inspired confidence.

The editors sought four dimensions of assessment in each chapter, agency, outcomes, focus, and context. Chapter 1 then runs through each chapter in useful summary, summarising specific insights which readers might draw from each, which are then unpacked in each chapter by the respective contributors.

In Chapter 2, Dorothy Spiller: (University of Waikato, New Zealand) examines co-construction in assessment for learning'. She discusses students as partners, and an emphasis on assessment for learning, rather than of learning, and acknowledges that despite much scholarship, the slow pace of change is detrimental. The chapter presents three case studies of co-creating assessment initiatives, each involving putting learners themselves in central positions in the design of assessment, and addressing ways of tackling the challenges that are likely to arise. One of the main points arising from this chapter is the need for conversational dialogue between students and teachers about learning and assessment, to be able to respond to learners' thinking about both processes.

Chapter 3 moves us to Latvia, with a pan-Baltic student group including students from Estonia and Lithuania, and latterly Belarus, Georgia, Moldova, Russia and Ukraine. Diana Pauna and John Branch discuss 'Student Development at the Stockholm School of Economics at Riga, and their journey beyond traditional learning objectives to include students' personal development. They describe how an Orientation programme helps students in their transition to university education, also giving early warning of students who may be at risk. The chapter describes the use of a hybrid model consisting of 7 main activities: academic interventions, peer support, academic advising, social counselling, career advising, alumni-student mentoring, and student self-evaluation.

In Chapter 4 'Introducing Visualisation into the Assessment of Learning in Legal Studies' Christa Tobler explores the benefits of bringing decision trees and diagrams into study of law, where the traditional text-driven approach in the discipline poses challenges, particularly for international students. It is posited that the use of visualisation as a complementary learning tool is not only possible, but beneficial, including within a traditional exam setting. Feedback from international students includes that the use of decision trees can improve their time-management during exams, as well as help them structure their own learning more effectively. It is good to see the hypothesis that 'language is the *only* lawyer's tool' being so roundly refuted. It is even suggested that the use of concept maps in assessment can be extended to 'ill-structured subject areas such as educational psychology, psychiatry, teaching, leadership, and marketing'!

In Chapter 5 'Effective Assessment Strategies for Higher Education Online Courses' Leon Cygman (Mount Royal University, Calgary, Canada) moves us to e-assessment, increasingly used in online and distance learning programmes today. The author reminds us that online learning is growing in usage at over six times the rate of growth of the entire higher education student body, and that the importance of feedback to online learners is critical. The techniques for assessment and feedback of online work need to be quite different to those traditionally used in face-to-face contexts, and formative feedback becomes more important than ever. The chapter presents strategies to enable accurate assessment of students at a distance, embracing the four e-assessment principles of Tinaco *et al*, and transactional distance considerations of Moore.

In Chapter 6, 'Peer Assessment: A Learning Opportunity for Students in the Creative Arts' Katja Fleischmann (James Cook University, Australia) presents a strong case for using peer-assessment, and illustrates how it helps first year creative arts students to develop the ability both to critically assess the creative output of others and to self-reflect. 'Crits' have long been used in creative arts disciplines, and peer-assessment allows the benefits to be realised with larger numbers of students. The case study illustrates a rubric where students are helped to peer-assess using a detailed rubric, allowing them to allocate grades 'exceptional', 'very good', 'adequate' or 'poor' to each other's' 'work for each dimension of 'content knowledge', confidence and organisation', 'public speaking', and 'quality of presentation slides and handout'. Data show very strong student agreement in using the rubric, remarkably for distinguishing between 'exceptional' and 'very good' for a really good piece of work, but more mixed for a sample that was less than exceptional. The data illustrate that peer assessment can be just as reliable as tutor assessment, but saves the tutor considerable time, and increases the quality of student work and interaction in class.

In Chapter 7 'Student Self-assessment: ePortfolios and Learning in Higher Education', Lori L. Hager (University of Oregon, US) argues convincingly for the benefits of not only enabling students to integrate their learning in and beyond the classroom, but deepen their critical reflection competences using self-assessment. The skills students acquire through developing and posting ePortfolios not only enrich their parallel studies in other disciplines but relate strongly to future employability.

In Chapter 8 'Transformative Power of Assessment: Implementing a Student-centred Methodology in a Culturally Constraining Context', Maja Hunter (now at Ermitage International School of France) presents work undertaken over a five-year period in Oman, to enhance transformative learning, using a problem-based learning approach in the challenging cultural context prevailing there. This is another fine example of how the contributors to this volume champion the benefits of self- and peer-assessment as deepening students' learning and enhancing the value of the feedback they receive.

In Chapter 9 'The Trust Issue: Implementing Peer-Assessment in an Undergraduate Professional Development Context' Michael Peters and Paul Bartholomew (both from Aston University, Birmingham, UK) illustrate how student-focused and student-led assessment practice can contribute to the empowerment of students in engineering as autonomous learners. Here, peer-assessment is strengthened by getting the students themselves to formulate the assessment criteria in the first place, and benefit from appropriate training and rehearsal of peer-assessment.

In Chapter 10 'Using Assessment Couplings to Engage Stakeholders in Co-Curricular Activities' Jesper Piihl and Kristin Balslev Munksgaard (both at the University of Southern Denmark) focus on helping students in business disciplines to develop abilities to connect academic learning to real-life problem solving, and thereby their employability. A 'camp' model is discussed, where in one or more intensive days, over 500 students (from 1st year to Masters level) work in groups, with faculty and external stake-holders including CEOs of companies, on real-life problems.

Some learning outcomes are non-negotiable. Pharmacists have to get calculations completely right – error-free calculations must be a 'given' in related assessment. In Chapter 11 'Assuring Achievement of Learning Outcomes Through Assessment: A Case Study in Pharmacy', Ieva Stupans (University of New England, Australia) posits challenges, including that 'online testing does not assure learning', 'students view assessment differently than staff', and that 'we haven't really started to think about "compensation" in terms of assessing learning outcomes in examinations'.

The next contribution addresses roles of student learning and assessment in the validation accreditation of programmes, providing case-studies in the discipline of translation, spanning the Arabian Gulf and Geneva. Chapter 12 'More Than a Mirage: The Role of Assessment Design in International Accreditation' is from Nicholas Cifuentes-Goodbody (Hamad bin Khalifa University, Qatar) and Andreas Karatsolis (now at MIT, US), explores the challenges and benefits of curriculum mapping as a basis for accreditation in a global environment.

The volume ends with Chapter 13, which probably bears the most challenging title in the book: 'Deconstructing Constructive Alignment: How to Make Relational Knowledge and Dialectical Assessment in Higher Education' by Jens Smed Rasmussen and Grethe Heldbjerg (both from the University of Southern Denmark). They suggest that 'managerial instrumentation logic' has spread from the business world into higher education institutions, losing much of the intended benefits of clearly articulated intended learning outcomes, and learning oriented assessment. It is refreshing to see some of the accepted 'givens' of learning and assessment being challenged, rather than just cited, and the chapter provides much food for thought for our continuing journey to make assessment 'fit for purpose' for all involved.

This is a truly international volume about assessment, and embraces several different cultures. I congratulate the editors for their achievement in bringing it all so well together, and all of the contributors for sharing their wisdom, expertise and experience so well.

Phil Race
Emeritus Professor: University of South Wales and
Leeds Beckett University
Visiting Professor: University of Plymouth and
University Campus Suffolk

Chapter 1

# An introduction to Assessment

Paul Bartholomew, John Branch & Claus Nygaard

## Into the Unknown

In February 2002 at a U.S. Department of Defense press meeting, the
then American Secretary of Defense Donald Rumsfeld was asked a question about the lack of evidence regarding Iraq's development of weapons
of mass destruction. Confidently, Rumsfeld responded:

> *"Reports that say that something hasn't happened are always interesting
> to me, because as we know, there are known knowns; there are things
> we know we know. We also know there are known unknowns; that is to
> say we know there are some things we do not know. But there are also
> unknown unknowns – the ones we don't know we don't know".*

Rumsfeld went on to suggest that it is the unknown unknowns which
figure prominently in human history, thereby intimating that an invasion
of Iraq was justified despite, even because of, the lack of evidence.

Rumsfeld's clumsily-worded response became the butt of many jokes,
and was widely criticised for its intimation that a 'pre-emptive strike' was
warranted. And this anthology is certainly not a champion of war. But his
seemingly illogical response might actually serve as an interesting framework for thinking about assessment. Indeed, as highlighted in the call for
chapters for this anthology, student learning is invisible – almost ethereal

in nature – and consequently assessment is rather like jumping into the unknown. Moreover, assessment is anything but straightforward, and the controversy which surrounded Rumsfeld's response hints at the innovations which assessment has witnessed in recent years.

As background, assessment has traditionally been considered as part of a kind of 'holy trinity' of teaching activities: curriculum design, instruction, and assessment (See Figure 1.). Curriculum design specifies the learning objectives of a programme or course of study. It addresses what the student must learn. Instruction focuses on the methods for learning. It addresses how the student will learn. Assessment aims at measuring the learning? It addresses if the student has learned. As highlighted in Figure 1, these three activities are interrelated – self-reinforcing and self-informing – suggesting an iterative improvement in the teaching.

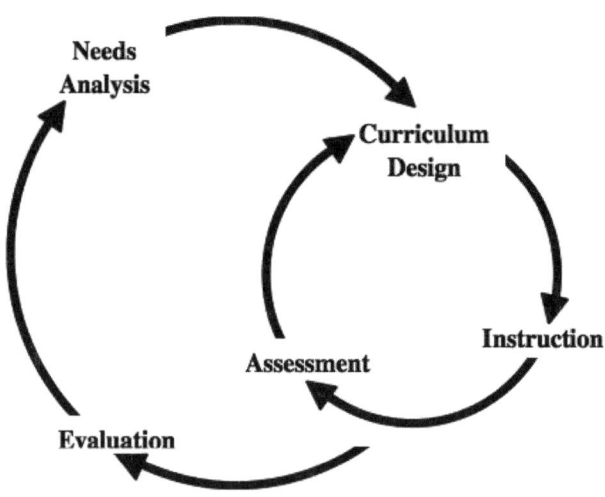

*Figure 1. A Model of Pedagogy.*

The other 2 activities in Figure 1 are less prominent in higher education (although no less valuable). They are worthy of attention, however, especially because the terms assessment and evaluation are often used interchangeably. Needs analysis identifies the motivation for the teaching.

It addresses why the student must learn. Evaluation gauges the impact of the teaching. It addresses the so what. As before, there is also an inter-relationship between needs analysis, the holy trinity of teaching, and evaluation, likewise suggesting the iterative improvement in the pedagogy overall.

An example here might help to clarify the model. Consider a company which has had falling sales. Needs analysis – think of it as a diagnosis of sorts – reveals that customers are not satisfied with the service which they have been receiving, thereby leading to the conclusion that the company's customer service agents require training. This training programme (the teaching), however, would point to decisions about which knowledge, skills, and attitudes would need to be learned by the customer service agents. It would require specific teaching methods – cases, role plays, or lectures, for example – to be created and implemented. And it would mean that the degree to which the customer service agents had indeed learned the requisite knowledge, skills, and attitudes would be measured. After the training had been completed, the company would then need to evaluate if sales had improved.

According to the model, therefore, with this traditional view of assessment as the measurement of learning, assessment is seemingly focused on the known knowns. Indeed, curriculum design specifies the learning objectives; assessment measures against them. In other words, instructors know those things which they want their students to know. And assessment measures if they know them.

In the current parlance, however, a distinction is made between assessment *of* learning and assessment *for* learning, commonly referred to as summative assessment and formative assessment respectively. Assessment *of* learning measures if the student has learned the intended learning objectives. It is backward-facing, aimed at reporting on the student's achievement. Assessment *for* learning, on the other hand, is forward-facing. It attempts to determine the student's progress toward the intended learning objectives, thereby allowing an instructor to alter instructional methods mid-stride. In either case, however, the intended learning objectives are known knowns.

But undoubtedly students are learning more than just the intended learning objectives. Students who have been assigned a semester-long project which must be completed in a group, for example, will surely develop their communication, negotiation, and teamwork skills… learning outcomes which were not necessarily specified in the curriculum design. These could be considered the known unknowns.

Claus identifies closely with this notion, proposing that technology has the ability to move assessment 'from big brother to big data'. Rather than a professor dictating the learning objectives (the known knowns), new modes of assessment, new types of assessment, and new assessment techniques have all resulted in mounds of learner-specific data, which allows for the ex-post identification of learning. Known unknowns indeed.

Paul has been contemplating a different innovation in assessment which has been proposed in recent years, that assessment be liberated from specific learning objectives. This proposition argues that assessment need not be aimed at measuring learning against pre-defined codified expectations, but instead be aimed at triggering, encouraging, facilitating learning. In other words, assessment is process-oriented, rather than product-oriented – with 'claims for learning' be made where and when they occur. The unknowns, therefore, are unknown.

When the unknowns are unknown, therefore, assessment becomes about student growth. Indeed, it *"is based on the conviction that students are capable of becoming adaptable, flexible, and independent in their learning, their thinking and their decision-making"* (Earle, 2015:67). This focus on student growth has led to the term assessment *as* learning, which John dubs generative assessment in contrast to summative assessment and formative assessment.

Assessment as learning occurs when students reflect on and monitor their progress to inform *their* future learning goals. It is regularly occurring, formal or informal (e.g. peer feedback buddies, formal self assessment) and helps students take responsibility for their own past and future learning. It builds metacognition as it involves students in negotiating and understanding the criteria that might define learning; in setting and monitoring their own learning goals; and in developing strategies for working towards achieving them.

Whatever the focus of assessment – the known knowns, the unknown knowns, or the unknown unknowns – assessment has become an important activity in higher education. We do understand too though that the central feature of many accreditation agencies, for example, is the notion of 'assurance of learning'. Professional bodies hold institutions and members to very specific standards which must somehow be demonstrated. And new competency-based diplomas and degrees demand sophisticated and valid corroboration of the competencies. This anthology is about assessing learning in higher education, in all its guises.

## LiHE

The anthology is the product of *Learning in Higher Education* (LiHE), an academic association which, as intimated by its name, focuses entirely on learning at the post-secondary level. The focus of the association reflects the shift from a transmission-based philosophy to a student-centred, learning-based approach. And its scope is limited to colleges, universities, and others institutions of higher education.

The main activity of the association is a symposium. About 10 years ago, Claus noted that professors attend conferences at which they present their scientific research in a 10-20 minute session, receive a few comments, then very often 'head to the bar for a drink'. He proposed an alternative, therefore, which *au contraire* returns to that ancient Greek format – the symposium – at which co-creation is key.

So, about 16 months prior to a symposium, a call for chapter proposals which has a relatively tightly focused theme is announced on the Association's website and on various electronic mailing lists. The June 2014 symposium, for example, had the theme *Technology Enhanced Leaning in Higher Education*; previous themes have revolved around games and simulations, classroom innovations, and learning spaces (in higher education).

Authors submit chapter proposals accordingly, which are then double-blind reviewed. If a proposal is accepted, its author is given 4 months to complete it. The whole chapter is then double-blind reviewed, and if it is accepted, the author is invited to attend the symposium. There, all authors revise their own chapters, work together to revise each other's chapters, and collaborate to assemble an anthology which, about a month later, goes off to the publisher.

## The 2015 Aegina Symposium

For this symposium, we (the editors) sought chapters which explored assessment within the domain of higher education and with an emphasis on learning, as per the focus of LiHE. We aspired to publish an anthology which was diverse in nature and which showcased concrete examples of assessment of learning in higher education from around the world. We welcomed chapters from all scientific disciplines and which followed any methodological tradition. We were guided by the following criteria:

1. does the chapter show a clear example of *assessment of learning in higher education?* It is required that a chapter not only describes the assessment method, but also documents an example of its application in higher education;

2. is the chapter grounded in *contemporary theory* of both assessment and learning? It is important that a chapter not only describes the assessment method, but also situates it theoretically; and

3. does the chapter demonstrate how assessment enhances student learning? It is expected that a chapter moves beyond speculation, instead providing evidence of the enhanced student learning which results from the assessment.

The call for chapter proposals resulted in 35 submissions from around the world which explored a variety of different aspects of assessment of learning in higher education. The subsequent review and re-submission process, however, whittled these down to the 12 chapters which follow in this anthology. The LiHE symposium at which the chapters were revised and the anthology was assembled was held in June 2015 on the Greek Island of Aegina, off the coast of Athens. In addition to the academic symposium activities, authors explored the ruins of the 5th century B.C.E. Temple of Aphaea, visited the monastery of Saint Nektarios, and, naturally, sampled the culinary delights of the Mediterranean.

## The Editors and Assessment of Learning

As editors, of course, we bring our own perspectives to the role, which are based on our own experiences with assessment. We each have our own disciplinary backgrounds, which come with their own specific approaches to assessment. And we have our own philosophical assumptions about pedagogy which, in turn, influence our views about assessment.

*John*

My first experience with assessment as an instructor – as distinguished from my many years of experiencing assessment as a student – occurred in my first years as a lecturer at École Supérieure de Commerce de Rennes in France, a business school which had opened its doors only 3 years prior to my arrival. The Dean of the Business School was quite entrepreneurial, and had decided that we also ought to attempt to get the French 3-year business school diplôme recognised in the United Kingdom, thereby giving our graduates an international 'leg-up' over their compatriots. Thus began a painful 2-year process with the Open University Validation Services (OUVS).

As my first experience with assessment, it could not have been much better… despite the pain. Indeed, in order to receive OUVS validation, we had to prepare very precise processes for assignment submissions. We were pushed to create a syllabus template which not only enumerated learning objectives, but also linked clearly the assessment activities to all learning objectives. We were required to develop an elaborate external examination system to ensure grading fairness. And so on and so on. I had moved to France to become a teacher… but it seems that my teaching career began with an apprenticeship in assessment!

The dean at the business school was also convinced that an official co-curricular programme for our students might likewise separate them from graduates of the other French grandes écoles. The resulting programme was dubbed PEI (the pedagogy of experience and initiative), and, as suggested by the title, was focused on student growth through real-life (meaning out of the classroom) and student-driven experiences. For example, in my first year I had a student whose passion was not-for-profit, mission-driven organisations. During her year under my mentorship, she launched a student branch of Médicins sans Frontières (Doctors without Borders), and led a 9 person team to Hungary and Ukraine, delivering medical supplies to orphanages, hospitals, and refugee camps. Experience and initiative indeed, and my initiation into assessment *as* learning.

In my third year in France, the Dean decided to launch a new MBA programme, which, like the undergraduate diplôme, would be validated by the OUVS. The validation process, however, triggered a very philosophical debate in assessment, which stemmed from discussions about minimal competence. The OUVS required that we set standards in the MBA for minimal competence. My French colleagues suggested that students could fail entire MBA modules (accounting or finance, for example) but still demonstrate minimal competence overall. My Canadian and American colleagues, however, were adamant that by failing specific modules students were not demonstrating minimal competence (in business administration) at all. They argued that minimal competence ought to be applied within module – that is to say, within subject – and not across the entire degree. My 2 German colleagues remained quiet!

Interestingly, this issue reared up again in a faculty meeting last year at the Ross School of Business, during which the issue of minimum grade point average (GPA) was raised. The MBA office had proposed a number, 2.7/4 if I remember correctly. My argument was that there ought not to be a minimum GPA. Well in fact, I argued that our grading nomenclature (F-fail, LP-low pass, PS-pass, GD-good, and EX-excellent) already had a built-in minimal competence; the term 'pass' itself intimates that a student has indeed demonstrated the basic requirements for a module.

Another interesting philosophical issue in assessment reared up when I was contemplating a move from England to the United States. I was about to finish my Ph.D. and was 'on the market' for a position at an American business school. In one interview, while explaining my Ph.D. dissertation to a hiring dean, he interrupted to ask me about my Ph.D. programme. I explained that in Europe (in fact, most everywhere in the world part from Canada and the United States), a Ph.D. student is assessed on his/her ability to 'demonstrate a significant and original contribution to knowledge'. "But what about the programme?" he asked again. I reiterated that a Ph.D. programme is not really a programme per se, but instead a demonstration of significant and original thought through independent research. He was not buying it. So I mirrored the question back to him. "About five years." was his response.

Recently, I have been thinking a lot about assessment, as part of a larger flipped classroom project with which I have been tasked by my dean. He is concerned about the efficiency (and effectiveness, to be fair) of our faculty members. And rightly so. We have two professors, for example, who teach the introduction to statistics module to first -year MBA students. The module is 6 weeks in length. They both teach 3 of the 6 sections of the MBA cohort. That is their entire annual teaching requirement. And they both make about 200 000 USD per year. You can see the reasoning for his concern.

I have been asked, therefore, to think about flipping the classroom – to think about which bits can be moved out of the classroom – in order to get more teaching out of people at the same cost. I am developing a syllabus-maker tool, therefore, which instructors can use to design and document their courses. For example, say an accounting professor wants her students to know the definitions of debits and credits, and the process of entering them in a T-account. Can any or all of these things be learning outside the classroom? Does it make more sense to have the students learn this on their own, from a video or a reading, then practice T-accounts in the classroom with some sort of experiential, action-based method? In developing this syllabus-maker tool, however, I continue to face the same basic question 'But how will I know if the student has learned?' As much as I love teaching – and I entered this business to become a teacher – I always seem to get pulled back into assessment.

## Paul

My first role in higher education was in a healthcare education context – I had just moved from a clinical career working in hospitals to begin working at a university within my subject discipline of Diagnostic Radiography. Healthcare subjects carry with them the 'responsibility' to equip students for safe clinical practice and thus, unsurprisingly, assessment is often bound to notions of (clinical) competence than of notions of what might be referred to as 'learning'. Although the two concepts are not completely divorced from one another, a focus on 'competence' does rather define the dominant assessment paradigm as one characterised as assessment *of* learning – whereby the focus is on assessment-as-test where the test is regarded as a tool to measure competence for which there is a threshold level.

Sometimes, that threshold level can be set very high – I remember undertaking a postgraduate certificate in radiographic image interpretation where the pass mark (for a 5-hour exam) was 95% – write diagnostic reports on 100 x-ray sets, 3 minutes per report – get 5 wrong = pass, get 6 wrong = fail. Put like that (and take a patient perspective), perhaps a 95% pass mark is too low!

As I moved into academic staff development and my understanding of, and aspirations for, assessment changed and grew I began to become interested in assessment design – I was already teaching a module/course to university academics that taught them how to be innovative in their teaching practice (Bartholomew and Bartholomew, 2010) and noted that although academics were willing and able to innovate in relation to their teaching practice, they were much less likely to innovate with their assessment practice. Broadly, academics felt that what they did in 'their' classrooms was their own business but changes to assessment practice were within the legitimate purview of those who administered university quality processes. It was perceived as risky to make changes to assessment – and often regarded as too cumbersome and time-consuming to 'jump through the requisite hoops'.

In response to this agenda, and as a consequence of my growing conviction that assessment was centrally important to they way students approach their learning, I designed and ran a new academic staff development module/course entitled *Effective Assessment Design and Feedback*. This course encouraged academics to consider what they believed 'good assessment' and 'bad assessment' to look like, to revisit broader notions of assessment design – particularly constructive alignment and outcomes-based curriculum models – and to become more critical of assessment design. Indeed, *their* assessment for the course was to redesign an assessment for one of the courses they taught. They first of all had to identify an assessment 'issue' that needed 'fixing', they then explored assessment literature and examples of cited effective practice from across the sector and select a new assessment regime that would address the 'issue' they had chosen. They then had to write a full assessment brief and a full set of marking criteria (often through the use of a rubric) and submit these documents together with a reflective document that explained their design choices.

The course was transformative for many academics and led to some movement and innovation in assessment design when there had previously been considerable inertia. Such (relatively) innovative methods included the introduction of peer-assessment, the use of video (as a student-produced artefact), the use of posters and greater use of technology to facilitate electronic submission and feedback.

## Claus

My first experience with assessment was as a Primary School pupil in Denmark in the 1970's and early 1980's. Twice a year all pupils were assessed by teachers and given what is best described as a continuous assessment mark in each course. One mark was given for our academic knowledge of the subject, and another mark was given for how orderly we did our work. Apart from these continuous assessment marks we were pretty much left in the dark, when it came to feedback on our progress. My understanding of the marks given to me was indeed as limited as were the marks themselves. Judging from my lack of progress, the fact that I took all courses at the lowest possible level, and often inhabited the back row, I did not have a promising career before me. All (including myself) seemed to agree I was destined to work with my hands once the school years were over. My grades were often 5 (hesitant and not satisfactory), 6 (just acceptable) or 7 (mediocre, just below average). Then something strange happened when I was 13 years old and had two years left in school. I got a new math teacher, who was also the principal of the school. I have to admit I knew him well, because I had occasionally been in his office for detention. Well, the first semester went by, and when I received my continuous assessment marks, he gave me 13 in math (exceptionally independent and excellent performance) which was a very rare mark to give. It completely turned my self-awareness around. Maybe I was good at math? Maybe I was good at other subjects too? Maybe I had always been good, but just been assessed poorly due to other factors? Maybe my behaviour in school had influenced teachers' assessment of me? Maybe teachers had shared their opinions of me as a child and that had influenced their assessment of me? I passed my two final written math exams in my final year of school with another 13 and a 11 (independent and excellent performance). I improved slightly in other subjects, but my marks in Danish were still 6 and 7. All my other school mates, who decided to continue studying, went to the college that shared the facilities of our primary school. That was the obvious choice.

Despite my odds, I decided to go my own way and enter a trade college in a larger city 30 kilometres from my hometown. I wanted to break out of the social group I was in, and I wanted to find new friends, new teachers, and new challenges. There I experienced wonderful teachers, who were educated at university and had a solid academic background. Assessments were more frequent and came in the form of tests and assignments and there were more efficient feedback loops to students about their progress. Two teachers were highly inspiring and motivating. One was my Danish teacher Ole Munksgaard. Not only did he hand me back my first written assignment with the mark 13, he also decided to read it to the class. His way of giving feedback was exceptional. He would stop you in the corridor or in the canteen or library and just let you know, how much he had enjoyed reading your work. Or giving you thumbs up for your participation in class. It was like he helped you steer in the right direction, and he motivated me to work even harder. The other was my ICT-teacher Edward, whose last name I have forgotten. He was so kind to all that sometimes he would have a hard time keeping us quiet. But his kindness towards his students and his expert knowledge of ICT made us respect him very much. He was passionate about his job. Not only did he assess our work on programming and binary coding, he also used his knowledge of how well we performed as students to give us individual career advice. Told us about the career paths we could follow. Based on his advice, I chose not to continue studying computer science, although I was a keen programmer, but instead a bachelor in business and administration. And that led to my master of science in Strategy, Organisation and Management, which led to my ph.d. in Business Administration, and many years later to my professorship in Management Education.

I tell these stories, because I do believe that they caricature how assessment takes place in many education institutions. And obviously inspires us to improve. During the ten years I worked under the excellent and inspiring leadership of the now late Ib Andersen at the Learning Lab at Copenhagen Business School, I had the privilege to be engaged in a variety of assessment projects. One was a student peer-assessment project, where I developed a template for peer-assessment that students would use when other students or groups of students did presentations in class. The peer-assessments were done on a single piece of paper and after the presentation all papers were passed onto the student or group who had just presented. That student or group would then work on improving their presentation based on the peer-assessment. If a student or group of students had another presentation coming up, they could come to me and do a pre-presentation, and I could help them improve based on the peer-assessments given. I ran this project five times with great results. My takeaways were:

1. the more precise your assessment is (in the sense that your assessment categories mirror the students' present learning activity) the more student's engage in the assessment and the more they learn from it;

2. the closer your assessment links to the possible progress of students (in the sense that your assessment informs students about concrete steps to take in order to improve) the more student's engage in the assessment and the more they learn from it; and

3. the better your feedback loop is (in the sense that students get valid feedback from using the assessment method itself, such as peer-assessment or assessment by the teacher) the more student's engage in the assessment and the more they learn from it.

I have worked with another peer-assessment project, where students had to grade other students work, while teachers graded the same work, and all students could see all grading and commenting online at the same time. This transparency in assessing academic quality led to very high quality of work from students. On an institutional level, I have worked nationally in Denmark and internationally in Europe with quality enhancement and quality assurance. Both disciplines have resounded some of the important aspects of assessment as I see it:

1. assessment is about development of students – not judgement of students;

2. assessment needs to rest on a clear strategy of learning;

3. assessment has to follow an explicit assessment method that links to students' learning activities;

4. assessment has to use clear categories so students and teachers know what is assessed in which way; and

5. assessment has to have a well-defined feedback loop, so students and teachers can have a dialogue about the assessment that leads the student forward.

I am pleased to see, that those five aspects of assessment are well represented in the excellent assessment practices at universities reported in this anthology.

## A Framework for the Anthology

A significant challenge when editing an anthology is developing a device for structuring its chapters, even when they all share a common theme. During the symposium, therefore, together with the authors we attempted to identify the common features of the chapters. We teased out the different dimensions of assessment. We considered 2×2 matrices, triangular models, and even a Greek-inspired framework with 4 columns and pediments. In the end, however, we settled on four dimensions which capture some of the complexity of assessment.

1. assessment agency – whether the chapter describes a student-driven or a teacher driven approach to assessment – or both;

2. assessment outcomes – whether learning outcomes to be assessed were conceived as being fixed or flexible – or both;

3. assessment focus – whether the focus of the assessment is related to process (an assessment *for* learning approach) or related to outcome (an assessment *of* learning approach) – or both; and

4. assessment context – whether the assessment practice was highly specific and heavily bound to a subject or cultural domain or whether it was transferable across subject or cultural domains – or both. We open each chapter by signposting its position using this figure below.

| Assessment Agency | Student-driven | Teacher-driven |
| Assessment Outcomes | Fixed | Flexible |
| Assessment Focus | Process | Outcome |
| Assessment Context | Specific | Transferrable |

# The Anthology, Chapter by Chapter

In chapter 2, Dorothy Spiller examines the learning potential of model of assessment based on co-construction and shared ownership of assessment processes, and the conceptual barriers to its implementation. Her concern is that much current assessment practice in higher education is teacher-driven and managed, which can restrict student ownership of discipline ideas and limit the development of learner autonomy. Reading her chapter, you will: 1) see the learning potential of co-construction in assessment and the conceptual barriers that make it challenging to implement; 2) learn that co-construction or partnership between teachers and learners in all aspects of the assessment process is integral to student ownership of the learning and the development of learner autonomy; 3) understand that introducing this model of assessment needs to include dialogue and a process of re-education with both teachers and students.

In chapter 3, Diana Pauna & John Branch push assessment beyond learning objectives to also include a student's personal development. Reading their chapter you will gain the following insights: 1) assessment can be generative in nature; 2) assessment as learning requires a heavy commitment; and 3) assessment as learning can pay big dividends, both for students and an institution of higher education.

In chapter 4, Tobler shows how visualisations through the use of charts add value to assessment of law students' learning outcomes. Reading her chapter you will gain the following insights: 1) that visualisation through charts can be usefully employed in legal studies, not only as a complementary tool for teaching but also in the context of assessment, even in the setting of a traditional law exam; 2) that using visualisation through charts in legal studies assessment is not only possible in practice but also adds value to the traditionally verbocentric approach in the legal field, notably through formative potential; and 3) that students not only find it easier to study and to perform in a traditional, summative exam but also subsequently are able to create their own visualisation, which proves a lasting learning effect that goes beyond the content and meaning of the law itself and relates to analytical abilities crucial for legal practice.

In chapter 5, Leon Cygman provides assessment strategies for distance education courses. The chapter offers and discusses four suggested strategies that will result in not only an accurate overall assessment of distance education students but also enhanced online learning. Reading his chapter, you will gain the following four insights: 1) why using the four strategies for assessment in distance education courses is necessary; 2) how using these strategies can improve learning and retention in distance education courses; 3) how these strategies can strengthen the relationship between the students and the professor; and 4) how to increase the student integrity in distance education courses.

In chapter 6, Katja Fleischmann shows how peer assessment helped first year creative arts students develop the ability to both critically assess the creative output of others and self-reflect – essential in the development of a creative practitioner. Reading her chapter, you will gain the following three insights: 1) peer assessment displays several benefits and potentials for creative arts education; 2) peer assessment can facilitate a powerful reflective practice for students in creative arts education; 3) peer assessment is a reliable and valid assessment strategy to add or replace the traditional studio critique.

In chapter 7, Lori Hager presents findings from a long-term project integrating ePortfolios into graduate education, where it describes a process of supporting students' self-assessment. Reading her chapter you will gain the following insights: 1) knowledge of how students value ePortfolios as a way to integrate, apply, and make learning visible across courses and in complementary learning activities; 2) reflection on the values and goals of student self-assessment in contemporary and future learning in higher education; 3) how one comprehensive learning environment, organised around a digital commons, fostered and harnessed student centred learning and assessment, and how this might inform own practices; 4) thinking "outside the box" about ePortfolios as process and product in 21st century learning spaces.

In chapter 8, Maja Hunter describes a process of implementing an innovative – within the local Omani cultural context – teaching and learning methodology with emphasis on the embedded transformative assessment. Reading her chapter there are at least three insights to be gained, both for teacher practitioners and for educational researchers: 1) the knowledge that a culturally constrained environment plays a significant role and might even act as a brake on the introduction of innovative approaches to the classroom and, more particularly, to assessment; 2) the introduction of such innovations as Problem Based Learning and transformative learning, which entail specific approaches to assessment in order to be successful, require considerable sensitivity and cultural awareness on the part of the teacher, regarding issues such as gender in approaches to teamwork which entail young men and women working alongside each other; and 3) assessment has the power to be one of the means of enhancing student learning only under the condition of being an integral part of the learning process, aligned with the learning objectives, and in itself serving as a pedagogical tool.

In chapter 9, Mike Peters and Paul Bartholomew show how, in a specific UK context, student-focused and student-led assessment practice contributed to the empowerment of students as autonomous learners. They discuss how a module within a Foundation Year programme of study was developed to follow the constructive alignment model as proposed by Biggs and Tang (2007). This model proposes that teaching and learning activities and assessment should align with the intended learning outcomes of the programme via a process of knowledge construction. By reading their chapter you will: 1) gain an insight into the design of preparatory programmes in higher education; 2) learn of a structured technology-supported approach to the deployment of peer-assessment and the introduction of reflective writing to students who have never experienced it before; and 3) receive a narrative evaluation as to the efficacy of the approach.

In chapter 10, Jesper Piihl and Kristin Balslev Munksgaard develops a framework for coupling learning activities with indeterminate learning outcomes to curriculum through assessment. Thus, the framework will be of interest to readers who are seeking stronger stakeholder engagement (students, faculty, business, external bodies, etc.) in co-curricular activities. Reading their chapter you will gain three important insights: 1) knowledge of how to integrate learning activities at camps into curriculum while bridging interests of many stakeholders (such as faculty, firms, and students); 2) how to design assessment activities that links camp activities with curriculum through purposes of feeding forward, out and back – to make camp activities closely or loosely coupled to existing courses; and 3) inspiration for ways to discuss how assessment and learning activities can be linked to development of students' competencies in metacognition.

In chapter 11, Ieva Stupans argues that multiple iterations of assessments which integrate a number of learning outcomes may be required in order to assure a non-negotiable learning outcome. She presents a case in which learning outcomes are not assured through a single non-invigilated online test. Reading her chapter you will gain the following four insights: 1) online test does not assure learning; 2) programs need iterative integrated assessments to assure learning; 3) student view of assessment is not the same as staff's; and 4) we haven't really started to think about "compensation" in terms of assessing learning outcomes in examinations.

In chapter 12, Nicholas Cifuentes-Goodbody & Andreas Karatsolis show the important role that assessment must play in accreditation. Reading their chapter you will gain the following insights, as they discuss the role that assessment played in the accreditation process at their university: 1) some background on how student learning has come to occupy a central place within the accreditation process generally; 2) how the faculty at their university used accreditation to reconcile the realities of their classrooms with the outcomes that were built into the original programme proposal; and 3) insight into the outcomes of the accreditation process at their university, paying special attention to improvement in the programme's curriculum and its assessment of student learning.

In chapter 13, Jens Smed Rasmussen & Grethe Heldbjerg argue that teachers and academics responsible for assessment of modules and programmes will benefit from substituting their managerial logic of standardisation and modularisation with a new logic of learning. They propose that assessment demands the use of advanced combinations of multiple perspectives on assessments in an effort to enhance learning and to fully assess actual learning and educational outcome, but also to communicate and convey educational outcomes to stakeholders. Doing this they deconstruct the notion of constructive alignment and propose a dialectical approach to assessment of learning. Reading their chapter you should gain the following insights: 1) theoretical insights into the current case of assessment in research based learning processes of students doing research in HEIs under external institutional pressure for standardization; 2) theoretical insights into different perspectives on assessment integrated into a theory of learning orientated dialectical assessment; 3) initial practical insights on how to eventually use the constructed concept of learning orientated dialectic assessment.

We are pleased to present this book of inspiring chapters, which all address important issues of student assessment and reflect those on interesting cases. Happy reading.

## About the Authors

John Branch is Academic Director of the part-time MBA programmes and Assistant Clinical Professor of Business Administration at the Stephen M. Ross School of Business, and Faculty Associate at the Center for Russian, East European, & European Studies, both of the University of Michigan in Ann Arbor, U.S.A. He can be contacted at this e-mail: jdbranch@umich.edu

Professor Dr. Paul Bartholomew is Director of Learning Innovation and Professional Practice at Aston University, Birmingham, England. He can be contacted at this email: p.bartholomew@aston.ac.uk

Professor, Dr. Claus Nygaard is executive director of LiHE, and executive director of cph:learning and the Steelcase Active Learning Centre in Copenhagen. He can be contacted at this e-mail: info@lihe.info

## Bibliography

Bartholomew P. and N. Bartholomew (2010). Learning Through Innovation, in Nygaard, C., N. Courtney, C. Holtham (Eds.), *Beyond Transmission – Innovations in University Teaching*. Oxfordshire, Libri Publishing.

Earle, L. (2009). Research interview. Online resource: http://www.education.vic.gov.au/Documents/about/research/rilornaearl.pdf [Accessed January 3, 2016].

Chapter 2

# Co-construction in Assessment for Learning: Possibilities and Prejudices

Dorothy Spiller

| Assessment Agency | Student-driven | * | Teacher-driven | * |
| Assessment Outcomes | Fixed | | Flexible | * |
| Assessment Focus | Process | * | Outcome | |
| Assessment Contexts | Specific | | Transferable | * |

## Introduction

This chapter examines the learning potential of a model of assessment based on co-construction and shared ownership of assessment processes, and the conceptual barriers to its implementation. It is widely recognised that assessment is a key determinant of student learning. Correspondingly, assessment practices and processes shape students' learning in their academic disciplines as well as their capacity for inquiry into, and engagement with, their work and society in the future. The concern is that much current assessment practice in higher education is teacher-driven and managed, which can restrict student ownership of discipline ideas and limit the development of learner autonomy. The chapter outlines the theoretical imperatives for co-construction in assessment and then highlights the multi-layered conceptual challenges for both educators and learners to implementing assessment that is congruent with co-constructionist learning values and approaches. The next section reports on three case studies to illuminate possibilities for, and challenges to, involving students as partners in the assessment process. The cases are not presented as perfect exemplars of co-construction in assessment, but as instances of academics' efforts to make assessment more dialogical and collaborative. The case studies are explored in relation to the theoretical principles underpinning co-construction in assessment and the complex amalgam of factors that impedes movement away from a teacher-controlled model of assessment. The cases are discussed both to suggest practical strategies for assessment and also to emphasise the importance of engaging with academics' and learners' underlying belief systems when trying to shift assessment paradigms. Reading this chapter you will gain three important insights:

1. you will see the learning potential of co-construction in assessment and the conceptual barriers that make it challenging to implement;

2. you will learn that co-construction or partnership between teachers and learners in all aspects of the assessment process is integral to student ownership of the learning and the development of learner autonomy;

3. you will understand that introducing this model of assessment needs to include dialogue and a process of re-education with both teachers and students.

## Why co-construction?

There is considerable scholarship to support the conception of students as co-constructors in the teaching, learning and assessment processes, both for their engagement in and the meaningfulness of current academic learning, and to equip them for informed and critical partnership in the workplace and society. A number of case studies in this anthology testify to a growing recognition of the need for more active partnership by students in their learning and assessment processes and for their long term learning (Hager; Fleischmann; Peters & Bartholomew, all in this volume). The collaborative involvement of students in the making and shaping of their higher education learning experience is given a variety of labels including collaboration, co-creation and partnership (Healey *et al.*, 2014). In this chapter, the term co-construction of assessment is used because extending the realms and scope of student co-responsibility is seen as a natural corollary and development of an understanding of the learning process as *constructivist*. In the constructivist understanding of the learning process, each learner brings a unique mental map to his or her engagement with learning, which is the starting place from which he or she tries to make sense of new learning. Correspondingly, the learning space needs to be open and dialogical, so as to enable multiple understandings to be unpacked, voiced, and a shared new meaning created.

Buhagiar (2007) makes a direct link between the shift towards a constructivist understanding of learning and the evolution of the assessment to promote learning paradigm. The words dialogue, partnership and collaboration help to define the social, ethical and moral values that support the concept of co-construction in the learning and assessment process, because they all suggest a spirit of mutual respectfulness, inclusiveness and a sharing of authority that, it is argued, is vital to ownership of the learning in the short term and its long term value. In the course of the higher education learning experience, Healey *et al.* (2014:7) suggest that partnership *"offers the potential for a more authentic engagement with the nature of learning itself and the possibility for genuinely transformative learning experiences for all involved"*. The phrase "for all" is particularly pertinent in the case of assessment which has, historically and conceptually, often been linked to both gatekeeping and selection (Torrance, 1995; Delandshere, 2001; Buhagiar, 2007).

Not only is a co-construction of learning and assessment appropriate from a constructivist learning model and for principles of educational empowerment, but also, the conceptualisation of teacher and learners as partners has significant implications for students' future participation in work and society. If, as many argue, the role of universities is to prepare critical informed citizens (Barnett, 2007) who are capable of making autonomous, mature and discerning judgements and decisions (Baxter Magolda & King, 2004), the entire teaching, learning and assessment process needs to prepare learners for this role. Barnett suggests that the primary goal of higher education is the attainment of "authentic being" which he explains in this context as *"the state of being in which a student becomes her own person"* (2007:31). As assessment is at the centre of students' learning experience, keeping it as the prerogative of teachers denies students essential education in the journey towards personal authority. By contrast, active partnership in the assessment process, especially the development of the capacity to judge, can help to equip students for engaged participation in society beyond academia.

While significant changes in higher education, including technology, have opened new pathways for active learner partnership in the teaching and learning processes, assessment thinking and behaviours have lagged behind these trends (Ecclestone, 2000; Crisp, 2007; Buhagiar, 2007; Deneen & Boud, 2006; Weber & Tschepikow, 2013). Buhagiar observes that *"although assessment reform has now been a major educational issue for almost two decades, assessment practices inside these countries' classrooms have not changed that much"* (2007: 51). The slow pace of change around assessment is especially detrimental, as it is the assessment regime that, more than anything else, determines what students actually learn, and how they go about their learning (Ramsden, 2003; Boud & Falchikov, 2007; Gibbs, 2006). The quality of the assessment regime is consequently powerful in dictating the nature of students' engagement with learning. The difference between a teacher-imposed and controlled assessment regime and one in which students are genuine partners can have a profound impact on learning. In the former instance, learning can become a ritualised and mechanistic passage through a series of externally defined stages. Contrariwise, in a co-constructed approach to assessment, learning has the potential to be a *"searching, challenging, agonising struggle for meaning and growth"* (Boud, 1995) that will be valuable long after particular assessments have been completed (Boud & Falchikov, 2007).

The literature over the past decade strongly reinforces the paramount connection between assessment and learning, both in the widely recognised idea of alignment (Biggs, 2003), and in the assessment FOR learning movement (Carless, 2007; Rust, 2007). The notion of "learning-oriented assessment" is built on three core principles, one of which insists on the primacy of learner involvement at all stages of the assessment process. Principle two articulated by Carless (2007:60) states that *"assessment should involve students actively in engaging with criteria, quality, their own or peers' performance"*.

Carless's stand is supported by other expressions of a "counter discourse" to traditional assessment thinking in the literature (Boud & Falchikov, 2007) and scholars have argued for the importance of student involvement in assessment from a range of perspectives. The early work of Boud (1995) offers a significant catalyst for rethinking assessment beliefs and practices. Boud (1995) argues persuasively that traditional assessment practices impair independent learning and the quality of learners' long term participation in work and the community. Boud's thesis is that traditional assessments do not teach students to judge the quality of their own work (1995). Boud's position corresponds to Carl Rogers' dictum that the best learning occurs when judgements by the teacher are minimised and judgements by students are maximised (1969). Likewise, Boud and Falchikov (2007) note that the traditional unilateral model of assessment denies learner involvement in the determining component of their learning.

Ideas of dialogue, transparency and formative learning through assessment are also evidenced in the literature on feedback and feed forward (for example, Nicol & Macfarlane-Dick, 2006) and in the notion of "assessment literacy" so that students are better equipped for an active partnership in the assessment process (Rust *et al.*, 2003; Smith *et al.*, 2013). The "assessment literacy" discussion marks an important milestone in the efforts to engage students as collaborators because it moves the emphasis on the need for transparency in assessment to active training of students to equip them for partnership in assessment.

The challenge for those involved in educating for change around assessment practices and involvement of students as partners is to work with academics to bring practices closer to the "counter discourses" (Deneen & Boud, 2014; Carless, 2009). It is a process that has to address conceptual as well as practical and systemic barriers.

## Barriers to co-construction

My understanding of the depth, complexity and resilience of the barriers to co-construction in assessment is based on a long history of working as an academic developer as well as insights from the literature. Experience and the scholarship suggest that, while many educators can relate to the idea of the dialogical classroom, it appears to be much more difficult to transfer this idea of shared meaning-making to assessment. Such reluctance can be attributed to the long history of assessment for selection and certification purposes, the investment many stakeholders have in assessment, issues of power and control and the many fragments of unscrutinised ideas about assessment that are part of the higher education landscape. As Ecclestone (2002:142) observes, these issues include *"sociocultural aspects of students' motivation"* and *"issues of power"*.

It is suggested that a web of multiple strands has been spun around assessment and it is difficult for institutions, teachers and learners to free themselves from these tangled threads (Deneen & Boud, 2014). However, it is contended that unravelling these threads of thinking and the associated language must accompany any efforts to shift assessment practices to a more co-constructionist and dialogical model. Wittgenstein's words, noted by Ecclestone, aptly sum up this imperative when he notes: *"sometimes an expression has to be withdrawn from language and sent for cleaning – then it can be put back in circulation"* (Wittgenstein, quoted by Ecclestone, 2002:142).

## Three case studies

This section reports on three different assessment initiatives. These examples involve efforts to make the assessment closer to what the students bring to the learning and to integrate assessment and core course learning. None of the examples provides a complete model of a co-constructed approach to assessment, but each suggests possibilities that could be incorporated into a co-constructed model of assessment. Each example also suggests conceptual barriers that constrain ideas about assessment and the importance of encouraging dialogue about, and working with, these attitudinal constraints.

### Case study one: Students' personal understanding as the foundation of an assessment for learning process

The first example concerns a modest assessment change initiative by a colleague in Language Teacher Education and an associated research study (Daly & Spiller, 2008). The initiative was not originally conceptualised as co-construction of assessment, but was designed as a way of making the students' experiences, perceptions and views the starting point of their assessment and learning journey. In this respect, it involves the key principles of co-construction by placing the students' voices at the centre of the assessment design.

The catalyst for the initiative was twofold. Firstly, the teacher was unhappy with the quality of the students' first assignment, an essay involving reference to theories of second language teaching. Secondly, the teacher's reflective journal entries, during the first iteration of the course in 2007, revealed that students were most engaged in course ideas during discussion (both in class and online) and were particularly animated by a discussion about what makes for effective second language teaching. The teacher's journal reflections capture the socially constructed learning opportunities that can occur when students' voices are invited into the learning process. *"The discussion question about what makes a good language teacher worked really well. The students brought up lots of relevant characteristics and gelled [got on with each other] well."* (Teacher's reflective journal, 26 Feb 2007). The teacher's journal then goes on to note how the students, in effect, co-constructed the subsequent lecture. *"This group is very talented at co-constructing and participating and questioning. They covered so many issues that the lecture was relatively brief and easy to pin on their previous discussions."* (Teacher's reflective journal, 2 April, 2007). However, the teacher reflected that this animated involvement and personal meaning-making was not evident in the essay assessments. The teacher wanted to change the assessments so that they would be about the students' voices, which were so lively but entirely absent from the theoretical essay assessment.

While the initial goal was to rethink the assessment, discussion eventually led to a redesign of the course around a single core question about what makes an effective language teacher. Subsequent assessments invited students to revisit their original personal thinking about effective language teaching, using different lenses which were the curriculum documents, practical teaching experience and finally theoretical perspectives. The changes reflected the effort to work from the students' initial understanding, beliefs and interests. Correspondingly, the question that engaged students most strikingly became the framework for the course and the assessments. The changes reflected other key components of assessment FOR learning (Carless, 2007), including the notion that course design and assessment are interwoven and the recognition that learning is iterative. In terms of any initiatives to bring student voice and thinking into the assessment process, the example indicates how an assessment change needs to be connected with course design as a whole and with other course assessments.

In the course of dialogue around this case study, one specific challenge demonstrates how teachers' ingrained values can constrain assessment thinking and how important it is to allow these resistance notions to come to the surface and be addressed (Deneen & Boud, 2006). Previously, the first assignment required the students to summarise a journal article about theories of effective second language teaching. The students found the article difficult and most were unable to engage with the ideas. In keeping with the wish to place students' voices at the centre of the learning process, the assignment was changed to ask the students to talk about their personal views on this topic without recourse to other readings. The teacher acknowledged the appropriateness of starting course learning with the students' personal views but struggled with the notion that this might not be an academically acceptable exercise. *"We also touched on the feeling that I was having about not making the assignments really complicated and focussed on outside sources, that I might be making things too easy.... I was also struck by the idea that we need to make assignments difficult so as to sort the students out, a kind of elitism really."* (Teacher's reflective journal, 2 August 2007). The teacher's comments here capture some of the discourses that influence teachers' beliefs about assessment and that need to be articulated and discussed in order for academics to feel more comfortable with co-construction in assessment. The teacher's comments indicate the elitist traditions that underpin much of our thinking about assessment in higher education (Ecclestone, 2002), as well as the long-standing use of assessment for measurement, selection and certification (Torrance, 1995; Delandshere, 2001; Buhagiar, 2007).

Despite her previous recognition that the best energy in the course resided in the students' discussions, the academic was held back by inherited discourses about academic assessment. As Carless (2009) argues, trust is an essential component in dealing with resistance to assessment reform. A long process of collaborative dialogue and reflection between the teacher and myself as staff developer ensued and provided a safe environment for the teacher to rethink and shift her practice. Both parties kept reflective journals of the progress of the conversations, which offered them an additional opportunity to share aspirations, hopes, vulnerabilities and uncertainties. From a teaching development perspective, I argue that conversations about changes to assessment need to include broader discussions about teaching and learning goals. The teacher's comment suggests a therapeutic aspect to challenging beliefs and values, which then allows new conversations to happen. *"DS asked me what my conceptions of tertiary teaching were. I loved answering this. I loved having the chance to talk about my work at this level. It felt like allowing a stream to flow when it had been dammed up for a lovely clear stream in my depths."* (Teacher's reflective journal, 5 June, 2007).

When working with academic teachers to encourage a partnership model of learning and assessment, the nature of the change process needs also to be dialogical, collaborative and mutually respectful. It is not only that an environment of trust is important in dealing with change (Carless, 2009), but a more coercive approach would be entirely counter to the substance and spirit of the changes in learning and assessment thinking and practices that are being promoted.

## Case study 2: Using assessment to build student ownership of course learning and build dialogue in the large class setting

The second case study discusses how a lecturer in a third year course on the promotion of health matters tried to enhance student partnership in course learning and assessment. Her aim was co-constructed learning through the integration of assessment and core course learning (Forsyth & Spiller, 2013). In this instance, the assessment was designed to invite the students to initiate the learning conversation around a course topic and shape the subsequent large class learning experience.

In the assessment, students were asked to submit four electronic submissions on the topic of obesity to the lecturer prior to the scheduled date for the large class lecture on this topic. Students were invited to locate articles on the topic of obesity from a range of perspectives such as health, economic, social and political. They were encouraged to consult a variety of texts, such as newspapers, television, magazines, internet, peer reviewed journals and public health organisation resources. The exercise was carefully aligned with the course learning outcomes. In terms of the long term goals of co-construction in learning and assessment, it was also intended to give the students practice in negotiating and interpreting multiple perspectives on a social issue. This intention was in line with the view that co-constructed learning and assessment is an important way of developing *"authentic being"* (Barnett, 2007) and *"learner autonomy"* (Baxter Magolda & King, 2009).

The assessment task required students to submit four 250-word submissions on discussions of the topic from different sources. In their submissions, students were asked for a brief summary of what they had read and their personal opinion on the ideas expressed there. A small percentage of the overall course grade (7%) was given to students for completion of the four online submissions. The lecturer collected these submissions and designed the large class and tutorials around the themes that emerged.

The experiment aimed to involve the students in an authentic experience of co-constructed learning which would heighten both their ownership of and involvement in the assessment and class learning. In designing the initiative, the teacher/researcher was also using technology to disrupt perceptions about ownership of the learning space and demonstrate to students how their contributions provided the foundations for the construction of the learning experience when they came back into the class. The design was intended to make the progression from students' engagement with key course ideas in assessment to the lecture context as seamless as possible, in keeping with the assessment for learning model (Carless, 2007). It was hoped that this would send an important message to students about the relationship between assessment and their meaningful personal engagement with course learning. The teacher also chose to step back from determining lecture content, ascertain students' thinking on the topic and use these ideas to segue into some of the theoretical learning.

Evaluation of the initiative drew on multiple sources. These sources were the observation of the large class by an independent observer, a focus group conducted with students by an independent facilitator, teacher reflections and analysis of 40 randomly chosen scripts by the two researchers. In the analysis, the researchers were interested in identifying the source of the information, the focus of the content of the chosen piece and each student's personal response to what they had read. The researchers were particularly interested in seeing whether the students had demonstrated any critical questioning of the materials.

Evaluations indicated that the experiment led to some shift in students' personal engagement in their learning and a sense of satisfaction about their more active partnership in the learning. The observer noted, "*The comments made by the students showed that there was a high level of engagement overall, there was a great range and depth of discussion and about the different findings and views presented.*" (Forsyth & Spiller, 2013:159).This observation suggests the potential for richer learning that exists when the students are involved in co-construction of a learning process which was integral both to the assessment and the classroom experience. Not only did the strategy result in the students' personal engagement in the learning, but it was also a simple way for the lecturer to bring contested views around the topic into the classroom. The classroom became something of a rehearsal for genuine debate about socially constructed views of how a contentious health issue is promoted.

One problem noted by the observer was the domination of the discussion by some students. For future iterations the lecturer recognised that she would need to devise better strategies for managing this part of the process. While, to some extent, this problem was mitigated by the fact that every student had the opportunity to voice personal views through the online submission, the goal of partnership is endangered if the lecturer's dominance is going to be replaced by the domination of the learning space by a few students. It is a reminder that, for the patterns of interaction in assessment and learning to change fundamentally, extensive practice and re-education needs to occur for both teachers and students.

The focus groups reinforced the strengths and limitations of the initiative. Students' comments indicated that they enjoyed hearing different points of view and felt more connected to the learning. Comments included: "*The lecture time was interesting because it allowed everyone to share their personal perspective. The learning was different because it was interesting to hear other opinions. The submissions made prior to the lecture were things that struck something with you...they meant something to you.*" (Forsyth & Spiller, 2013:160). Again, some students' reservations suggest that there is considerable underlying re-education about how learning can happen that needs to underpin initiatives like this. For example, some students indicated that they "*weren't really bothered about sharing ideas*", and one focus group participant said "*some people need to learn that you are trying to share an idea rather than prove a point.*" (Forsyth & Spiller,

2013:160). A similar problem is noted in the lecturer's reflections when she commented that, in spite of the students' enhanced readiness to share ideas, there was still a strong tendency to direct comments to her and look to her as expert for confirmation of their views. The researchers felt that one reason for this was that this approach had only been followed in one part of the course and it needed to be embedded more deeply across the whole course so that everyone became more comfortable with shared ownership of the learning. More generally, this raises the larger question of whether it is possible for particular teachers and courses to shift the assessment and learning dynamic when the teacher-as-expert model and practice is still so powerful in higher education institutions.

Thematic analysis of the students' contributions showed that students had relied heavily on the internet and only a small percentage of the students had engaged critically with the ideas that they had sourced. This example suggests that some of the barriers to co-construction reside with the students as well as the lecturers. While active participation in the large lecture surpassed usual levels, the students' contributions and comments were generally at quite a surface level. Again, this outcome indicated that one problem was that the assessment and learning initiative were isolated occurrences and that co-construction was not embedded in the culture of the course as a whole. The unfamiliarity of this way of working led many students to superficial commentaries.

Furthermore, the students did not have opportunities to practise critical evaluation of source material in this course. Throughout the paper, the authors suggest that this particular skill needed to be coached and practised to enable students to be more effective partners in the learning and assessment processes. These findings point to a major problem around developing assessment partnerships with learners: the need to assist students in acquiring the specific and the generic competencies to participate as collaborators and partners in the assessment and learning process. It is argued this "assessment literacy" is essential for authentic co-construction (Smith *et al.*, 2013:44). Developing students' "assessment literacy" may also help combat student reluctance to engage in such assessment activities as the development of assessment criteria, as noted in a case study in this anthology (see Peters & Bartholomew, this volume).

## Case study three: Inquiry-based assessment for learning

The third example involves assessment in the Postgraduate Certificate in Tertiary Teaching where the learners are all academic teachers. When this programme was initiated in 2001, it was designed on traditional lines and the assessments were essays and small research studies. While self-assessment was a topic in the programme, generally the assessment was teacher designed, implemented and evaluated. Interestingly, during that phase of the programme, in the module on self-assessment, it seemed logical to invite the group to develop the essay criteria in dialogue with the course teacher. The attempt was an abysmal failure, with the group declaring that these decisions were "your job" and refusing to engage in the exercise; this is a reluctance that we often see from students (Peters & Bartholomew, this volume) but it was certainly surprising and disturbing in this context. In part, the reaction could be attributed to the fact that a culture of co-construction had not been established and that the exercise needed to be part of a broader scheme of co-construction in all aspects of course learning and assessment.

There was an assumption that the academic teachers would readily take shared responsibility for the standards that were going to be used to evaluate their work. The reaction of these academics points to deeply-held ideas in academia that the teachers need to be in charge of assessment. It is one of the significant discourses around assessment that cause resistance to change and that needs to be addressed if co-construction practices in assessment are to become a reality (Deneen & Boud, 2014).

In this early iteration of the Certificate, the course teachers had fallen into the content transmission trap in spite of teaching contrary educational theories. When the paper was redesigned, an effort was made to ensure that it was informed by the practice of academics. This is evident in the two main assessments for one of the courses: participants are invited to select some aspect of their current work (teaching and assessment) to examine more systematically and conduct a small action research project on it.

The key learning occurs in individual conversations between the course teacher and each student, which have the development of these action research initiatives as their focal point. Both the learning process and the conversations are shaped around the inquiry initiated by the teachers themselves. There is no grading for the assessments, but there is regular conversation around drafts of sections of the work as they progress until the task is completed to agreed-on standards. Many learners report a fundamental shift in thinking and beliefs and subsequently adopt the habit of systematic investigation of teaching. Contrariwise, some participant responses illustrate the traditional thinking that clusters around assessment. For example, many participants struggle with the notion of submitting regular chunks of writing in draft form as a basis for the learning conversations.

It is argued that some of this resistance stems from the traditional culture of assessment that focuses on a product and the associated expectation that this product should be well-constructed and communicated coherently. The academic teachers, like other learners, have been trained in a model of assessment that emphasises measurement of performance and, by implication, evaluation of self-worth. For example, one of the academic teachers studying on the Certificate expressed these fears when writing in her personal portfolio. *"There is a little part of me that worries that I will fail at this. It's a non-intellectual idea, but I suspect it's a hangover from undergraduate days when I worried so much about failing assessments. The idea of failing seemed the worst thing in the world to me."* (Spiller & Ferguson, 2014:np).

The intensity of the emotions that underlies the language used in these reflections suggests how academics bring the weight of their own learning histories into their academic practice, and that these may form significant barriers to change. It is sometimes challenging to persuade learners to write these draft segments and recognise that the entire assessment process is the learning, not the end product. As we have been working this way for a while now, I have to remind myself to unpack these assumptions and values with each new cohort of students in the interests of transparency and dialogue. There have also been some participants who are so focused on the idea of imposed assessment deadlines, that they find it difficult to produce anything in writing before a final due date. Again, this is about assessment as performance and can be difficult to deal with, when there is considerable and deliberate flexibility around dates to accommodate the learners.

# Conclusion: Towards co-construction in assessment

The scholarship and these case studies illuminate both the desirability of co-construction in assessment and learning to bring the assessment FOR learning notion (Carless, 2007) closer to a reality for students and teachers, and to coach students in ways of being and participating that will equip them to engage authentically, critically and purposefully in work and society (Barnett 2007, Baxter Magolda & King, 2004). At the same time, it is evident that there is considerable work that needs to be done with learners and teachers to create spaces and opportunities for assessment to become more closely associated with meaningful personal learning and growth. Some of this involves ongoing dialogue with both teachers and learners as, for both groups, ingrained ideas about assessment are part of past learning and experiences.

Dialogue needs to be conducted in a respectful way in a safe environment. Such collaborative conversation needs to invite exploration of underlying beliefs and assumptions about assessment and learning, as well as carefully scaffolded conversations about the rationale for particular changes in assessment design and processes. If we are involved in change management, it needs to be done with openness to, and respect for, the histories and reservations that both teachers and learners bring into the assessment conversation (Carless, 2009; Deneen & Boud, 2014). It is not only that an environment of trust is important in dealing with change (Carless, 2009), but a more coercive approach would be entirely counter to the substance and spirit of the changes in learning and assessment thinking and practices that are being promoted.

Congruent with this approach to change that involves exploration of underlying thinking and practice, is a need to try and embed co-constructed assessment initiatives in the design of a course as a whole and to give learners plenty of opportunities to practise and talk about this kind of learning. One of the difficulties here is that many of the messages about who owns the learning are communicated subliminally by contradictory messages suggested by learning spaces, institutional norms, and individual behaviours. Furthermore, students need opportunities to develop assessment literacy attributes through exercises like developing criteria practice marking, so that they are better equipped for authentic partnership in assessment (Rust & O'Donovan, 2003; Smith *et al.*, 2013).

As educators or people involved with trying to motivate change in assessment and learning processes, it is clear that this is only possible if done in an integrated way. Inevitably, the battle is not only about teachers and learners, but also about institutions and society and employers and the way in which we conceptualise the purposes of higher education. The collaborative conversations about partnership in assessment that are advocated for promoting teachers' and learners rethinking need to occur at a much wider level, both within institutions and beyond, not least in relation to assessment for selection and the kinds of assessments that are used for these purposes.

## About the author

Dorothy Spiller is Senior Lecturer at the Teaching Development Unit at University of Waikato, New Zealand. She can be contacted at this email: dorothy@waikato.ac.nz

## Bibliography

Barnett, R. (2000). *Realising the university in an age of supercomplexity.* Buckingham, UK: SRHE

Barnett, R. (2007). Assessment in higher education. An impossible mission? In D. Boud & N.Falchikov (Eds.) *Rethinking Assessment in Higher Education*, London & New York: Routledge, pp. 29-40.

Baxter Magolda, M. & P. M. King (Eds.) (2004). *Learning partnerships: Theory and model of practice to educate for self-authorship.* Stirling, V.A: Stylus.

Biggs, J. (2003). *Teaching for quality learning at university.* Great Britain: Society for Research into Higher Education and Open University Press.

Boud, D. (1995). *Enhancing learning through self-assessment.* London: KoganPage.

Boud, D. & N. Falchikov (2007). Assessment for the longer term. In D. Boud & N. Falchikov (Eds.) *Rethinking Assessment in Higher Education*, London & New York: Routledge, pp. 3-13.

Buhagiar, M. A. (2007). Classroom assessment within the alternative assessment paradigm: revisiting the territory. *The Curriculum Journal*, Vol. 18, No. 1, pp. 39-56.

Carless, D. (2007). Learning-oriented assessment: conceptual bases and practical implications. *Innovations in Education and Teaching International*, Vol. 44, No. 1, pp. 57-66.

Carless, D. (2009). Trust, distrust and their impact on education reform. *Assessment & Evaluation in Higher Education*, Vol. 34, No. 1, pp. 79-89.

Crisp, G. (2007). *The e-Assessment handbook*. New York: Continuum

Daly, N. & D. Spiller (2008). Motivating teachers of additional language by design: The use of reflection in the development and design of an additional language teacher education paper. In *Proceedings of the NZALTInternational Biennial Conference*, 6-9 July.

Delandshere, G. (2001). Implicit theories, unexamined assumptions and the status quo of educational assessment. *Assessment & Evaluation in Higher Education*, Vol. 8, No. 2, pp. 113-133.

Deneen, C. & D. Boud (2014). Patterns of resistance in managing assessment change. *Assessment & Evaluation in Higher Education*, Vol.39, No 5, pp. 577-591.

Ecclestone, K. (2000). Assessment and critical autonomy in post-compulsory Education in the UK. *Journal of Education and Work*, Vol. 13, No. 2, pp. 141-162.

Forsyth, G. & D. Spiller (2013). Reconceptualising the lecture space so that student voices matter. In *Research and Development in Higher Education: the place of learning and teaching*, Milperra, NSW, Australia: HERDSA, pp.153-163.

Gibbs, G. (2006). How assessment frames student learning. In C. Bryan & K. Clegg (Eds.) *Innovative Assessment in Higher Education*. London & New York: Routledge.

Healey, M.; A. Flint & K. Harrington (2014). Engagement through partnership: Students as partners in learning and teaching in higher education. *Higher Education Academy*

Nicol, D. & Macfarlane-Dick, D. (2006). Formative assessment and self-regulated learning: A model and seven principles of good practice. *Studies in Higher Education*, Vol. 31, No. 2, pp. 199-218.

Ramsden, P. (2003). *Learning to teach in higher education*. London & New York: Routledge Falmer.

Rogers, C. (1969). *Freedom to learn*. Columbus: Merrill

Rust, C.; M. Price & B. O'Donovan (2003). Improving students' learning by developing their understanding of assessment criteria and processes. *Assessment & Evaluation in Higher Education*, Vol. 28, No. 2, pp. 147-164.

Rust, C.; M. Price & B. O'Donovan (2007). Towards a scholarship of assessment. *Assessment & Evaluation in Higher Education*, Vol. 32, No. 1, pp. 229-237.

Smith, C.D.; K. Worsfold; L. Davies; L. Fisher & R. McPhail (2013). Assessment    literacy and student learning: the case for explicitly developing students' 'assessment literacy'. *Assessment &Evaluation in Higher Education*, Vol. 2, No. 1, pp. 44-60.

Spiller, D. & P.Bruce Ferguson, P. (2014). The head and the heart: The personal portfolio and the development of identity as an academic educator. Presentation at the 4*th* *Academic Identities Conference*. Durham University, England.

Torrance, H. (1995). The role of assessment in educational reform. In H. Torrance (Ed.) *Evaluating authentic assessment: problems and possibilities in new approaches to assessment*. Buckingham: Open University Press.

Webber, K. L. & K. Tschepikow (2013). The role of learner-centred assessment in postsecondary organisational change. *Assessment in Education: Principles, Policy and Practice*, Vol. 20, No. 2, pp.187-204.

Chapter 3

# Student Development at the Stockholm School of Economics in Riga

Diana Pauna & John Branch

| Assessment Agency | Student-driven | * | Teacher-driven | |
|---|---|---|---|---|
| Assessment Outcomes | Fixed | | Flexible | * |
| Assessment Focus | Process | * | Outcome | |
| Assessment Context | Specific | | Transferrable | * |

## Introduction

This chapter pushes assessment beyond learning objectives to also include a student's personal development. At its core, assessment is about measuring a student's learning. Indeed, it is a kind of comparison between a student's performance and the learning objectives of a given course of study. Simply stated, assessment answers the question "Has the student learned what was intended to be learned?".

When conducted at the conclusion of a course of study, assessment is summative in nature. This type of assessment is often referred to as assessment of learning (See the chapters by Stupans and Cygman in this volume for examples of summative assessment.). When conducted during a course of study, on the contrary, assessment serves a more formative purpose. This type of assessment is often referred to as assessment for learning (See the chapter by Fleischmann for an example of formative assessment.).

Many experts, however, have suggested that assessment ought to move beyond learning objectives to also include a student's personal development. According to Palomba & Banta (1999), "[a]ssessment is the systematic collection, review, and use of information about educational programs undertaken for the purpose of improving student learning *and development*" (p. 12, our emphasis). Similarly for Erwin, "[a]ssessment is the systematic basis for making inferences about the learning *and development* of students" (p. 8, our emphasis). With this broader perspective, assessment views the student as a whole person, not only as a knowledge 'vessel', and assessment, therefore, assumes a more generative role. This type of assessment is often referred to as assessment as learning.

Since its founding in 1994, the Stockholm School of Economics in Riga has followed the broader perspective on assessment, by considering both a student's academic success and personal growth. Specifically, it has created and implemented a hybrid model for student development, in concert with the more traditional summative and formative assessments within the curriculum. The hybrid model for student development employs various activities, including peer support, social counselling, and alumni-student mentoring, which together aim to:

1. smooth the transition from secondary school to university;

2. ensure progress throughout the 3-year bachelor degree;

3. lay the foundation for career success; and

4. instill a passion for life-long learning.

The purpose of this chapter, therefore, is to document the creation, implementation, and evaluation of the hybrid model for student development at the Stockholm School of Economics in Riga. The chapter begins by overviewing the Stockholm School of Economics in Riga. It then describes the hybrid model for student development. Finally, the chapter presents an evaluation of the hybrid model for student development. Reading this chapter you will gain the following three insights:

1. assessment can be generative in nature;

2. assessment as learning requires a heavy commitment; and

3. assessment as learning can pay big dividends, both for students and an institution of higher education.

# The Stockholm School of Economics in Riga

The Stockholm School of Economics in Riga (hereafter referred to as SSE Riga) was founded in 1994 by the Stockholm School of Economics in Stockholm, Sweden, with the support of the Swedish government and the Latvian Ministry of Education and Science. It responded to the need for modern economics and business education in Latvia, following the dissolution of the Soviet Union. And, it aimed to contribute to the economic and social development of Latvia and of the larger Baltic region, including Sweden.

The first programme to be offered at SSE Riga was a bachelor of science (BSc) degree in economics and business. In 2002, a 2-year modular executive master of business administration (EMBA) degree was introduced. SSE Riga also has an executive education department, which conducts open-enrollment and customised training programmes on its own and with partner institutions, for public and private organisations from Latvia and elsewhere. The BSc degree, however, remains the flagship program of SSE Riga.

## The BSc Degree

The BSc degree in economics and business is a 3-year, 180 ECTS credit programme with a focus on economics and business, but with a solid social science foundation. It is comprised of five main components: core courses, specialisation courses, elective courses, an internship, and a bachelor thesis. Students also have an opportunity to spend a period of study at an international partner school. All courses are structured in a modular fashion, with a maximum of two modules running simultaneously. The language of instruction is English (except at partner institutions which might teach in local languages).

The first cohort of students in 1994 consisted of 56 students, all of whom were from Latvia. A year later, enrolment of students from Estonia and Lithuania began, leading to a 'pan-Baltic' cohort of 100. Today, the BSc degree enrolls 120 students in each of the 3 years. Since 2011, efforts have been made to internationalise the cohort further, and thanks to generous financial aid from the Swedish government, scholarships are now available for students from Belarus, Georgia, Moldova, and Ukraine.

Russian students have also been attracted to SSE Riga, although they must pay full fees.

Admission to the BSc degree has remained unchanged at SSE Riga over its 2 decades of existence. Prospective students first sit an admissions examination which aims to gauge their academic preparedness/potential. The examination has 3 components: a test of logical aptitude, a test of the English language, and a test of mathematical skills. The top 200 prospective students as identified from the admissions examination are then invited for personal interviews. The interviews are conducted by 1 instructor/staff member and 1 alumna/us who attempt to gauge the independence, life 'involvement', and inquisitiveness of the prospective students. Based on the results of the interviews, 120 offers are made. According to admissions data, one of five prospective students has been admitted for the last 3 cohorts (2012, 2013, and 2014).

## The BSc Orientation Programme

In order to help admitted students in their transition from secondary school to university, SSE Riga conducts an orientation programme which runs immediately prior to the first semester of the 3-year BSc degree. This orientation programme was introduced in 1994 for the first cohort of the BSc degree, and ran for a total of 8 weeks. In 2003, it was reduced to 6 weeks in length.

During the orientation programme, the new SSE Riga students participate in acculturation exercises, learn academic skills, and follow business English, applied mathematics, and basic economics lessons. The acculturation exercises and academic skills learning are considered especially important, given the diversity of the new students in terms of both nationality and secondary school experiences. The more theoretical lessons help to level set all students, preparing them for the subjects of the first semester.

The orientation programme also serves as a kind of 'early warning system' for students at risk. Indeed, the results of both the formal and informal assessments implemented in the orientation alert SSE Riga of students who are not adjusting well to the added rigours of university level studies, are in danger of falling behind, or might even be suffering from emotional or social problems. In these cases, SSE Riga can intervene before the first semester begins, which, in most instances, begins with a meeting between a student at risk and the SSE Riga Rector or Pro-Rector.

The perceived success of the BSc orientation – as a means of easing the transition from secondary school to university, as a level setting device, and as an early warning system – triggered SSE Riga to consider the addition of other non-curricular activities which could be implemented throughout the 3-year BSc degree, and which would serve a similar student development function. The number, the nature, and the scheduling of the activities have varied over the years at SSE Riga, but together they constitute that which is now known as the hybrid model for student development at SSE Riga.

## The Hybrid Model for Student Development

The roots of the hybrid model for student development can be traced to 2002 when one-to-one conferences between students and the Pro-Rector were added to the second year of the BSc. These conferences morphed into self-evaluation conferences in 2008. Social counselling was introduced in 2006, conducted at first by a professor of business psychology and, as of 2008, by a professional counsellor. A peer support programme was introduced to Year 1 students in 2011 and to Year 2 students in 2012. Based on discussions with both students and instructors, SSE Riga introduced an academic advising programme in 2014. Recently, the mentoring of students by alumni was also introduced.

As the hybrid model for student development has evolved in terms of activities, so have the facilitators. Indeed, early on, the Rector and Pro-Rector were heavily involved, serving as the primary student-SSE Riga interface. More recently, however, upper year students, instructors, staff members, and alumni have begun to participate. For example, academic advising is now conducted by a team which consists of six instructors and staff members, each advisor serving 20 students. During the period 1994 to 2010, student self-evaluations were run by an instructor/staff member duo; in 2010, one of these was replaced with an alumnus/alumna.

Today, the hybrid model consists of 7 main activities: academic interventions, peer support, academic advising, social counselling, career advising, alumni-student mentoring, and student self-evaluation (See Table 1 for a summary.). Each activity has a different focus of development, is aimed at a different group of students, and is conducted by a different set of facilitators. Each of the activities is described below.

| Activity | Focus | Students | Facilitators |
|---|---|---|---|
| 1. Academic Interventions | Early warning | Year 1 students | Academic Advisors |
| | Interventions in cases of students at risk | Year 1, Year 2, Year 3 students | Rector & Pro-rector |
| 2. Peer Support | Group or individual tutorials before exams or retakes | Year 1and Year 2 students | Year 2 and Year 3 students, Education Committee of the Student Association, Teaching Assistants |
| 3. Academic Advising | Review of progress and identification of problem areas | Year 1 students | 6 academic advisors (each academic advisor working with 20 students individually) |
| 4. Social Counselling | Support of emotional needs | Year 1, Year 2, Year 3 students | Social Counsellor |
| 5. Career Advising | Employability, life and career decisions | Year 1 students | Mentor-Entrepreneur and a Career Development Instructor |
| 6. Alumni-Student Mentoring | Life and career guidance | Year 2 and Year 3 students | On average 40-50 students mentored by 40-50 alumni |
| 7. Student Self-Evaluation | Individual development | Year 2 students | Duo of an instructor or staff member and an alumnus/alumna approximately 10 teams each meeting 12 students individually |

*Table 1. Activities of the hybrid model for student development at SSE Riga.*

## 1. Academic Interventions

Academic interventions are targeted towards students at risk, and such interventions are provided as a remedial service to assist students either to advance in a particular course or to maintain appropriate academic standing. Academic interventions take place after each semester to monitor the overall class performance. However, given the modular course sequence at SSE Riga, academic interventions can take place after a course if there is a larger number of underperforming students, or if some course results are unusually low. Early warning is of particular importance for Year 1 students who struggle with the transition from secondary school to university. Meeting underperforming Year 1 students after their first examinations allows SSE Riga to identify individual reasons for failure, to learn more about the instruction and student individual learning styles, and to ask students to develop a learning strategy in preparation for a retake. It is especially useful for students who were accustomed to being top-performers at secondary school and now find failure a confusing experience. Compared to other activities of the hybrid model, academic interventions are perceived as fairly negative, and students generally find the experience unpleasant and emotionally painful.

## 2. Peer Support

Student-led peer support is provided to increase student academic confidence in a collaborative learning environment. Peer support is conducted in an informal and unstructured way along with a support scheme which is coordinated and supervised by the Education Committee of the Student Association. First, students form their own informal study groups to work collaboratively on problem-solving and prepare for seminars. Similarly, when preparing for examinations, students often form informal study groups. Sometimes, students who are more advanced in the subject area volunteer to form study groups in order to assist their peers in studying for an examination. Second, structured peer support is provided by the Education Committee of the Student Association. At SSE Riga there are four retake periods: the end of December/early January, the pre-Easter week, the end of June, and a week prior to the new academic year that starts in the fourth week of August. On average, students retake two to three exams during a week. Prior to each retake period, junior teaching assistants who are either their classmates or senior students run study seminars. For example, for a retake of the mathematics examination (Year 1), six senior teaching assistants from Year 2 work together as a team and consult with the course director to prepare six study seminars, each of the teaching assistants preparing one seminar. Compared to peer support experiences at other universities (Scott, 2012), volunteer peer leaders at SSE Riga do not receive comprehensive training; instead, support from the instructor is provided to teaching assistants during the seminar preparation phase. Based on student feedback, it is worth implementing a training program for teaching assistants to enhance the productivity and quality of seminars. In contrast to academic interventions, peer support is the most supportive and non-threatening form of student support, and it serves well in assisting peers. Finally, peer support allows students to identify their weaknesses as seen by others or compared to others; peer leaders can also serve as role models.

## 3. Academic Advising

Compared to previous generations, the current student population is more advanced at using technologies and information searching systems. Yet, they still need guidance to understand the context, requirements, relationships and the application of knowledge and skills. Therefore, a structured academic advising programme for Year 1 students has been designed to review progress, identify problem areas, and provide advice. The six advisors of the advising team have different and complementary professional experiences. In order to coordinate their work, academic advisors have regular meetings, and they apply standard templates for recording and reporting their progress. Each advisor works with twenty students and in parallel with the four tutorials which run in August, October, January, and May. Students can approach their advisors for advice throughout the academic year. The first two tutorials are mandatory for all students; the remaining two are left for students to choose unless they are underperformers, in which case they are mandatory. Making the first two tutorials mandatory is based on the notion that students need to learn and experience what academic advising means. During the first two tutorials, advisors also follow up on the student individual development plans which were designed during the orientation programme.

## 4. Career Advising

Career advising as a one-on-one service for Year 1 students was introduced in 2011 after SSE Riga adopted Racing Towards Excellence by Muzaffar Khan and Jan Sramek (2009) as a required textbook in the orientation programme. After students have read and discussed the four accounts which are outlined in the textbook (mental, emotional, physical, and material), Muzaffar Khan himself provides a guest lecture for the 120 Year 1 students, followed by a one-on-one meeting with each of the students.

As of 2015, a week-long intensive programme in early February entitled Introduction to Internship has also been added to Career Advising. It consists of six career development sessions and three 60-minute group sessions which are run by a career advisor. The focus is on employability and corporate social intelligence skills.

## 5. Social Counselling

Social counselling has an important place in the hybrid model for student development, serving international students when they experience homesickness related issues, for example, or any student who is struggling during the transition from secondary school to university. Social counselling is also common for underperforming students who need to 'regain their strength', and for students who must manage personal and family problems. Social counselling is introduced to Year 1 students during the orientation programme when the counsellor runs an information session explaining the meaning of counselling, the different kinds of counselling available, and the tell-tale signs of which students ought to be aware. Explanatory material, a statement on confidentiality, and a letter from the counsellor are published on the e-learning platform; a listing of common problems which are treated by the social counsellor is also available there. Academic advisors might also encourage students to seek help from the counsellor.

## 6. Alumni-Student Mentoring

Alumni-student mentoring was launched in 2012 with five broad goals:

1. to help students realise their potential as students;

2. to prepare students for the world of work;

3. to encourage alumni to remain engaged with SSE Riga;

4. to provide an opportunity for alumni to practise their mentoring skills; and

5. to facilitate the building of networks among students and alumni.

Mentoring is only available to Year 2 and Year 3 students, based on the assumption that they would benefit more from a mentor after having solidified their career choices from Year 1 experiences, their summer internships, an additional year of maturity, etc. On average, 40-50 students are mentored by 40-60 alumni. The students and alumni are paired in a matching process in September of Year 2. Interaction between students and alumni occurs approximately twice a month, with each session having clear aims and outcomes. Typically, the relationship is evaluated at the end of Year 2, and continues into Year 3 if the student and the alumnus/alumna are in agreement.

This programme is administratively-challenging, considering students' schedules (and their agenda) and alumni family and career demands. With some careers being more popular than others, it is also sometimes difficult to provide a good match between the student and the alumnus/alumna for all students. In the case of finance, for example, there are too few mentors. And in some instances, as expected, the mentor-mentee relationship begins with great enthusiasm, but dissolves after a few months.

## 7. Student Self-Evaluation

Student self-evaluation conferences with Year 2 students were introduced in 2002 to encourage students to reflect on and review critically their personal development, the output of which is then a set of goals for their final year at SSE Riga. Self-evaluation conferences with Year 2 students take place in early June. The academic year finishes on June 20 at SSE

Riga. Prior to attending the conference, students must submit a Student Self-Evaluation Report (SSR). The report consists of five major parts: academic performance; personal development elements; social involvement; expectations and outcomes; and future plans. In the academic performance section, students reflect on their overall academic performance, compare their performance in Year 1 and Year 2, and identify the core and elective courses which they have found most attractive. In the personal development section, students reflect on their successes and/or failures in mastering self-management, efficiency in structuring work processes in relation to the results, practicing time management, and being open to innovation and change. In the social involvement section, students report on their engagement in the SSE Riga community, by enumerating the co-curricular activities in which they have participated and by identifying the benefits of these activities. In the expectations and outcomes sections, students reflect on the degree to which their studies and 'life' at SSE Riga have served their personal goals. Finally, in the future section, students share their plans regarding the upcoming summer internship, the specialization courses which they are considering for Year 3, and their proposed Bachelor Thesis.

The SSR is discussed with the facilitators during a 20-minute individual conference, with a view towards any conflicts or challenges and, of course, possible solutions. Students are also required to rate their performance against expectations in each of the sections, not unlike employee evaluations which are conducted between an employee and his/her supervisor in a human resources setting. As a conclusion to the conference, the facilitators provide additional academic and career advice, based on both the report and the conference discussion.

## Evaluation

As highlighted above, the hybrid model for student development at SSE Riga was created (and continues today) with a singular purpose: student development. Indeed, its activities are intended to be generative in nature – the idea of assessment as learning which was mentioned in the introduction. Student development, therefore, when viewed at the highest level, really means 'learning to learn'. As defined in the recommendation of the European Parliament and of the Council of Europe (2006), the eight key competences for lifelong learning are:

1. communication in the mother tongue;

2. communication in foreign languages;

3. mathematical competence and basic competences in science and technology;

4. digital competence;

5. learning to learn;

6. social and civic competences;

7. sense of initiative and entrepreneurship; and

8. cultural awareness and expression.

Indeed, the overarching goal of the hybrid model for student development is to engender in students the ability to self-regulate their own learning, by examining critically the inputs, throughputs, and outputs of their efforts. It is hoped that through each of the activities of the hybrid model, specific meta-cognitive skills rise to the surface; skills such as self-awareness, self-evaluation, and self-empowerment. Moreover, it is intended that the activities also contribute to the students' resilience, confidence, and identity. But does the hybrid model for assessment student development work? And what are its specific outcomes?

## Characteristics of the Activities

To begin, it is clear that the seven activities of the hybrid model for student development vary dramatically in terms of scope, features, and potential (See Table 2 for a summary.). Indeed, some activities are mandatory, with a very top down approach to their implementation. Consider the student self-evaluations, for example. Other activities, like the peer support, are optional and almost entirely student-initiated. Some activities are very remedial, while other activities are intended to be transformative. Compare student interventions and career advising, for example. Consequently, each of the activities of the hybrid model for assessing student development has both pros and cons which cannot be overlooked.

| Activity | Approach | Specific features | Pros | Cons |
|---|---|---|---|---|
| 1. Academic Interventions | Top-down, mandatory for under-performing students | Remedial function; applies to students at risk | Allows monitoring academic performance and opportunity for early warning | Painful, threatening, with a negative connotation |
| 2. Peer Support | Bottom-up | Collaborative learning, applies to students who are willing to participate | Friendly, supportive, and non-threatening learning environment | Vaguely structured, teaching assistants are not trained |
| 3. Academic Advising | Top-down and bottom-up | A personal development plan prepared during the orientation programme; two mandatory one-on-one tutorials | Assisting in making a transition from high school to university, monitoring progress, assisting in identifying weaknesses<br><br>Links together other support services (encourages students to see the social counsellor, seek for peer support, etc.) | Students, especially top-performers, do not recognise academic advising as value added for the first session or two |
| 4. Social Counselling | Bottom-up | Students in need, one-on-one, confidential | Takes care of student wellbeing | In many cases still perceived as a medical/health problem |

| Activity | Approach | Specific features | Pros | Cons |
|---|---|---|---|---|
| 5. Career Advising | Top-down, mandatory for Year 1 students, bottom-up for Year 2 and Year 3 students | Introducing career development concepts | Bridging and balancing academic and career aspirations | Difficult to schedule both 120 individual sessions and three sessions for 12 groups |
| 6. Alumni-Student Mentoring | Bottom-up | Promote interaction between the alumni and students | Increases alumni participation, provides advice in both academic and career progression | Some of the alumni are willing to contribute their time, but then cannot manage time-wise because of work-related obligations, complicated to coordinate |
| 7. Student Self-Evaluation | Top-down, mandatory for each student | A self-evaluation report combined with a 20 minute conference, including comparison to his/her own best performance | Trains reflection and critical thinking, helps to outline a plan for the final year of studies, valuable feedback for school regarding the study program and the learning environment | Time consuming to read 120 reports and have individual conferences 120x20 minutes, no follow-up in Year 3 except for the cases of under-performers |

*Table 2. Characteristics of the activities of the hybrid model for assessing student development at SSE Riga.*

## Advantages and Disadvantages of the Hybrid Model for Student Development

The hybrid model for student development also has clear advantages and disadvantages (See Table 3 for a summary.). The advantages stem from the variety and diversity of facilitators, exercises, and deliverables. Students benefit from a range of opinions, approaches, and experiences of academics and professionals. Compared to a centralised model with a fixed number of professional advisors, the hybrid model for student development also allows more flexibility. Most importantly, the hybrid model brings together all types of advising (academic, social, and career advising), thereby helping students to improve their performance, enhance learning, and graduate successfully from SSE Riga.

The disadvantages of the hybrid model for student development relate to the lack of professional background in advising and administration of all activities. Except for the social counsellor, no facilitators are trained. Arguably, this lack of professional qualification is overcome by experience, but nevertheless it is a concern. Coordination between the facilitators, the students, and SSE Riga is also critical. This is especially true in Year 1 which has so many top-down activities. Finally, the hybrid model for assessing student development is resource intensive, in terms of time, energy, finances, humans, organisational focus, etc. Now, do the benefits of the hybrid model for student development justify its expense?

| Advantages | Disadvantages |
|---|---|
| A decentralized model with a range of advisors: faculty and staff members, and alumni | Except for the social counsellor, none are professional advisors or mentors |
| Students are exposed to a variety of opinions, approaches and experiences of academics and professionals | Coordination between advisors, mentors, and administrators |
| With a range of components and activities, engaging various facilitators, students have more opportunities for matching their individual needs | Time consuming, financial and human resources demanding |

*Table 3. Advantages and disadvantages of the hybrid model for student development.*

## Benefits to SSE Riga

To begin, the hybrid model for student development informs the SSE Riga about the overall 'temperature' within the learning environment, and points squarely to areas which demand attention. Similarly, the hybrid model for student development also serves as a means of data validation – of triangulation so to speak – when course evaluations allude to problems in the School. Indeed, compared to anonymous and rather superficial course evaluations, the various activities of the hybrid model for student development lead to detailed feedback, which can subsequently drive corrective measures.

The hybrid model for student development has also helped SSE Riga tighten both its summative and formative assessments. During the first Academic Advising session, for example, SSE Riga Regulations and Procedures are reviewed, and academic performance and expected learning outcomes are delineated. The consequence was a clarification of the expectations and educational standards at SSE Riga, on the part of both students and the School. During student self-evaluation conferences, deficiencies in report-writing were also uncovered, thereby leading to changes in academic writing instruction and in course summative assessments.

The hybrid model for student development also benefits SSE Riga greatly by providing opportunities for keeping alumni engaged, in a meaningful and rewarding way. They practise their own mentoring skills. They furnish summer internship and full-time career opportunities. And, not to be overlooked (especially considering that SSE Riga has recently changed it legal status and now charges tuition fees), they begin to view SSE Riga as a possible target for donations and philanthropic support. But what about the students?

## Benefits to Students

To a large degree, SSE Riga faces the old 'pharmaceutical dilemma' – patients will not switch pills if they believe that their current medicine is working. And SSE Riga believes that the current medicine is working. That is not to say that the School is closed to innovations. On the contrary, the evolution of the hybrid model demonstrates clearly that SSE Riga has embraced change. But absent comparative data which demonstrate that student development would occur without the activities, SSE Riga will continue to embrace (and modify) the hybrid model for student development.

Anecdotally, the hybrid model for student development is effecting change in the students. Indeed, the activities require dialogue between students, instructors, staff members, and alumni, which subsequently leads to a culture of openness and trust. They kindle a culture of learning, rather than a culture of grades. They push students to take responsibility for their own learning, a welcome notion in today's generation of students who suffer from an 'entitlement complex'.

Beyond anecdotes, however, data do suggest that the activities of the hybrid model for student development have had an impact on students. Each year, SSE Riga surveys the graduating students, measuring in particular the four attributes of self-confidence, critical thinking, team-work, and social interaction (See Table 4 for a summary of recent year results). The questionnaire uses self-reporting, but the data are also borne out in course formative and summative assessments. In the Laboratory of Entrepreneurship course, for example, the students are required to keep and reflect on a diary of their entrepreneurship activities. The instructor noted the students' ability to provide critique of their own work. John's experience teaching at SSE Riga is that the students there are far more confident than his own students at the University of Michigan, or at other universities at which he teaches.

| Attribute | 2010 | 2011 | 2012 | 2013 | 2014 |
|---|---|---|---|---|---|
| Self-confidence | 5.4 | 5.4 | 5.4 | 5.0 | 7/32.7% |
| | | | | | 6/30.9% |
| | | | | | 5/16.4% |
| Critical thinking | 7/33.9% | 7/21.7% | 7/21.1% | 7/31.4% | 7/38.2% |
| | 6/32.1% | 6/32.6% | 6/43.9% | 6/34.3% | 6/38.2% |
| | 5/19.6% | 5/32.6% | 5/24.6% | 5/14.3% | 5/14.5% |
| Teamwork | 7/37.5% | 7/37.0% | 7/31.6% | 7/11.4% | 7/21.8% |
| | 6/28.6% | 6/28.3% | 6/33.3% | 6/40.0% | 6/38.2% |
| | 5/16.1% | 5/23.9% | 5/22.8% | 5/28.6% | 5/21.8% |
| Social interaction | 6.1 | 5.8 | 5.9 | 5.7 | 5.6 |

*Table 4. Metacognitive skills the graduating class (using a Likert scale in which 1 indicates strongly disagree and 7 indicates strongly agree).*

Viewed in terms of team work and social interactions, the hybrid model of student development exposes students to a much wider array of people and situations. And that cannot be a bad thing, not only in terms of new experiences and new challenges, but also with respect to the skills of social interaction.

## Moving Forward

The hybrid model for student development in its current form dates to 2014. But it has already revealed a few needed changes, due to some unsolved issues inherited from the previous model and some new issues arising. As described previously, advising and mentoring provides feedback about the hybrid model for student development as such. It seems that a significant challenge is to make students understand the importance of academic advising. In particular, it is difficult, especially during Year 1, to keep well-performing students engaged and interested in academic advising. They do not suffer from any academic problems, and consequently perceive academic advising as support for underperforming students. It raises the question, therefore, if academic advising ought to be mandatory for all Year 1 students or if students themselves ought to be able to choose.

Generally, summative assessment is perceived by students as more significant than formative assessment. And what about generative assessment? It remains unknown, but experience would suggest that it is likewise under-valued. Kumar (2007) recommends aligning summative and formative assessments. It would follow, therefore, that the generative assessments of the hybrid model for student development should also be linked more closely with curricular assessments. Similarly, there ought to be tighter communication between the instructors, advisors, and mentors. For example, the e-learning platform is currently available only to academic advisors; access ought to be extended to other appropriate facilitators who are involved in the hybrid model for student development. Moreover, it suggests that a common metrics might also increase the effectiveness of the activities of the hybrid model for student development. As suggested by advisors and mentors, templated reports would allow the establishment of a framework so that student development can be compared.

SSE Riga is also aware that the mentor programme could be improved. Indeed, although there is a great demand from alumni to be mentors (a good problem to have), there is no preparatory training for mentors, except for a short introduction to the program. A communication channel is available in case mentors need support or additional information. But a more structured and mindful approach to mentoring would doubtless increase both its efficiency and effectiveness.

## Conclusion

Assessment has traditionally been very summative in nature, with its purpose essentially to rank students; to identify the 'winners and losers' in education. Formative assessment arose in response, with the goal of adjusting instruction mid-stride in service of those students who were not on track to achieve success. A more modern take on assessment, however, takes a very holistic approach, mandating the education of the 'whole child', in the language of elementary education. Indeed, assessment need not be limited to learning objectives, but also ought to include student development.

The Stockholm School of Economics in Riga, since its founding in 1994, has used a hybrid model for assessing student development, which employs various activities, including peer support, social counselling, and alumni-student mentoring. The hybrid model has benefitted the school by creating a more open atmosphere between students, instructors, and staff members, and by helping to identify areas for improvement in curriculum and school infrastructure. More importantly, the hybrid model has benefitted students, by developing in them an ability to self-regulate their own learning.

## About the Authors

Diana Pauna is the Pro-Rector of the Stockholm School of Economics in Riga, Latvia. She can be contacted at this email: diana.pauna@sseriga.edu

John Branch is Academic Director of the part-time MBA programmes and Clinical Assistant Professor of Business Administration at the

Stephen M. Ross School of Business, and Faculty Associate at the Center for Russian, East European, & European Studies, both of the University of Michigan in Ann Arbor, U.S.A. He can be contacted at this email: jdbranch@umich.edu

## Bibliography

Boston, C. (2002). The concept of formative assessment. Practical Assessment, Research & Evaluation, Vol. 8, No. 9.

CADQ (2013). CADQ Guide: Formative assessment and feedback. Nottingham Trent University, Centre for Academic Development and Quality..

EC (2006). Recommendation of the European Parliament and the Council of 18 December 2006 on key competences for lifelong learning. Official Journal of the European Union.

Erwin, C. (1991). Assessing Student Learning and Development: A Guide to the Principles, Goals, and Methods of Determining College Outcomes. San Francisco, U.S.A.: Jossey-Bass.

Krase, H. & E. Osei-Mensah (2012). Effective Strategies for Supporting Students on Academic Probation. The Advisory Board Company, Washington DC

Kumar, A. (2007). Personal, Academic and Career Development in Higher Education. SOARing to Success. Routledge.

Nicol, D. J.; D. Macfarlane-Dick (2006). Formative assessment and self-regulated learning: A model and seven principles of good feedback practice. Studies in Higher Education, Vol. 31, No. 2, pp. 199-218.

OECD-CERI (2008). Assessment for Learning Formative Assessment. Organiation for Economic Co-operation and Development.

Palmoba, C. & T. Banta (1999). Assessment Essentials: Planning, Implementing, and Improving Assessment in Higher Education. San Francisco, U.S.A.: Jossey-Bass.

Scott, K. (2012). Enhancing Student Support. Peer Support Report. Edinburgh University Students' Association.

Chapter 4

# Introducing Visualisation Into the Assessment of Learning in Legal Studies

Christa Tobler

| Assessment Agency | Student-driven | x | Teacher-driven | |
|---|---|---|---|---|
| Assessment Outcomes | Flexible | x | Fixed | |
| Assessment Focus | Process | | Outcome | x |
| Assessment Context | Transferrable | x | Specific | |

## Introduction

This chapter shows how visualisations through the use of charts add value to assessment of law students' learning outcomes. Law is a highly text-driven field where learners have to digest large amounts of text and where teaching and assessment have traditionally relied exclusively on text. This poses a particular challenge for learners studying in a foreign language, such as international students. Some calls have been made for visualisation to be incorporated into teaching and assessment in the field of legal studies. The purpose of this chapter is to document two practical examples where visualisation through charts was used in legal studies assessment and to discuss the outcome of these against the background of the reactions voiced by the learners themselves. The chapter is based on the hypothesis – rather daring in the legal field – that the use of visualisation as a complementary learning tool is not only possible but indeed beneficial, even in a traditional exam setting.

The chapter begins by describing in more detail the challenge posed by law as a text-driven field, in particular for international students. It then addresses visualisation in legal studies and its notable lack in the realm of assessment. Thereafter, the practical examples are discussed. More specifically, these examples concern the use of two visualisation approaches in different settings and with different groups of learners; first, the creation of charts by the learners in a high-level conference attended by legal experts and, second, the use of decision trees in a written examination taken by international post-graduate students. While this chapter specifically deals with the use of visualisation in the assessment process in legal studies, it suggests that the basic findings are transferrable to other fields where the use of text poses a challenge for learners. Reading this chapter you will gain the following three insights:

1. that visualisation through charts can be usefully employed in legal studies, not only as a complementary tool for teaching but also in the context of assessment, even in the setting of a traditional law exam;

2. that using visualisation through charts in legal studies assessment is not only possible in practice but also adds value to the traditionally verbocentric approach in the legal field, notably through formative potential; and

3. that students not only find it easier to study and to perform in a traditional, summative exam but also subsequently are able to create their own visualisation, which proves a lasting learning effect that goes beyond the content and meaning of the law itself and relates to analytical abilities crucial for legal practice.

## The challenge posed by law as a text-driven field

To work in the field of law means to work with text. Indeed, law as we know it today is based on text and, as such, it relies on language. When I studied law at Zurich University in the 1980s, it was impressed upon the students that the lawyer's tool is language (in the German language of our classes: *"Die Sprache ist das Werkzeug des Juristen"*). Accordingly, we were urged to accept the paramount importance of this tool for our studies and our future profession. At the same time, we were also introduced to the specificities of the legal language, which is often quite particular, both in terminology and style. Indeed, Schmidt-Wiegand (1998) notes that the German legal language has developed into something so specific that it is markedly different from both the language of literature and the standard high-level language. To varying degrees, the same applies to other languages as evidenced, for example, by the fact that there is an abundance of special courses on "Legal English" for non-native speakers.

In addition, as law students we learned quickly that to work in the field of law means to work with a very large amount of text. For example, in European Union (EU) law, the field in which I teach and research, our students are shocked to find that the leading English-language textbooks on the basics of EU law that are used on the graduate and the postgraduate level contain more than a thousand pages of text. A further challenge lies in the fact that, as a rule, these books contain text only, without any helpful additional elements and, in particular, without any visualisation other than certain parts of text underlined with a different colour. As for the law that is being discussed in these books and that forms the primary material of EU legal studies, it is much larger than the textbooks. It not only includes a very large body of Treaty and statutory law but also an even larger body of case law, i.e. court decisions on the validity, the meaning and the application of this law. Moreover, this extensive body of legal materials is constantly evolving, generating ever more text for students to navigate.

It is obvious that this situation, in which there is a strong focus on lots of text in a highly specialised language, poses a challenge for both teachers and students. As Holzer (2011) notes, this is particularly true for international students who simultaneously struggle with a foreign language and a different culture of teaching and learning. My own practical experience confirms this, in particular in postgraduate study where, over the past years, an increasing number of Asian students have enrolled in programmes offered in Europe. Many of these foreign language students find that the verbocentric nature of the law, the sheer volume of text to be digested and the traditionally text-driven approach to teaching and assessment make things extra difficult for them.

This raises the question of whether students could be helped and whether learning could be enhanced through the use of elements other than text. Some seem to think that this is not possible. Several decades after my law studies at Zurich University, Schnapp (2004:39), in his "Style guide for Lawyers", again reverts to the adage of language as the lawyer's tool; adding, however, and emphasising this even graphically, that language is the lawyer's *only* tool (*"Die Sprache ist nicht nur das Werkzeug des Juristen, sie ist das einzige."*). Others disagree, and I am part of this school of thought. In the following section, the discussion of the broader framework of visualisation within legal studies will lead to a hypothesis on the use of visualisation in the specific context of assessment.

## Visualisation in legal education: context and hypothesis

### Visualisation in legal teaching and the "charts approach"

Writing about law in a digital world, Katsh (1995:154) stated already 20 years ago that we live *"in an increasing visual world and are exposed to ever-growing quantities of pictures, images, icons, charts, figures, graphs, scales, tables, diagrams, maps, sketches blueprints, and colourful and animated graphics."* The author then raised the question of what impact this will have on a text-oriented enterprise such as law. Indeed, authors such as Röhl & Ulbrich (2007), Bergmans (2009) and Brunschwig (2014, with further references to this author's previous writing) have long argued in favour of moving beyond verbocentrism in order to conceive law as a textual phenomenon that may also include visual elements.

To some degree, a practice of visualising law has already emerged. Brunschwig (2014) distinguishes different modes, both outside the legal context such as in art (for example, pictures of Justice) and within, such as in legislative texts, court judgments, research and education. With respect to education, the author mentions a number of concrete examples, among them a teaching tool developed for legal education in the field of EU law by the author of this chapter together with a colleague (Tobler & Beglinger, 2013).

This tool is based on what we term the "charts approach". As we explain on our project website and also in an article on the making of charts (http://www.eur-charts.eu/project/understanding-the-charts-method; Beglinger & Tobler, 2008), the charts approach is grounded in the conviction that, in a changing world, teaching and knowledge sharing methods must cater to a new generation's needs. In this context, we refer to the "Generations Internet, iPod, Executive Summary and Global Village" in the following manner:

+ the Generation Internet expects to find the most relevant information on a single page and then to follow hyperlinks to suit individual needs;

+ students of the Generation iPod are used to exercise control through hierarchic menus and thus understand and memorise graphic structures faster than mere texts;

+ in the business community, the Generation Executive Summary expects short and concise documents, which easily present the most relevant information;

+ finally, the Generation Global Village appreciates graphic representations because they use less textual language and are therefore more suitable to use for cross-border communication.

It seems obvious that these new generations of learners are not well served by the purely textual approach that has characterised legal materials and teaching resources. The charts approach therefore attempts to include visualisation by using pictures and graphic elements in presenting legal content and the relation between legal concepts. Charts show certain commonalities with concept maps, defined by von der Heidt (2015:288) as *essentially a graphical tool for organising and representing knowledge* (see further Kinchin, 2014). In our charts, legal concepts are visually put into a logical relationship to each other, based on the underlying logic within the law itself (Hoogwater, 2009).

Charts typically present content moving from top to bottom and from left to right. Mielke & Wolff (2010) note that this manner of visualisation corresponds to the Latin way of reading and writing. In this context, the question may be raised of whether the charts are equally accessible for students who in their mother tongues read from right to left. However, in practice I have found that my Chinese and Japanese students have no problems with the approach reflected in the charts. One reason for this might be the fact that – unlike, for example, Arabic speakers – Chinese and Japanese students are used to the left to right approach from writing in their own languages (when they write Chinese characters or Japanese kanji, they also construct the character from top to bottom and from left to right).

The following is an example of a chart from our book that makes use of a metaphor. The chart deals with the function of, and the relationship between, the foundational texts of the EU. The topic sentence that accompanies the chart states: "Following the Lisbon revision, there are three fundamental EU texts of equal value, namely two treaties (the Treaty on European Union [TEU] and the Treaty on the Functioning of the European Union [TFEU]) and one Charter (the Charter of Fundamental Rights). In the picture of a planet, they represent the core, the mantle and the crust of the planet." In a previous chart in the book, the EU is described as a planet around which the European Atomic Energy Community, a separate organisation that is institutionally linked to the EU, circulates like a satellite.

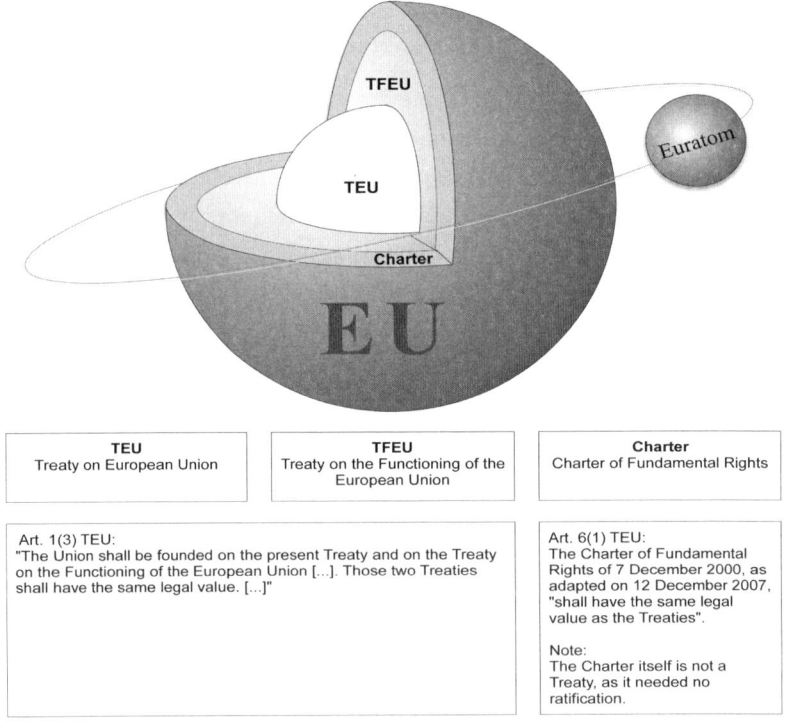

*Figure 1: Tobler & Beglinger 2013:Chart 2/23*

Charts making use of metaphors are intended to use visualisation for memory, i.e. to extend cognition, through the use of a visual artefact, of the relevant issue on a level where the metaphor helps shape understanding and promote the recollection of the legal issue (here the relationship between the three foundational texts of the EU).

A further and particularly common type of chart in our book puts the focus on structure. The following is a simple example.

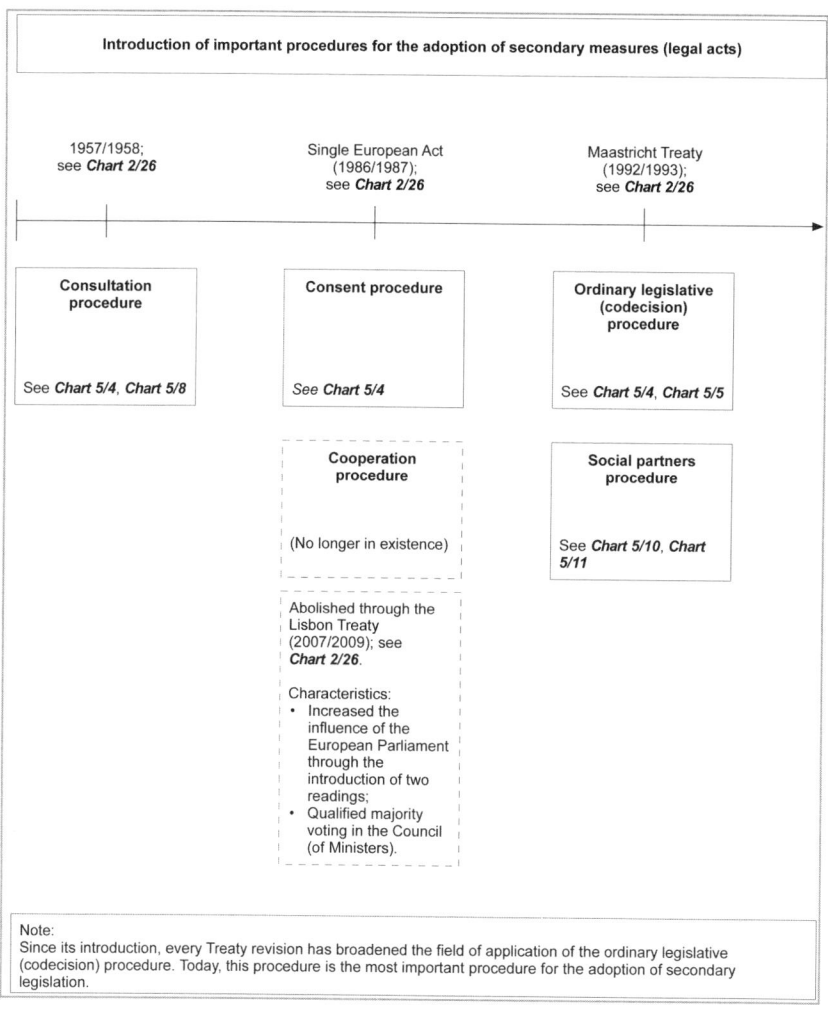

*Figure 2: Tobler & Beglinger 2013:Chart 5/2*

It deals with the development over time of different procedures for the adoption of so-called secondary measures by the EU's institutions, i.e. measures that are intended to complement the EU's primary law (i.e. in particular the above-mentioned foundational texts). The topic sentence that accompanies the chart states: "The procedures for the adoption of secondary measures have developed over time." On a timeline, the chart mentions important Treaty revisions that led to the creation of new procedures, most of which remain in existence today. The information in the chart indicates that this development led to a modernisation of the procedures, for example, with respect to the degree of democracy (such as through an increased influence of the European Parliament). The details are further explained in subsequent charts (namely those to which this chart refers).

Charts such as these are actively used in the classroom during our teaching.

Another specific type of chart, a decision tree, is not actively used in class but given to the students to use when preparing for the exam and when writing the exam. This will be discussed further below, where two practical examples of using charts in assessment are documented. There, the specific nature and function of a decision tree will be explained. Before turning to these examples of innovative assessment, the next section deals with the traditional framework of legal studies assessment. This will lead to my hypothesis, which is that value can be added through visualisation not only in teaching in the field of legal studies but also in assessment.

## The traditional framework of legal studies assessment

Stolker (2014:185), himself a law professor and at present the Rector of Leiden University in the Netherlands, has called assessment "an underestimated topic in our law schools". In saying so, he echoes numerous others (e.g. Sullivan *et al.*, 2007; Rees, 2007; Dedek, 2011; Dany *et al.*, 2008). Indeed, before I embarked on proposing a chapter for the present anthology, I never encountered an academic discussion on this matter within the law faculties where I teach. I therefore first had to situate such assessment within the general theory of assessment, before considering visualisation in its context.

According to Joughin's (2009:16) self-professed "simple definition", assessment is the process of *"[making] judgements about students' work, inferring from this what they have the capacity to do in the assessed domain, and thus what they know, value, or are capable of doing."* Even simpler is the definition by Oakleaf (2009:539) as *"the process of understanding and improving student learning."* Within the range of different types and functions of such assessment, I have come to realise that legal studies assessment has traditionally been summative rather than formative, more individual than collective and to some extent performative, if not authentic.

Stolker (2014) has drawn attention to the present strong summative culture of legal studies assessment and pointed to the need to add formative elements. While in the summative context the assessment process is used to measure what students have learnt at the end of a given unit, formative assessment refers to *"frequent, interactive assessments of student progress and understanding to identify learning needs and adjust teaching appropriately"* (OECD/CERI, 2008:2). According to William (2010:148), the formative method has *"the potential to improve instructional decision-making by teachers, learners and peers"* because it helps the teacher to measure students' understanding while the material is being taught. Dedek (2011) has raised the question of how this could be achieved in the field of legal studies (without, however, proposing an answer).

Legal studies assessment is mostly individual but sometimes collective. The prime example for the latter is the seminar format where presentations and papers are done by groups of students and graded by the professor collectively for the entire group. Where the papers are finalised after the seminar meeting, there is also a formative element in this approach. On an informal level, exercise sessions provide another collective and formative element in law studies but they are usually not linked to a formal assessment of learning. As for the traditional law exam, it remains strictly individual, requiring students to individually produce responses to exam questions.

One favourable element in legal studies assessment is that it often includes performative elements. On this issue, I follow Whitlock & Nanavati (2013) who distinguish between performative and authentic assessment. In the case of the former, students' skills are measured in simulated scenarios. This occurs in particular when students have to deal with case problems or when they engage in moot courts (which also have a formative function). In contrast, authentic assessment, i.e. measuring students' skill acquisition when the need for the skill arises from a real life situation, rarely happens (for example, in law clinics, where students engage in giving advice to people with real legal problems or questions and where there is normally no formal assessment).

Finally, it must be added that, within the above framework, the field of legal studies is just as verbocentric in its assessment as it is in its teaching, as already stated. Assessment is typically based entirely on text, requiring students to respond to questions or tasks by producing text in return. At the same time, even within this traditional framework, the declared aim of law exams has always been to go beyond the testing of a mere superficial knowledge and to ensure that students, when preparing for assessment, adopt a deep approach to learning. Could the use of visualisation in assessment help achieve this aim?

## Hypothesis: added value through visualisation

The hypothesis underlying this chapter is that visualisation through charts can be usefully employed in legal studies, not only as a complementary tool for teaching but also in the context of assessment, even in the setting of a traditional law exam. In addition, such an approach can have a formative effect, thus promoting deep rather than merely superficial learning, as advocated by Marton & Säljö (1976). This is based on the argument that visualisation warrants that both the learner's expectation and the teacher's approach are focused towards stringent and meaningful learning and assessment, which recognises that *"meaning is not something imparted or transmitted from teacher to learner, but is something learners have to create for themselves"* (Biggs, 2003:2). Accordingly, teaching students to visualise and to use visualisation also in the context of assessment may act as a catalyst for learning by adding a complementary learning tool that is beneficial, in particular for those learners who are helped by a visual approach. In the next section, these arguments are analysed against the background of two practical examples.

# Using visualisation in legal studies assessment

## Introductory remarks

While the use of visualisation is regularly advocated for the purposes of learning and teaching in legal studies, as noted above, it is much more rarely suggested or even mentioned in the context of assessment. Indeed, there is virtually no theoretical discussion of this matter: I have been able to find no more than two examples of practical use mentioned in academic writing. The first is the "image exam" mentioned by Röhl & Ulbrich (2007), where the task put to the students includes a picture that illustrates the question put to them. As for the second example, Basak (2011) reports the creation of "wall journals" by groups of students, asking them to show their knowledge through a creative, graphic and pictorial approach.

The present chapter documents, as a further variation, the introduction of charts into the assessment process. As was noted above, charts show certain commonalities with concept maps. According to von der Heidt (2015), the use of concept maps in assessment has been found to be particularly useful in ill-structured subject areas such as educational psychology, psychiatry, teaching and leadership, and her own field, marketing. I would submit that while law is not an ill-structured subject area, there is still the challenge of understanding the (often complex) relationship between different legal concepts, as well as the structure underlying a particular legal issue – skills that are essential for professional legal work.

In the following, two practical examples of attempts to introduce charts as visual elements into the legal studies assessment process, rather than relying exclusively on language, are documented. These examples include, on the one hand, the creation of charts by learners of the highest level (namely experts) and, on the other hand, work with decision trees as a particular type of chart by advanced learners (i.e. university students on the postgraduate level). In the first of these examples, the use of visualisation is very ambitious, on a level that, for practical reasons, is not feasible when working with students in a traditional exam setting. In contrast, the use of visualisation in the second example may appear rather modest at first sight. However, our students' feedback shows that its effect on learning should not be underestimated.

## Example I: assessing knowledge and understanding through the creation of charts by high-level learners

In my experience, one of the best and most sustainable strategies of assessing learning and, by doing so, of securing enhanced learning is to ask learners to create their own charts visualising what they have learned. However, this is an intellectually demanding and very time consuming exercise and using it in a traditional exam setting is simply impossible for reasons of time constraints. Even outside an exam setting, I have found it difficult to use this approach with students, in particular if the student cohort includes international students who are faced with challenges over and beyond those of domestic students, as stated previously. At the beginning of their study programme, to which the second example described in the next section relates, some of our students work practically day and night just to reach the point where they understand the textual meaning of the legal materials they are asked to study. It is difficult for them at the same time to grasp the relationship between concepts and to reflect critically on the broader implications of what they are reading. For students in that situation, the creation of free-roaming graphical representations of concepts is beyond their capabilities, at least in the early stage of their study.

Instead, the first practical example offered in this chapter for assessing knowledge and understanding by creating charts concerns a high-level seminar for academic experts in the field of EU non-discrimination law from various European countries. Held in Giessbach, Switzerland, in September 2009, its purpose was to learn about and discuss the subject of "Equal opportunities in a time of crisis." This example is discussed here only briefly as it does not relate to a traditional setting of learning by students, but rather to learning by high-level experts.

The seminar began with presentations and discussions on the economic crisis (which was in full swing at the time) and on challenging new issues of non-discrimination law against this background. In addition, the programme included a presentation on the subject of "visualising legal concepts through charts", i.e. the concepts behind this approach, its design methods (e.g. the use of graphic structures, pictures and pictogrammes) and the digital tools needed to create charts on a professional level. Following this, the participants formed groups that met several times throughout the seminar to create charts on different subjects related to the seminar theme. The following is an example of the outcome of this collective exercise:

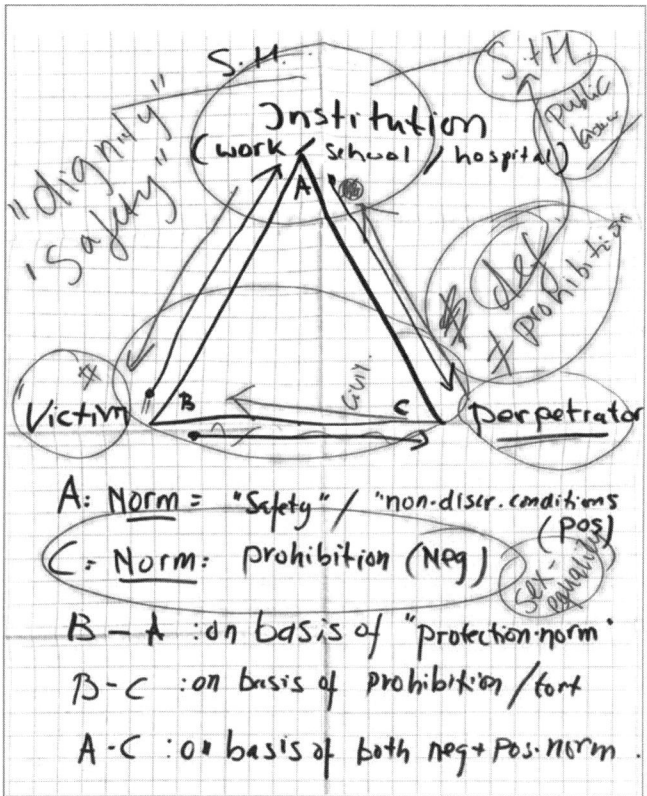

*Figure 3: output of the seminar on "Equal opportunities in a time of crisis"*

In the evaluation, only one participant stated that she preferred not to use this charting technique. The other participants agreed that the process of making charts enhanced their learning experience and at the same time gave them a valuable tool for their own work. However, they also commented on the difficulty of the exercise. One participant found that "*it was much more difficult to do than I had expected beforehand.*" Another commented: "*I did not find the exercise with drafting a chart easy, but certainly useful as it obliges you to focus on the main points of the relevant law and the relations between different subjects.*"

## Example 2: using decision trees in a traditional law exam

In comparison to the above seminar, the second example of using visualisation is much more modest in its attempt to include visual elements in the assessment process. It concerns the written examination for the course "The Internal Market and Harmonisation" (i.e. the core of EU economic law) in the English-language postgraduate study programme on European and International Business Law offered by Leiden University in the Netherlands. The students who enrol in this programme are from all over the globe, including an increasing number of Asian, particularly Chinese, students. For virtually all of the students, the programme is in a foreign language.

The examination comes after ten weeks of intense teaching. It is a traditional law exam where students, at the end of the course, are asked to individually formulate answers in writing to questions put to them in writing. Since "The Internal Market and Harmonisation" course is one of two foundational courses that lay the groundwork for further course work in the programme, it is important to assess the individual students' knowledge and abilities not only during the course (namely through discussions and oral assignments) but also at the very end, to make sure they have indeed acquired the knowledge necessary for the subsequent courses. In other words, it is important to ensure that students actually know and understand certain things (similar for the field of pharmacology, Stupan, this volume). For that latter purpose, the programme board has always felt that there is no valid alternative to the traditional framework of summative, individual assessment in the form of a written examination for these two first courses.

It is obvious that this framework does not leave much room for changes in the style or approach of the exam. However, when I considered how things could be made easier for our international students and how the exam could contribute to a more lasting learning effect at the same time (as advocated by Boud & Falchikov, 2006), the idea arose of giving decision trees a place in case questions.

In legal studies, working with cases (i.e. court cases or case questions) is the closest one can get to learning that approximates the requirements of the students' future legal practice. Case questions are based on fictional but realistic legal problems (an example will be given below). In our class, students are told that working with case questions will be practised in exercise sessions in group discussions and that they should be used in preparing for the exam, which will include them. This is in line with Biggs's (1996) alignment principle according to which the qualities of learning that we are looking for and the performances that need to be confirmed in assessment should be answered already in the curriculum objectives and the teaching activities. At the same time, this approach also includes self- and peer-assessment, the importance of which has also been underlined by Biggs (and also by Boud & Falchikov, 2006).

As for decision trees (also called flow charts), they are a special type of chart that describes the logical structure of a particular legal issue by guiding the user through decision boxes. In logic design, a decision box is defined as a diamond shaped symbol with input path(s) and output paths, the latter being true or false branches (e.g. Kumar, 2008). As such, a decision tree is different from a mere checklist: it adds a visual element that is absent in a mere list of words or sentences.

The approach that lies behind decision trees is crucial for almost any legal rule, as there will always be a logical structure for approaching a given issue, and doing it otherwise will lead to mistakes. Also, it is essential for any lawyer to be able to identify where (i.e. on the level of which element) the legal challenge of a particular case lies. In practice, this knowledge is instrumental for decision-making.

This is where decision trees are intended to help. The following example lists the analytical steps to be taken when applying two fundamental economic law rules of the European Union in the area of the free movement of goods, namely the prohibition of customs duties between EU Member States (Art. 28 TFEU) and the prohibition of quantitative restrictions to the importation of goods between EU Member States

(Arts. 34 and 36 TFEU; this issue is relevant for the exam question quoted below):

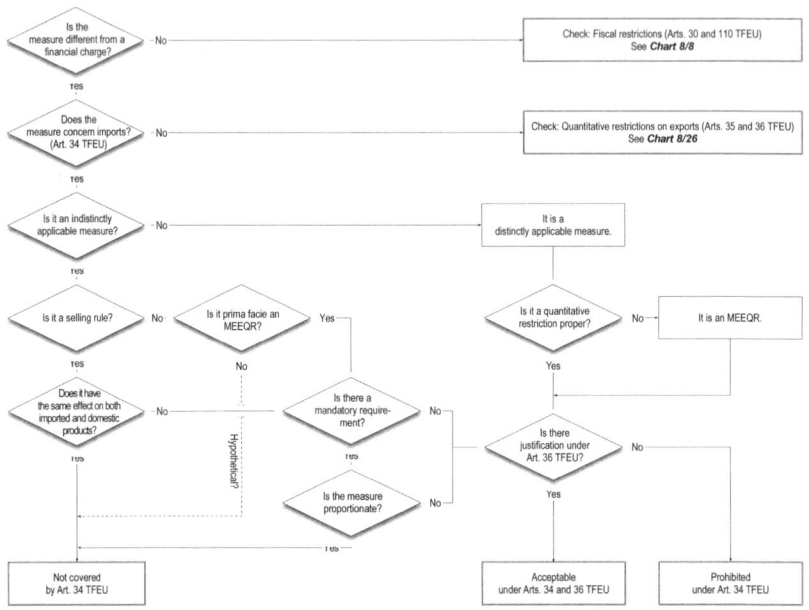

*Figure 4: Tobler & Beglinger (2013:Chart 8/8).*

In academic writing, criticism is sometimes directed at the use of checklists and schemata, including decision trees. The argument is that they may tempt students to rely on the decision tree rather than on the law itself, which should be their primary material (e.g. von Dauner-Lieb *et al.*, 2011). However, while it is essential that students work with the relevant legal texts, I would reiterate that the step-by-step approach reflected in a decision tree corresponds to what is also needed in legal practice. Evidence for this is the fact that employment tribunals in England work internally with charts, in particular to help lay members of the bench understand the structured approach demanded by any particular case in a specialised area of law, but also more generally to train judges and members in structured decision-making.

At the same time, and in line with the above-mentioned criticism, it needs to be emphasised that the flowcharts are not treated by the English judiciary as an authoritative statement of the law. It would seem that our students have understood this, as evidenced in the following statement by one of our Chinese students in the evaluation of our case study (as mentioned below): "For the use of the chart book, students including myself should keep in mind that the chart book is not the primary source of law, as rightly pointed out by our professors. Indeed, it is a very useful tool to understand EU law, but we should always refer back to Treaties, Regulations, Directives and case-law to examine what is really written there. The appropriate reference to the primary source of law would maximise the usage of the charts."

In the above-mentioned "The Internal Market and Harmonisation" course, the function and use of decision trees is explained in class, but active work with them is left to the students. In particular, students are encouraged to use the decision trees when preparing for the exam, both in order to practise case questions and as a form of self-assessment before the exam, to check whether they know and have understood what is "behind" each diamond shaped box. Exams are open book, which implies that the decision trees can also be consulted in the exam. In a recent written retake exam, in order to give visualisation an explicit (though modest) place in assessment, I expressly pointed the students to the possibility of working with the relevant decision tree in the exam setting itself. In other words, I encouraged the students to actively use the decision trees in dealing with case questions, hoping in this manner to give them an additional, not exclusively verbal element to deal with these questions. Here is an example of such a case question, including a reference to the decision tree at its very end:

> *"Stefano and Domenico, two brothers originally coming from the South of Italy, are passionate about football and wine growing. Stefano lives in Greve, a small village close to Florence in the Chianti region, where he produces Solaya wine. For a couple of years, his wine has been receiving the "Gallo Nero" label, a quality mark reserved to the best Chianti wines. Domenico lives in the countryside outside Venice, where he makes Amarone, a wine characterised by its bitter taste and its high alcohol percentage. The wine of Domenico reaches peaks of 16% alcohol. Both Solaya and Amarone are highly appreciated wines, not only in Italy, but*

*also in the rest of Europe. Nevertheless, in some countries, the brothers are confronted with a number of problems when trying to market their wines:*

   *a)   in the Netherlands, the law requires the following label to be attached to all alcoholic drinks sold in the country: 'Drink moderately: too much alcohol is bad for your health', even though there is no EU legislation on this subject;*

   *b)   in Sweden, in order to avoid too high consumption of alcohol during the week, alcoholic drinks may only be sold at the weekend, from Friday 19 hours until Sunday 21 hours;*

   *c)   the Maltese law prohibits the sale of any wine with an alcohol percentage over 14%.*

*Discuss the legal issues raised, with reference to the applicable legal provisions and the relevant case law of the Court. In doing so, explain which element in the various steps of the legal analysis of the question in particular is at issue. You may do so by identifying in your Charts book the relevant element (diamond shaped box) of the decision tree that applies to the present question of your exam."*

The legal issue raised by this question is whether the national rules infringe the EU law on the free movement of goods and, more specifically, the rules on quantitative restrictions on imports, as mentioned in the decision tree reproduced above. Within this framework, each of the above sub-questions relates to a different sub-issue in the decision-tree. For example, sub-question b) concerns a selling rule which, if it meets certain conditions, is outside the field of application of Art. 34 TFEU and, therefore, not forbidden under EU free movement law. On the decision tree reproduced above, this corresponds to the fourth and fifth boxes on the very left hand side. It would be legally wrong to deal with boxes further to the right before having arrived at a no-path of any of one of the two boxes based on selling rules.

In grading the exams, I found that most students correctly identified the relevant legal framework of the question (i.e. Arts. 34 and 36 TFEU) and the relevant legal sub-issue (e.g. the issue of the selling rule). However, in terms of the latter, most students simply referred to the relevant legal concept by giving its name, without referring to the relevant box(es) of the decision tree. I could therefore not see from the answers whether the decision tree had actually been used in the retake exam and whether it had been helpful to the students. When I asked our class (i.e. the full class, as opposed to the smaller number of students who sat the retake exam) about the actual use of decision trees in the exam, the overwhelming majority reported that they had indeed worked with decision trees in the exam and that this had helped them better to understand the case questions and to deal with them. Only one student reported that she preferred to work with traditional checklists without visual elements.

From this, we can conclude that, in an exam setting, the large majority of students were glad to make use of a visual instrument, rather than working with text only. This also emerges from the students' individual comments (put in writing at our request). From the following comments, three distinct issues emerge: first, the usefulness of decision trees in the exam as such; second, their importance for self-assessment when preparing for the exam; and third, the lasting effect of working with charts for subsequent studies and work.

With respect to the usefulness of decision trees in the exam setting, the student comments highlight different functions of this tool. Thus, some students see decision trees as a memory retrieval tool:

+ student from Spain: *"During the exam, I used the decision trees to check that I hadn't missed any step in the analysis. In my opinion, the charts and decision trees are especially useful for people with visual memory, as is my case. I have found it very easy, not only to understand and process the data contained in the charts, but also to store it in my memory and particularly to retain it easier and for a longer period of time than when I study by just reading a text";*

+ student from China: *"In the exam, the decision trees provide us with the outline and steps of analysis, which are straight and clear. In my view, it is an interesting and innovative way to learn law by charts. Charts make complicated theories become visual and easy to grasp. Decision tree is a good tool to recall and summarise relevant knowledge".*

Others appreciate decision trees as a time saving tool that helps avoid time-consuming navigations through the very large textbooks:

+ student from Ukraine: *"When solving the case, I followed the structure of the decision tree provided for in the relevant charts. It made it much easier to understand what the next step would be should the answer to the current question be yes or no and using the charts also saved me a lot of time during exam comparing to the time I would have spent if I had to look for the answers in the textbooks";*

- student from China/Japan (born in Japan of Japanese parents and raised in China): *"One of the biggest challenges in an exam is time management. Without the chart book, I will spend too much time trying to figure out what subject matter is in this case and what exactly shall I write down in the question. In that sense, the decision trees are super helpful. Moreover, they enabled me to provide a comprehensive legal analysis structure efficiently in both challenging EU Law exams";*

- student from China: *"We have open-book exams but time is very limited. Knowing the structure by heart and go back to the decision tree for checking specific points can be efficient and helpful for exams".*

Yet other comments suggest that using decision trees leads to a higher order of learning:

- student from Indonesia: *"For purposes of the exam, I have used decision trees and found that they are very helpful indeed. I personally view that the emphasis of the charts is on depth of understanding much more than breadth of detail. The decision trees are particularly useful because they can provide a quick and easy understanding of the key points of the structure and functioning of the EU law, particularly the free movement issues. They created a quick visual guide through the subject for my learning aid to understand the EU law in a general context. The charts have proven, at least to me, as an effective learning tool in preparing and during the exams. In my view, the Charts book represents a new approach to the study of the EU law. It is different compared to previous years, as stated by some graduates of the programme where they learnt the EU law based on the textbook only (and it was quite challenging they say). Therefore, I consider my generation very fortunate indeed for having this Charts book for our learning in this class. It helps in visualizing and mapping of the EU law, and makes it interesting to learn the EU law";*

+ student from the USA (in fact the only student in the class who studied in her mother tongue): *"For the Internal Market exam, the decision trees were particularly helpful. Each diamond-shaped box led me to a separate relevant chart to help in working through the problem. Each box represents a different level of analysis that requires deeper analysis in light of legislation, Treaty law and case law. In short, the decision trees served as a useful guide in how to structure solving a problem. For the Internal Market exam, I started every question by looking at the decision tree. I would take 2-3 minutes to outline my answer on a scrap piece of paper using the necessary steps from the decision tree to ensure I did not miss a crucial level of analysis. I am a visual and logical learner, and having the steps to work through the analysis is the most helpful form of studying tool for my personal use".*

Apart from the usefulness of decision trees in the exam setting itself, a second issue that emerges from the student comments is the importance of the decision trees in preparing for the exam and in assessing, by the students, whether they have understood what they need to know (i.e. in what we termed self-assessment in the exam discussion):

+ student from Japan: *"In my self-assessment process, the charts book was extremely useful. Because of my limited English ability, I sometimes could not understand all the textbook and cases. In addition, I used the chart book when I discussed with my classmates about the EU law. The decision trees were very useful because they taught us the right track. Without this, our discussions could lead to a wrong place";*

+ student from China: *"The chart book is pretty good in preparing for the exam. It gives me a systematic image of the relevant knowledge instead of lengthy articles, which is very "user-friendly", especially to the non-native speakers, like me. The decision trees are helpful when reviewing the lessons, I like using it after I went through relevant other charts, it helps me to make a good summary and knowledge integration";*

+ student from Belgium: *"The Charts book is in general very helpful. It is the first time in my student career that everything was visually so clear to understand. Normally, I try myself to get the books I need to study and to prepare for the exam, but I never succeeded to make it so pleasant and easy to absorb all the information".*

A third issue is the lasting effect of working with charts for subsequent studies and work. When introducing the charts approach and, in particular, decision trees to our students, we explained to them that though many of them might find it difficult to create their own charts from the beginning, we would hope that through the use of the charts provided by us, they would eventually learn to make charts themselves, for example for future courses and for legal practice. Characteristically, our only native speaker, who was also one of the top students of the class in question, reported that in her previous studies she already used to make her own charts and that, with respect to EU law, she intended to keep and use our charts throughout her practice.

While most of our students had never encountered the instrument of charts or decision trees before, several of them reported that, in the course of their exam preparations, they had taken our decision trees as a starting point and worked to develop them further.

One Chinese student wrote: *"I imitated the charts and drew new detailed decision trees (including references to cases and specific charts and Articles) during my preparations for the exam. I think it is really a good method which is worth learning. There is a Chinese proverb: Teach one to fish is better than giving him a fish. I think we get both fish and fishing from the Charts"*.

Finally, I was particularly pleased to see that, when submitting a proposal for Ph.D. studies, a Chinese/Japanese student created her own charts. The proposed research is a comparative analysis of the law on the free movement of persons within the EU, on the one hand, and the law on migration within China, in particular of the agricultural population, on the other hand. The following is an example of a chart created by this student:

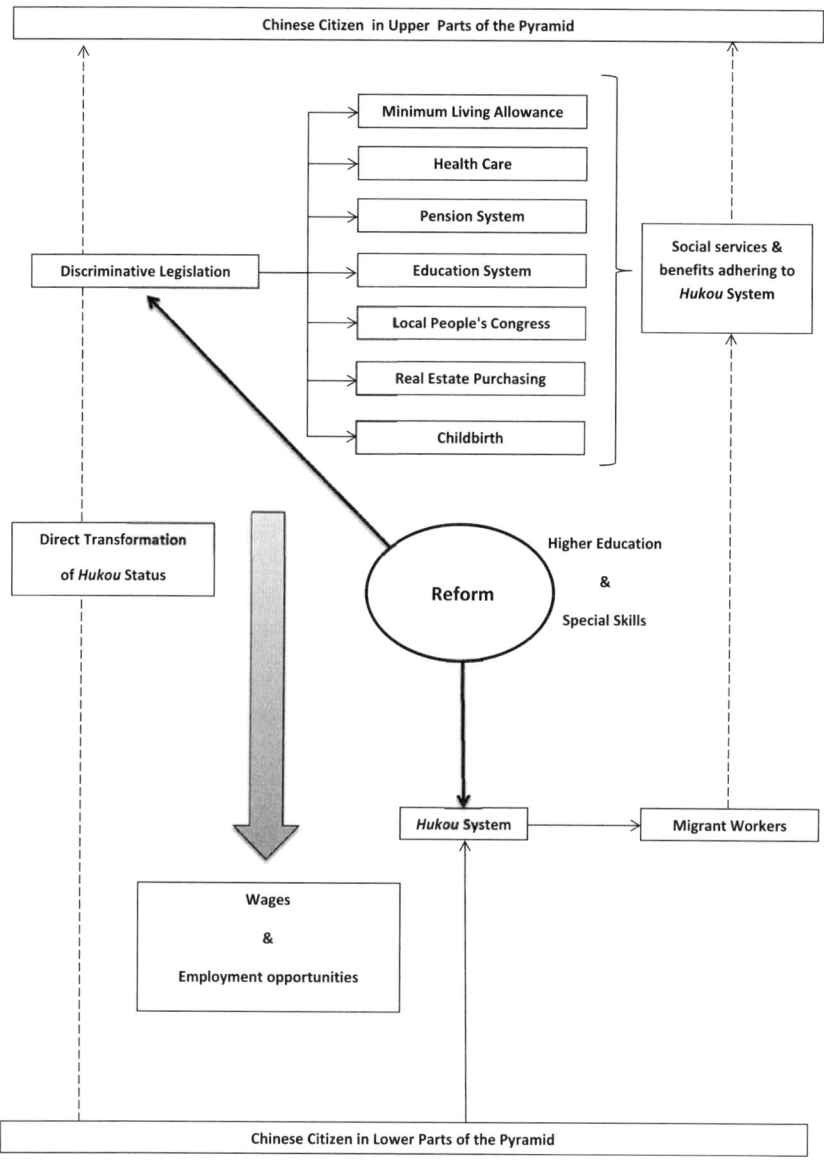

*Figure 4: Chart from the PhD proposal of one of our students.*

# Evaluation and discussion

Overall, I must admit that I have found it difficult to introduce even modest elements of visualisation, through the use of charts, into the process of legal studies assessment. Gibbs (2006) has argued that assignments that are larger, more complex and open-ended, requiring *"performances of understanding"* are more likely to induce the desired approach to study than are short-answer tests or multiple choice questions. However, what I consider the most promising strategy in the context of using charts as visual tools, namely that learners externalise their knowledge by creating their own charts, in my experience is too difficult for the average student at the beginning of a new study programme; in particular for the average international student who, as stated previously, is faced with many more challenges than a domestic student in the same situation.

Moreover, even on the highest level of learners, that of high-level experts, the process of creating charts is perceived as demanding and difficult, though at the same time also as useful to promote deeper understanding. In addition, the process of having learners create their own charts is very time-consuming and it requires a professional introduction that allows learners to develop the specific assessment literacy they need to perform the task (Price *et al.*, 2012). All of this does not seem to fit into an average law course with its structural constraints. In addition, there are other constraints, such as cultural issues (the idea that legal study is text only) and student issues (such as the particular challenges for international students). In their combination and interaction, such constraints may amount to very considerable obstacles to using the creation of charts as an assessment method.

In order to reach its objective, innovation in assessment must take account of such constraints (Hunter, this volume). In this context and in view of the future, it is suggested that more favourable circumstances for the use of visualisation in legal studies assessment could be created. First, new approaches have to be taught. Thus, the students in the second example described in this chapter were able to use decision trees only after having been introduced to them. Similarly, room for the use of visualisation in assessment on a more ambitious level could be created by actively preparing law students through general training on visualisation, and by making such training a part of the curriculum (as tried out by Musumeci & Schmidt, 2011). Second, students could be asked to create their own charts in a collaborative effort outside the class. This would have the double benefit of a collective approach and of avoiding the time constraints of a traditional exam setting or law class (Kinchin, 2014, with respect to concept maps). Finally, even though the majority of the students might not be able to produce very polished charts from the beginning, constructive feedback by the teacher, further coaching and constant practice by the students should help them to improve and refine their work, and to benefit from it for future learning and professional practice.

This latter expectation appears all the more justified, given the experience with our international students when working with charts on a much more modest level and, more specifically, with decision trees, as a complementary tool in the context of (self-)assessment. The example described shows that even such a modest use of visualisation is able to overcome some of the above-mentioned constraints. In particular, it has been found to be helpful for students who are faced with special challenges related to language and culture. In addition, the use of visualisation sows a seed that might come to full fruition at a later point in time. In that context, it is gratifying for a teacher to see that students not only find it easier to study and to perform in a traditional, summative exam, but also subsequently are able to create their own visualisation. This proves a lasting learning effect that goes beyond the content and meaning of the law itself and relates to analytical abilities crucial for legal practice.

## Conclusion

The hypothesis underlying this chapter is that using visualisation through charts in legal studies assessment is not only possible in practice but also adds value to the traditionally verbocentric approach in the legal field, notably through formative potential. The chapter confirms that using charts in assessment is indeed possible, though its form may depend on the level of the learner involved and the framework of assessment. While high-level experts are able to create their own visualisations, our average international student is not able to do this right away. However, practice in class, exercise sessions, exam preparations and the exam itself enables students not only to better deal with the exam but – ideally –to develop the skill to create their own charts.

Visualisation challenges the traditional approach to both learning and assessment. Overall, it may be concluded that working with charts, and in particular with decision trees, helps students to develop what Bork (2011) calls well-versed problem strategies and a general problem solving competence in legal practice. In that sense, I believe that using visual elements in the assessment process is a valuable tool towards assessment for learning in that it engages students in a productive learning activity (Gibbs, 2006) and helps create the life-long, autonomous learners needed to meet the challenge inherent in any living legal system, namely its ever-evolving nature (Sambell *et al.*, 2013).

## Bibliography

Basak, D. (2011). Lern- und methodenorientierte Arbeitsformen. In J. Brockmann; J.-H. Dietrich & A. Pilniok (Eds) *Exzellente Lehre im juristischen Studium*. Baden-Baden: Nomos, pp. 141-153.

Beglinger, J. & C. Tobler (2008). Das EUR-Charts-Projekt oder: The Making of „Essential EC Law in Charts" – Visualisierung eines Rechtsgebietes am Beispiel des Rechts der Europäischen Union. In E. Schweighofer; A. Geist,; G. Heindl & C. Szücs (Eds) *Komplexitätsgrenzen der Rechtsinformatik. Tagungsband des 11. Internationalen Rechtsinformatik Symposions IRIS 2008*, Stuttgart et. Al: Richard Boorberg Verlag, pp. 531-539.

Bergmans, B. (2009). *Visualisierungen in Rechtslehre und Rechtswissenschaft. Ein Beitrag zur Rechtsvisualisierung*. Berlin: Logos.

Biggs, J. (1996). Enhancing teaching through constructive alignment. *Higher Education*, Vol. 32, pp. 347-364.

Biggs, J. (2003). *Aligning teaching for constructing learning*. York: The Higher Education Academy.

Bork, R. (2011). Rahmenbedingungen der Juristenausbildung für eine rechtswissenschaftliche Fachdidaktik. In J. Brockmann; J.-H. Dietrich & A. Pilniok (Eds) *Exzellente Lehre im juristischen Studium*. Baden-Baden: Nomos, pp. 59-65.

Boud, D. & N. Falchikov (2006). Aligning assessment with long-term learning. *Assessment & Evaluation in Higher Education*, Vol. 32, No. 4, pp. 399-413.

Brunschwig, C.R. (2014). On Visual Law: Visual Legal Communication Practices and Their Scholarly Exploration. In E. Schweighofer; M. Handstanger; H. Hofmann; F. Kummer; E.G. Primosch; G. Schefbeck & G. Withalm (Eds) *Zeichen und Zauber des Rechts: Festschrift für Friedrich Lachmayer*. Berne: Weblaw, pp. 899-933.

Dany, S.; B. Szczyrba, & J. Wildt (2008). *Prüfungen auf die Agenda! Hochschuldidaktische Perspektiven auf Reformen im Prüfungswesen*. Bielefeld: Bertelsmann Verlag.

Dedek, H. (2011). Didaktische Zugänge zur Rechtslehre in Nordamerika. In J. Brockmann; J.-H. Dietrich & A. Pilniok (Eds) *Exzellente Lehre im juristischen Studium*. Baden-Baden: Nomos, pp. 41-57.

Gibbs, G. (2006). How assessment frames student learning. In C. Bryan & K. Clegg (Eds) *Innovative Assessment in Higher Education*. London: Routledge, pp. 23-36.

Holzer, F. (2011). Visualisierung im rechtswissenschaftlichen Studium. In J. Brockmann; J.-H. Dietrich & A. Pilniok (Eds) *Exzellente Lehre im juristischen Studium – Auf dem Weg zu einer rechtswissenschaftlichen Fachdidaktik*. Schriften zur rechtswissenschaftlichen Didaktik. Nomos: Baden-Baden, pp. 155-170.

Hoogwater, S. (2009). *Beeldtaalvoorjuristen. Grafische modellenom juridische informatietoegankelijkertemaken*. Den Haag: Boom.

Joughin, G. (2009). Assessment, Learning and Judgement in Higher Education: A Critical Review. In G. Joughin (Ed) *Assessment, Learning and Judgement in Higher Education*. Berlin: Springer, pp. 13-28.

Katsh, E. M. (1995). *Law in a Digital World*. Oxford and New York: Oxford University Press.

Kinchin, I.M. (2014). Concept Mapping as a Learning Tool in Higher Education: A Critical analysis of Recent Reviews. *The Journal of Continuing Higher Education*, Vol. 62, No. 1, pp. 39-49.

Kumar, A. A. (2008). *Switching Theory and Logic Design*. New Delhi: Asoke K. Gosh.

Marton, F. & R. Säljö (1976). On qualitative differences in Learning. I – outcome and process. *British Journal of Educational Psychology*, Vol. 46, pp. 4-11.

Mielke, B. & C. Wolff (2010). Wie sieht man das Recht? Blickanalyse von Rechtsvisualisierungen. *Jusletter IT* 1 September 2010. Online Journal: http://jusletterit.weblaw.ch/en/issues/2010/IRIS/article_82.html [Accessed 31 March 2015].

Musumeci, L. & M. Schmidt (2011). Lernen durch Visualisierung: Ein Erfahrungsbericht aus der Lehre. In Vereinigung Deutscher Rechtslehrender (Ed)*Rechtslehre. Jahrbuch der Rechtsdidaktik*. Berlin: Berliner Wissenschaftsverlag, pp. 173-178.

Oakleaf, M. (2009). The information literacy instruction assessment cycle: a guide for increasingstudent learning and improving librarian instructional skills. *Journal of Documentation*, Vol. 65, No. 4, pp. 539-60.

OECD/CERI (2008). *Assessment for Learning. Formative Assessment,* OECD/CERI International Conference "Learning in the 21st Century: Research, Innovation and Policy". Online Resource: http://.oecd/org/dataoecd/19/31/40600533.pdf [Accessed 31 March 2015].

Price, M.; C. Rust; B. O'Donovan; K. Handley & R. Bryant (2012). *Assessment literacy: the foundation for improving student learning.* Oxford: Oxford Centre for Staff and Learning Development.

Rees, C.A. (2007). The "Non-Assessment" Assessment Project. *Journal of Legal Education,* Vol. 57, pp. 521-529.

Röhl, K.F. & S. Ulbrich(2007).*Recht anschaulich. Visualisierung in der Juristenausbildung.* Köln: Halem.

Sambell, K.; L. McDowell & C. Montgomery (2013). *Assessment for learning in higher education.* London: Routledge.

Schmidt-Wiegand, R. (1998). Deutsche Sprachgeschichte und Rechtsgeschichte seit dem Ausgang des Mittelalters. In W. Besch (Ed) *Sprachgeschichte: ein Handbuch zur Geschichte der deutschen Sprache und ihrer Erforschung,* 2nd ed., 2nd Vol., 1st partial Vol. Berlin & New York: De Gruyter, pp. 87-98.

Schnapp, F.E. (2004). *Stilfibel für Juristen.* Münster: LIT VERLAG.

Stolker, C. (2014). *Rethinking the Law School: Education, Research, Outreach and Governance.* Cambridge: Cambridge University Press.

Sullivan, W.M.; A. Colby; J. Welch Wegner; L. Bond & L.S. Shulman (2007). *Educating Lawyers: Preparation for the Profession of Law.*San Francisco: Wiley.

Tobler, C. & J. Beglinger (2014). *Essential EU Law in Charts.* 3rd ed. Budapest: HVG-Orac.

von Dauner-Lieb, B.; H. Wessel & S. Pernice-Warnke (2011). Das Projekt „Recht Aktiv" – Ein ganzheitliches Konzept für exzellente Lehre im juristischen Studium, In J. Brockmann; J.-H. Dietrich & A. Pilniok (Ed) *Exzellente Lehre im juristischen Studium – Auf dem Weg zu einer rechtswissenschaftlichen Fachdidaktik.* Nomos: Baden-Baden, pp. 185-204.

von der Heidt, T. (2015). Concept maps for assessing change in learning: a study of undergraduate business students in first-year marketing in China. *Assessment & Learning in Higher Education,* Vol. 40, pp. 286-308.

Whitlock, B.&J. Nanavati (2013). A systematic approach to performative and authentic assessment. *Reference Services Review,* Vol. 41, No. 1, pp. 32-48.

William, D. (2010). The role of formative assessment in effective learning environments. In H. Dumont; D. Istance & F. Benavides (Eds) *The Nature of Learning. Using Research to Inspire Practice.* Paris: OEDC, pp. 135-159.

# Chapter 5

# Effective Assessment Strategies for Higher Education Online Courses

Leon Cygman

| Assessment Agency | Student-driven | * | Teacher-driven | * |
|---|---|---|---|---|
| Assessment Outcomes | Flexible | | Fixed | * |
| Assessment Focus | Process | | Outcome | * |
| Assessment Context | Transferrable | | Specific | * |

## Introduction

This chapter provides assessment strategies for distance education courses. The chapter offers and discusses four suggested strategies that will result in not only an accurate overall assessment of distance education students but also enhanced online learning. When reading this chapter, you will gain the following four insights:

1. why using the four strategies for assessment in distance education courses is necessary;

2. how using these strategies can improve learning and retention in distance education courses;

3. how these strategies can strengthen the relationship between the students and the professor;

4. how to increase the student integrity in distance education courses.

In the fall of 2002, there were over 1.6 million students taking at least one online course from degree granting post-secondary institutes in the United States of America. Ten years later, this number has grown to over 7.1 million. This represents a compounded growth rate of 16.1% and is over six times faster than the overall growth rate of the higher education student body (Allen & Seaman, 2014). This large growth in student numbers requires careful thought and informed principles in student management, course design and reliable assessment techniques. Unlike standard face-to-face courses, students may be allowed to digest the course materials at their own pace and take assessments when they feel they are ready, possibly without the scrutiny of a proctor. These issues pose many pedagogical concerns not found in face-to-face classrooms. There must be a radical change in the e-assessment strategies to support the exponential delivery of online courses (Tinoca *et al.*, 2014).

Assessing students is an important aspect of the teaching/learning cycle. Students are judged on how well they have comprehended the objectives in a course. Whether using a percentage scale, letter grade or grade point average, students receive feedback on their work. This feedback should be used as part of the learning so that the student is well aware of their strengths and weaknesses in the understanding of course material. It is of vital importance that the feedback received is a true reflection of the student's knowledge and abilities because the overall assessment may be used to judge pre-requisite knowledge, entry for graduate studies, scholarship and employment opportunities. *"By facilitating the creation of innovative assessment practice, student engagement and motivation can increase and the timely feedback offered by these forms of assessment can enable students to identify their weaknesses, reflect on their performance and improve their study skills"* (Marriott, 2009:239).

As with face-to-face courses, it is important to devise a plan to accurately measure student knowledge in a distance education course without the opportunity to meet the student in person. Professors who may not have taught in this modality may try to use the same instruments and techniques being used in a face-to-face cohort of the same class. The assessment of online coursework will not lend itself to the same assessment tools used in a face-to-face class. Both professors and course designers must understand how best to approach the new paradigm of assessing an online student. They must also understand that e-assessments can be used as a tool to keep students engaged with distance education course materials. Effective online assessment strategies *"must be carefully and systematically planned to require students to demonstrate that learning has occurred by completing a specific piece of work at various stages in the course and be given meaningful feedback"* (Gaytan & McEwen, 2007:126).

## The Challenge of E-Assessments

Assessment techniques used in online courses encompass a wide variety of techniques. These methods vary depending on the course, the professor's comfort level with Internet technologies and the expertise of the teaching assistant. In distance education courses, assessment vehicles must be designed to assess the student, taking into consideration the technologies available. The subject matter expert must decide on the correct number and type of e-assessments to be used. It is then the course designer who will choose the appropriate learning management tools to measure the knowledge of the student from a distance.

Fuegen (2011) recognises the value and flexible option provided by distance education but has concerns with some of its limitations. One of these limitations would be providing a fair assessment of the student that is not only an accurate reflection of the student's abilities but is beyond reproach in terms of the ethical issues involved in assessing students at a distance. The *"age-old concerns about ethical practices in assessment (i.e. cheating) take on new twist in the distance-learning environment. The issue of authorship of student work has always been one that is difficult to resolve, even when the course is taught with traditional methods"* (Abbott *et al.*, 2000:1129). This poses many challenges and creates new opportunities for the student learning experience.

Even though many universities are offering online courses and there is much literature on e-assessments, as shown by the literature reviews compiled by Ridgway *et al.* (2004) and Stödberg (2012), many institutions are using suboptimal methodologies. In a study of distance education courses at both the undergraduate and graduate level, these researchers found that none of the courses in the study were following advice found in literature with respect to distance education assessments. The reason for this finding is the fact that all the courses displayed a low overall usage of the authentic assessment techniques as defined by Meyen *et al.* (2002) such as, collaborative projects, team assessments, individual projects, simulations, case studies, discussions, portfolios, and peer assesment (Kim *et al.*, 2008). If more of these types of assessment techniques were used, the students would have a richer learning experience. In another survey of online assessments, Gaytan and McEwen (2007) found similar results and concluded that many courses did not use a variety of assessment techniques and provided little mechanism for feedback. *"Elements of e- or on- line learning receive less attention by academics and courseware developers alike. One such problematic area is that of assessment"* (Karran, 2004:127). The purpose of this chapter, therefore, is to propose an approach for effective and accurate assessment of students in distance education courses. It begins by discussing the challenges of e-assessment. It then continues by outlining two significant distance education theories. Finally, it describes four strategies that should be used in distance education courses in order to assess students.

## Theoretical Background

To best understand the appropriate assessment strategy for distance education modalities, it is best to frame it within the context of two distance education theories. The first refers to creating an optimal environment in distance education and the second provides a structure for e-assessments.

### *Theory of Transactional Distance*

Moore's (1991, 2007) theory of transactional distance suggests that if learning outcomes in any distance education course are to be maximised, transactional distance needs to be minimised. The theory postulates three interrelated components:

1.  structure – flexibility or rigidity of the instructional methods and strategies used in an e-learning experience (Moore, 1993);

2.  dialogue – a series of interactions having constructive qualities (Moore, 1993);

3.  learner autonomy – the extent to which, the learner rather than the teacher, determines the goals and the learning experiences and the evaluation decisions of the learning programme (Moore, 1993).

This theory defines distance education in terms of physical and psychological separation of professor and student. Transactional distance is impacted by the amount of dialogue present in the course between professors and learners. As communication between professors and students increases, transactional distance decreases (Park, 2011). Transactional distance is at its minimum when dialogue and structure are at their maximum (Moore, 1991, 2007). The challenge of physical distance in e-assessment, as stated by Kearns (2012), can never be completely solved because of the nature of distance education but can be mitigated by reducing transactional distance.

## Framework for E-Assessments

Tinoca *et al.* (2014) developed a framework for e-assessment intended to be used as a reference for instructors developing e-assessment strategies. This framework consisted of four proposed dimensions to be considered in competency-based e-assessment strategies. These four dimensions are:

1. authenticity – derived from the need to focus assessment on competencies;

2. consistency – related to the alignment of developed curricula and learning process;

3. transparency – centred around students and their engagement in the learning process;

4. practicability – assures that the students consider the assessment tasks as doable, relevant and contributing to their learning.

The authenticity dimension emphasises that online assessments are intricate, associated with real life concepts and recognized to be important by students, professors and employers. Consistency ensures that the competences being assessed are in line with the e-assessment strategies being used as well as with the assessment criteria, and the need to use a range of indicators. The transparency dimension encourages student engagement in online tasks and the visibility of the e-assessment strategies being used. Practicability is related to the need of assuring that a successfully implemented e-assessment design takes the needs of the learner into account (Tinoca, 2012).

# E-Assessment Strategy

Many researchers (Anderson & Dion, 2011; Garrison & Anderson, 2003; McConnell, 2006; Pereira *et al.*, 2009) are in agreement with the idea that a new assessment culture needs to be developed to support distance education courses rather than using traditional teaching and learning perspectives. *"Technology, although still under-utilised in assessment and feedback practices, offers considerable potential"* (JISC, 2010:8). Having been involved in the field of distance education for over three decades, as a professor, learner and distance education course developer, I am in the position of suggesting an e-assessment strategy based on my experience with this modality, using distance education-related theories as a foundation.

To illustrate the suggested e-assessment strategies, I will be using examples from a variety of courses and the tools of the learning management system (LMS) used at the university where I teach, BBLearn™. BBLearn™ is the LMS market leader. In a 2014 survey of over 2,500 US post-secondary institutions, BBLearn™ was found to be used at over 35% of the schools and by over 7.6 million students – more than double its nearest competitor (edutechnica, 2014).

## *Strategy 1 – Formative E-Assessments*

Distance education students must stay engaged with the learning process. If this is not achieved, there is the high likelihood that they will drop the course. The function of formative assessment is essentially to assist learners in *"closing the gap between actual and desired levels of performance"* (Black & Wiliam, 1996:543). Formative assessments are supported by the dimension of the authenticity in the e-assessment framework. Tinoca *et al.* (2014) relates authenticity to the similarities between the competences being assessed and the ones required in real/professional life. It should also provide cognitive challenges. This domain emphasises the need for online assessment tasks to be multifaceted, related to real life, and recognised as important by students, teachers and employers.

The autonomy of learners appears to be particularly important to their ability to work in interactive Web environments (Benson & Samarawickrema, 2009) where the opportunities have *"changed the way learners* can retrieve, share and evaluate information" (Benson & Brack, 2009:74). Formative e-assessments can also guide the direction of the course, allowing the student to aid in determining goals and thus supporting learner autonomy as defined by Moore (1993).

Formative e-assessments can be defined as *"the use of ICT [information communication technologies] to support the iterative process of gathering and analysing information about student learning by teachers as well as learners and of evaluating it in relation to prior achievement and attainment of intended, as well as unintended learning outcomes"* (Pachler et al., 2010:716). This is one of the techniques that may be used to keep students engaged and at the same time test their knowledge on course objectives.

Pachler *et al.* (2010) identified current practices relating to formative e-assessment of learning. In their survey, they found that a variety of formative e-assessments were being used by teachers and that the creative use of technology was able to enhance the learning experience. There are a variety of question types that can be facilitated through BBLearn™. In one of these questions types known as 'Fill in Multiple Blanks', students are presented with text containing up to 10 blanks. Each blank can have a maximum of 100 answers and can be scored by BBLearn™. Students complete the sentence by typing the appropriate word or phrase for each blank. For example, in the course, 'Business Statistics I', the formative questions shown in Figure 1 may be used to explore the students' knowledge of standard deviation:

1.  In statistics, the standard deviation, represented by the Greek letter
    _____, is a measure that is used to quantify

    _____.

2.  A standard deviation of zero implies that the data is
    _____ while a large
    standard deviation implies that the data is

    _____.

*Figure 1: Sample 'Fill in Multiple Blanks' questions.*

Karran (2004) compiled an extensive list of formative e-assessments along with their advantages, disadvantages as well as their use and application. A sample of those assessments is shown in Table 1 and provides the reader with examples of instruments that may be used in a distance education course.

| Instrument | Advantages | Disadvantages | Use and Application |
|---|---|---|---|
| Portfolios | Accommodate multiple intelligences; present a cross section of achievements and skills; capture performance data; require critical self-assessment. | Can emphasize presentation over content, require time to compile and assess; creators and assessors need technical skills. | Portfolios are developed using a variety of online tools or computer software products. LMS often have portfolio facilities where learners can gather a range of materials appropriate to the course. |
| Simulations | Require learners to construct knowledge and use metacognitive strategies; allow performance-based Assessment | Can involve complex programming and specific hardware and software. They are expensive tools to design and develop | Run a simulation where there is an aspect of safety involved. Students learning to fly jets or learning to repair elevators might benefit from a simulation. |
| Web publication | In addition to placing print-based texts online and allowing a 'high gloss' presentation medium, this facility could incorporate producing a journal of student work. | As with web page production generally, care is needed to ensure compliance with copyright regulations, and, if preferred, access limited through password protection. | Encourage learners to write and publish articles and assignments in web-based publications allowing for peer and faculty review. |

| Instrument | Advantages | Disadvantages | Use and Application |
|---|---|---|---|
| **Online quizzes** | Can be used as a diagnostic tool to assess the level of student knowledge prior to the course. Instant online feedback is given to learners. | Where quizzes require familiarity with a particular program, there is a danger that IT competence rather than subject knowledge is being measured. | Use regular quizzes online for a small component of final assessment. Quizzes can be used as formative assessment during the course, ensuring sufficient skills and knowledge have been attained. |

*Table 1: Examples of formative e-assessments (Karran, 2004)*

Formative e-assessment is used as a foundation of dialogic feedback with the goal of improving teaching and learning (Hargreaves, 2008). It is also an assessment for learning that occurs throughout the course of instruction with the objective of supporting learning (Oosterhof *et al.*, 2008; Vonderwell *et al.*, 2007). Marriott (2009) reported that over 82% of students surveyed preferred e-assessments testing small portions of the course materials. Formative e-assessment tools may be used to monitor learning and to allow for activities that create learning. Information gathered by formative assessments can not only be used to assess students but can be *"used by teachers, learners, or their peers, to make decisions about the next steps in instruction that are likely to be better, or better founded, than the decisions they would have taken in the absence of the evidence that was elicited"* (Black & Wiliam, 2009:9).

## Strategy 2 – E-Discussions

Keeping students involved in a discussion throughout the distance education course is of vital importance. Dialogue serves as a means to keep student interest in distance education courses and provides a method by which the professor can stay in contact. Dialogue must be purposeful, constructive and valued by each party (Moore, 2000) and used to establish meaningful engagement. Dialogue by learners to learners makes it possible for online students to share in the creation of knowledge. This shared learning, or collective intelligence, had been identified as the most advanced form of instructional process (Kowitz & Smith, 1987; Moore, 1993).

The use of e-discussion, supported by rubrics relate to the transparency dimension (Tinoca *et al.*, 2014), allows students to participate in their learning environment, increasing their commitment to the course and developing a responsibility to others. "*The transparency dimension intends to make the entire competence assessment program visible and comprehensible for all participants. For this reason, it is important that the students are able to understand the basis of their assessment, as precisely as their instructors, requiring them to have a complete knowledge of all assessment criteria and their relative weights*" (Tinoca, 2012:216).

The best technique to ensure student dialogue is through the use of Web-based discussion. Discussions serve as a means to keep student interest in the course and provide a method by which the professor can stay in contact. These discussions can be arranged in many different ways. There may be discussion questions posted by the professor based on each objective, major topic or at the beginning of each course week.

BBLearn™ provides a tool known as 'Discussion Board' to facilitate online discussions. The discussion board can be set up for the entire class to participate or the class can be divided into groups for more focused discussions. BBLearn™ refers to questions within the discussion board as a 'Forum'. A sample forum question from the midwifery course is shown in Figure 2.

---

**History:** H. is a G2P0101 who is at 37.2 weeks by a sure LMP and a 7 week ultrasound. Her cervix was checked yesterday in the office and was 3/60/-2, and the fetus was vertex.
**Subjective:** "I have not slept for 2 days because of all these contractions. I have just not been able to be comfortable. They are every 3 minutes without stop. The bathtub doesn't even help anymore. No, nothing else is going on. I do feel nauseous if I try and eat a large meal. The baby is moving well. I haven't had any headaches or swelling either. Everything is fine except these contractions!"
**Objective:** *Blood Pressure:* 127/78 *Pulse:* 89 *Temperature:* 98.5 *Respirations:* 16
*Contractions* palpate mild with a soft resting tone *External fetal monitoring- Fetus:* Baseline 128 with 5 accelerations of greater than 15 beats per minute for greater than 15 seconds *Woman:* Regular uterine contractions every 3 minutes lasting 40 seconds
**Questions for the discussion board:**
What is your assessment? What are the non-pharmacologic and pharmacologic options that can be given to her at this point? Include the rationale for your choices.

*Figure 2: Example of forum question (Phillippi et al., 2015)*[*]

---

[*] Reprinted from Nurse Education in Practice, Vol 15, Phillippi, J. C., Schorn, M. N. & Moore-Davis, T., The APGAR Rubric for Scoring Online Discussion Boards, Copyright (2015), with permission from Elsevier

It is imperative for the professor to monitor the discussion thread and move the topic forward, just as one would do in a face-to-face classroom. Swan (2002) studied the factors associated with student perceptions of satisfaction and learning in online courses. The results show that interaction with course content, interaction with course instructors and among course participants is of key importance. These discussions must be assessed and graded based on a rubric that includes demonstrating an understanding of core course concepts and an application of knowledge as well as responding to others.

Rubrics must be established to assist the facilitation and assessment of online discussions and will increase the cognitive quality of student postings to promote a deeper and more meaningful understanding of course content. A professor may choose to develop a rubric but many are found in literature. For example, Rovai (2001) provides a rubric based on the quality of the answer and showing evidence of collaborative learning. The online discussion rubric I used in my online courses was by Phillippi *et al.* (2015) and is known as APGAR. APGAR is based on five components: application, professionalism, group work, analysis and rationale, and provides scoring criteria for unacceptable, marginal and proficient performance. Application of knowledge in the course material is important to assess. Discussion boards give students an opportunity to apply the knowledge received from readings to carefully constructed discussion questions and to demonstrate their mastery of course content. The professionalism component of the rubric encourages students to respond to other students in a professional manner. Feedback to others must be substantive and demonstrate depth of understanding. The group work component scores timely and thoughtful participation in the discussion board. Students are expected to provide on-time and high quality submissions. The analysis component assesses whether students can analyze content in order to gain a better understanding. The rationale component of the rubric guides students to apply and cite high quality sources.

The APGAR rubric is easy to use, sets high expectations and provides clear indications of course objective knowledge. It lists grading criteria and establishes clear expectations that can be made consistent with curricular goals and encourages the students to meet course objectives. An excerpt of APGAR rubric is shown in Figure 3.

| Criteria | Unacceptable | Marginal | Proficient |
|---|---|---|---|
| **APPLICATION** Includes and applies relevant course concepts or materials correctly. | Did not explain course concepts or materials. | Summarized relevant course concepts, theories or materials. | Applied relevant course concepts or materials correctly. |
| **PROFESSION-ALISM** Responds to fellow learners, relates the discussion to relevant course concepts and provides substantive feedback. | Did not respond to fellow learners. Responded in a derogatory or deprecating manner. | Responded to fellow learners relating the discussion to relevant course concepts. | Encouraged depth of thought and interaction. Actively listened to & valued the opinions of others. |
| **GROUP WORK** Contributes to the group task. | Did not participate or did not offer substantive contributions to the group task. | Contributed to the group task, but work was minimal or inadequate. | Consistently participated in the group within provided time frames. |
| **ANALYSIS** Analyzes the application of knowledge with changing conditions and conflicting resources. | Stayed at knowledge and application level of content without analyzing changing conditions that influence management decisions | Course concepts or materials were analyzed through a variety of methods including compare/contrast based on changing conditions. | Included personal experience as a springboard for greater discussion & inquiry while placing emphasis on evidence. |
| **RATIONALE** Provides references to support position as applicable. | Citation of sources not provided. | Provided scholarly citations when indicated most of the time with few errors in citation format. | Regularly applied and cited scholarly sources. |

*Figure 3: APGAR discussion board rubric (Phillippi et al., 2015)*

_____

* Reprinted from Nurse Education in Practice, Vol 15, Phillippi, J. C., Schorn, M. N. & Moore-Davis, T., The APGAR Rubric for Scoring Online Discussion Boards, Copyright (2015), with permission from Elsevier

Reading and commenting on discussion board posts can significantly increase a professor's workload. BBLearn™ allows students to gain access to the course site with teaching assistant privileges, allowing them to moderate the discussion without the ability to alter any of the course materials. The use of students as moderators can help and has been seen to remove any hesitation from students who may be hesitant to respond to a professor. In some cases, having students as moderators has been seen to improve the quality of the discussion. *"It was found that such student involvement promoted increased cohesion and structure to the discussions. Furthermore, interaction and participation was increased"* (Zingaro, 2012:161). The professor acts as a guide to the student moderators and is available for clarifications and elaborations.

Online discussions have benefits of significant pedagogical value. *"Its ability to promote text-based communication for the purpose of discourse can support the construction of knowledge, as learners formulate their ideas into words and build on these ideas through responses from others. The opportunity for reflective interaction can be encouraged and supported, which is a feature not often demanded in traditional classroom settings"* (Rovai, 2000:146).

## Strategy 3 – Personalised E-Assessment Design

In the early days of distance education, assessments were designed to mimic those given in traditional face-to-face classrooms. These assessments were given to the entire cohort and it was the responsibility of the learner to use the results as a guide for further learning. Technology used to support distance education has changed vastly from the days of postal-based correspondence schools to modern Internet technologies. These technologies can be harnessed in such a manner that the results of e-assessments can be used to meet the learning needs of the student. A study by O'Donnell *et al.* (2012) found that the majority of academics surveyed agreed that the use of personalised e-learning activities would enhance the learning experience of students.

Relating the personalised e-learning activities strategy to the theories, the practicality dimension of the e-assessment framework fits with the personalisation. It dictates that the assessment takes into account the learners' prior knowledge and competencies (Tinoca *et al.*, 2014) and argues that *"this dimension is particularly important when designing a competence assessment program*" (Tinaco, 2012:216). Transactional distance theory states that greater structure results in more transactional distance (Moore & Kearsley 2005). Structure must be carefully crafted by course design experts so that the distance education course can accommodate and be responsive to each learner's individual needs without lessening autonomy and dialogue. Course structure was identified as one of the main considerations when designing distance education courses (Lister, 2014).

A personalised Web experience provides an environment that "*educational systems of the future must respond to learner differences dynamically as the learning process evolves and not necessarily be based on predetermined programs*" (Saba, 2005:264). As shown in Figure 4, technology can be used to create a personalised learning experience by providing feedback to the student based on the outcome of the assessment and lead the learner to the next appropriate module.

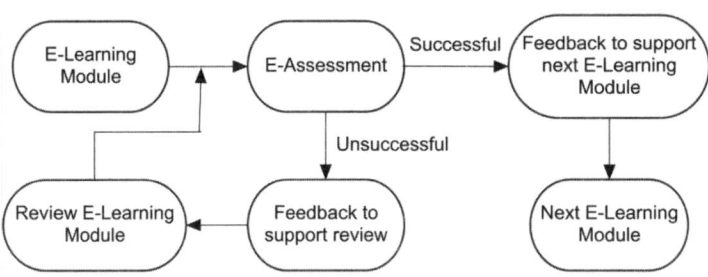

*Figure 4: The relationship between e-assessment and effective learning, (JISC, 2007 adapted)*

In the 'Canadian Air Law' course I teach, students are required to score a minimum average of 80% on a series of quizzes in any section of air law objectives without scoring less than 70% in any one quiz within a section. When these conditions are met, the student moves to the next section of laws. If these standards are not met, learners must review the section of laws by studying a remedial online unit and then re-take another quiz. BBLearn™ offers a facility known as 'Adaptive Release' that allows for the course designer to make content available to the student under a set of conditions. These conditions can be applied to specific users, groups or grade scores based on a range of values on any given set of assignments.

## Strategy 4 — Summative E-Assessments

Summative assessments are given at the end of an academic unit, after some defined period of the course or at the end of term. They are designed to judge the extent of students' learning of the material in a course, for the purpose of assessing student progress or for studying the effectiveness of a curriculum (Black & Wiliam 1996; Hargreaves, 2008).

A unit, midterm, final exam or other type of ending assessment is more than a method to test student knowledge. As the structure of a course sets the ways in which students can make their own interpretations of the what, how, and why questions with respect to the tasks they are asked to accomplish (Moore, 2007), a capstone assessment tool can add additional structure to help minimise the transactional distance. If the structure is loose, the students have greater opportunities for making their own interpretations.

Tinoca (2014) describes one of the criteria of the consistency dimension as instruction-assessment alignment, which is used to ensure that there is agreement between the work developed during the instruction and the assessment tasks being used. The dimension of consistency "*emerges as an answer to the traditional demands for validity and reliability ... It takes into account that the assessment of competences requires the implication of a variety of assessment methods, in diverse contexts ... as well as the adequacy of the employed strategies*" (Tinaco, 2012:215).

As assessment of students' work is always necessary, it should include summative assessment (Bergström, 2010) as a structured pillar in the course. In a study by Marroitt (2009), the majority of students said they preferred online summative assessments to traditional assessments and they favoured being tested on smaller sections of the material. Almost all of the students agreed that this type of testing improved their learning and encouraged them to study more throughout the course. Summative assessments ensure that the desired goals of learning have been met, or verify that the required level of ability has been achieved (Challis, 2005). It is also important that the vehicle used is as close as possible to the same assessment tool used in a similar face-to-face cohort. This will ensure that the distance education students are on par with the students studying in a traditional environment.

As honesty is an issue in distance education, it is very important that online students are given at least one major summative assessment in a proctored environment where their identity can be authenticated. This is supported by best practices for distance education developed by Western Cooperative for Educational Telecommunications (2002) on behalf of US regional accrediting associations. This document is used by many accrediting bodies within and outside the USA as a guideline for distance education programs. The document indicates that *"when examinations are employed (paper, online, demonstrations of competency, etc.), they take place in circumstances that include firm student identification"* (Western Cooperative for Educational Telecommunications, 2002:13). Although the UK education system thought there may have been a lack of venues to carry out these types of e-assessments, Mogey (2010) suggested that large examination venues be created so that cheating can be eliminated. In my own experience, approved proctors, local libraries or universities may be willing to authenticate the learner and provide a secure environment for the online student to write a summative e-assessment.

## Discussion

Face-to-face assessments have had the time to develop and have been refined to accurately assess the face-to-face student. The number of students enrolled in distance education classes is increasing and Internet technologies have been advancing at exponential rates. E-assessments must be carefully considered as it is important to have effective strategies to ensure fair, comprehensive and accurate assessments for online students. A variety of e-assessments should be used in distance education courses (see Stupans, this volume). These can include exams, quizzes, projects, portfolios, self-tests, peer assessments, and discussion boards. In order to maximise dialogue , there should be a high level of interaction between students and faculty and among peers. A study by Marriott (2009) found that over 70% of students agreed or strongly agreed that they prefer online assessments rather than traditional methods and that e-assessment has a positive impact on student engagement and in the practice of teaching and learning.

Rubrics need to be supplied to the learner and timely, meaningful feedback is of vital importance (Gaytan & McEwen, 2007). Employing rubrics can reduce professor workload and their use is strongly recommended.

Rubrics can also aid in providing timely feedback and are listed as one of the main considerations when designing distance education courses (Lister, 2014).

There are a many methods by which a professor can assess and stay in touch with an online learner outside the confines of a LMS. Social media has proven to not only allow users to communicate with each other but can also be used in distance education courses as an assessment platform. Technology for assessment purposes can use a variety of tools, some of which may already be in use by the professor. For example, Skype™ can be used to conduct face-to-face consultations, Pinterest™, Flickr™, and Instagram™ for picture repositories, SlideShare™, YouTube™ and Google Slides™ for presentations and Mahara™ for e-portfolios (see Hager, this volume).

E-learning technologies are advancing at a rapid pace. *"Because of the physical separation of students and the instructor, conscious efforts are required to engage students"* (Centner, 2014:234). Technology offers may advantages in online assessments including immediate feedback, efficient submission and marking systems, use of creative media, improved learner engagement and the ability to capture a wider set of skills that cannot easily be assessed by other means (JISC, 2010).

## Conclusion

Table 2 lists the e-assessment strategies and aligns them with their supporting theories.

| Strategy | E-Assessment Framework Dimension | Transactional Distance Component |
|---|---|---|
| Formative | Authentication | Autonomy |
| E-Discussion | Transparency | Dialogue |
| Personalisation | Practicality | Structure |
| Summative | Consistency | |

*Table 2: E-Assessment Strategy Summary.*

The four strategies presented in this paper will provide the distance educator with a robust set of tools that will enable an accurate assessment of students at a distance. The strategies support each of the four Tinaco *et al.* (2014) e-assessment framework dimensions and the three Moore (1991, 2007) transactional distance components. *"Formative assessments allows us to gauge the progress attained as far as objectives or competencies are concerned, it provides instructors and students alike with information about what needs to be improved and what is already known"* (Tinaco *et al.*, 2014:655). Employing formative assessments ensures important concepts are assessed and students have a sense of autonomy. E-discussion engages the students with the learning process and provides a facility to support dialog. Personalisation of the e-assessments supports the notion of tailoring the learning to the needs of the student and providing structure. Lastly, summative e-assessment confirms that course competencies are being assessed and provides a vehicle for authenticating the online student. *"Summative assessment performs a judgement about what the student learned enabling their accreditation"* (Tinaco *et al.*, 2014:655).

E-assessment technologies are still being advanced and therefore it is important to have strategies in place to ensure fair, comprehensive and accurate assessment tools and ensure authentication of the online student. *"Becoming knowledgeable about online learning and assessment is crucial at a time when there is an increased demand for accountability, growth, and excellence in educational institutions"* (Gaytan & McEwen, 2007:130).

## About the Author

Leon Cygman is the Chair of General Management, Human Resources and Aviation at Mount Royal University, Calgary. Alberta, Canada. He can be reached at this email: lcygman@mtroyal.ca

## Bibliography

Anderson T. & J. Dron (2011). Three Generations of Distance Learning Pedagogy. *The International Review of Research in Open and Distributed Learning*, Vol. 12, No. 3. Online Resource: http://www.irrodl.org/index.php/irrodl/article/view/890/1663 [Accessed on 25 March 2015].

Abbott, L.; H. Siskovic; V. Nogues & J. G. Williams (2000). Learner Assessment in Multimedia Instruction: Considerations for the Instructional Designer. In D. A. Willis; J. Price & J. Willis (Eds.) *Society for Information Technology & Teacher Education International Conference 2000*. Chesapeake, VA: Association for the Advancement of Computing in Education (AACE), pp. 1126-1131.

Allen, I. E. & J. Seaman (2014). *Grade Change: Tracking Online Education in the United States*. Babson Survey Research Group. Online Resource: http://www.onlinelearningsurvey.com/reports/gradechange.pdf [Accessed on 29 December 2014].

Benson, R. & C. Brack (2009). Developing the scholarship of teaching: What is the role of eteaching and learning? *Teaching in Higher Education*, Vol. 14, No. 1, pp. 71–80.

Benson, R. & G. Samarawickrema (2009). Addressing the Context of E-Learning: Using Transactional Distance Theory to Inform Design. *Distance Education*, Vol. 30, No. 1, pp. 5-21.

Bergström, P. (2010). Process-Based Assessment for Professional Learning in Higher Education: Perspectives on the Student-Teacher Relationship. *The International Review of Research in Open and Distributed Learning*, Vol. 11, No. 2. Online Resource: http://www.irrodl.org/index.php/irrodl/article/view/816/1544 [Accessed on 4 January 2015].

Black, P. & D. Wiliam (1996). Meanings and Consequences: A Basis for Distinguishing Formative And Summative Functions of Assessment? *British Educational Research Journal*, Vol. 22, No. 5, pp. 537-548.

Black, P. & D. Wiliam (2009). Developing the Theory of Formative Assessment. *Educational Assessment, Evaluation & Accountability*, Vol. 21, No. 1, pp. 5–31.

Centner, T. J. (2014). Structuring a Distance Education Program to Attain Student Engagement. *NACTA Journal*, Vol. 58, No. 3, pp. 230-235.

Challis, D. (2005). Committing to Quality Learning Through Adaptive Online Assessment. *Assessment and Evaluation in Higher Education*, Vol. 30, No. 5, pp. 519–527.

Pachler, N.; C. Daly; Y. Mor & H. Mellar (2010). Formative E-Assessment: Practitioner Cases. *Computers & Education*, Vol. 54, No. 3, pp. 715–721.

Edutechnica (2014). *LMSs by the Numbers – Spring 2014 Updates*. Online Resource: http://edutechnica.com/2014/05/26/lms-by-the-numbers-spring-2014-updates/ [Accessed on 15 March 2015].

Fuegen, S. (2012). The Impact of Mobile Technologies on Distance Education. *TechTrends*, Vol. 56, No. 6, pp. 49-53.

Hargreaves, E. (2008). Assessment. In G. McCulloch and D. Crook (Eds.) *The Routledge International Encyclopedia of Education*. New York: Routledge, pp. 37–38.

JISC. (2007). *Effective Practice with E-Assessment: An Overview of Technologies, Policies and Practice in Further and Higher Education*. Online Resource: http://www.webarchive.org.uk/wayback/archive/20140615085433/http://www.jisc.ac.uk/media/documents/themes/elearning/effpraceassess.pdf [Accessed on 31 January 2015].

JISC. (2010). *Effective Assessment in a Digital Age: A Guide to Technology-Enhanced Assessment and Feedback*. Online Resource: http://webarchive.nationalarchives.gov.uk/20140702233839/http:/www.jisc.ac.uk/media/documents/programmes/elearning/digiassass_eada.pdf [Accessed on 25 March 2015].

Garrision, R. & T. Anderson (2003). *E-learning in the 21-Century: A Framework of Research and Practice*. London: Routledge.

Gaytan, J. & B. McEwen (2007). Effective Online Instructional and Assessment Strategies. *American Journal of Distance Education*, Vol. 21, No. 3, pp. 117-132.

Karran, T. (2004). On-Line Assessment for E-Learning: Options and Opportunities. In T. Latomaa; J. Pohjonen; J. Pulkkinen; & M. Ruotsalainen (Eds). *eReflections – Ten years of Educational Technology Studies at the University of Oulu*. Oulu: Oulu University Press.

Kearns, L. R. (2010). Student Assessment in Online Learning:
Challenges and Effective Practices. *MERLOT Journal of Online Learning and Teaching*, Vol. 8, No. 3, pp. 198-208. Online Resource: http://jolt.merlot.org/vol8no3/kearns_0912.pdf [Accessed on 20 March 2015].

Kim, N.; M. J. Smith & K. Maeng (2008). Assessment in Online Distance Education: A Comparison of Three Online Programs at a University. *Online Journal of Distance Learning Administration*, Vol 11, No 1. Online Resource: http://www.westga.edu/~distance/ojdla/spring111/kim111.html [Accessed on 18 March 2015].

Kowitz, G. T. & L. C. Smith (1987). Three Forms of Instruction. *Journal of Educational Technology Systems*, Vol. 15, No. 4, pp. 419–429.

Lister, M. (2014). Trends in the Design of E-Learning and Online Learning. MERLOT Journal of Online Learning and Teaching Vol. 10, No. 4, pp. 671-690. Online Resource: http://jolt.merlot.org/vol10no4/Lister_1214.pdf [Accessed on 20 March 2015].

Marriott, P. (2009). Students' Evaluation of the Use Of Online Summative Assessment On An Undergraduate Financial Accounting Module. *British Journal of Educational Technology*, Vol. 40, No. 2, pp. 237–254

McDowell, L. (2006). *E-Learning Groups and Communities*. Berkshire, UK: Open University Press.

Meyen, E. L.; R. J. Aust; Y. N. Bui & R. Isaacson (2002). Assessing and Monitoring Student Progress in an E-Learning Personnel Preparation Environment. *Teacher Education and Special Education*, Vol, 25, No. 2, pp. 187-198.

Mogey, N. (2010). *What is it That is Really Acting as a Barrier to Widespread Use of Summative E-Assessment in UK Higher Education?* Proceedings of 13th CAA International Computer Assisted Assessment Conference. Southampton: University of Southampton. Online Resource: http://caaconference.co.uk/pastConferences/2010/Mogey-CAA2010.pdf [Accessed on 19 March 2015].

Moore, M. G. (1993). Theory of Transactional Distance. In D. Keegan (Ed.) *Theoretical Principles of Distance Education*. London, Routledge, pp. 22-38.

Moore, M. G. (2007). The Theory of Transactional Distance. In M. G. Moore (Ed.), *Handbook of distance education, 2nd Ed*. New York: Routledge, pp. 89-105.

Moore, M. G. & G. Kearsley (2005). *Distance Education: A Systems View*. Belmont, CA: Wadsworth.

O'Donnell, E.; M. Sharp; V. Wade & L. O'Donnell (2010). *Academics' Views on Personalised e-Learning in Higher Education*. ICEP 2012: International Conference on Engaging Pedagogy, Institute of Technology Blanchardstown, Dublin, Ireland, December, 2012.

Oosterhof, A.; R. M. Conrad & D. P. Ely. (2008). *Assessing Learners Online*. New Jersey: Pearson.

Park, Y. (2011). A Pedagogical Framework for Mobile Learning: Categorizing Educational Applications of Mobile Technologies into Four Types. *International Review Of Research In Open & Distance Learning*, Vol. 12, No. 2, pp. 78-102.

Pereira, A.; I. Oliveira; I. Tinoca; L. Amante; M.J. Relvas; M.C. Pinto & D. Moreira (2009). Evaluating Continuous Assessment Quality in Competence-Based Education Online: The Case for the E-Folio. *European Journal of Open, Distance and E-Learning*, Vol. 2. Online Resource: http://www.eurodl.org/materials/contrib/2009/Pereira_Oliveira_Tinoca_Amante_Relvas_Pinto_Moreira.pdf [Accessed on 25 March 2015].

Phillippi , J. C.; M. N. Schorn & T. Moore-Davis (2015). The APGAR Rubric for Scoring Online Discussion Boards. *Nurse Education in Practice*, Vol 15 [In Print].

Ridgway, J.; S. McCusker & D. Pead (2004). *Literature Review of E-Assessment*. Bristol: futurelab. Online Resource: http://archive.futurelab.

org.uk/resources/documents/lit_reviews/Assessment_Review.pdf [Accessed on 18 March 2015].

Rovai, A. P. (2000). Online and Traditional Assessments: What's the Difference? *Internet and Higher Education*, Vol. 3, No. 3, pp 141-151.

Saba, F. (2005). Critical Issues in Distance Education: A Report From the United States. *Distance Education*, Vol. 26, No. 2, pp. 255–272.

Smidt, E.; B. McDyre; J. Bunk; R. Li & T. Gatenby (2014). Faculty Attitudes about Distance Education. *The IAFOR Journal of Education*, Vol. 2, No. 2, pp. 181-210.

Stödberg, U. (2012). A Research Review of E-Assessment. *Assessment & Evaluation in Higher Education*, Vol. 37, No. 5, pp. 591–604.

Swan, K. (2002). Building Learning Communities in Online Courses: The Importance of Interaction. *Education, Communication & Information*, Vol. 2, No. 1, pp. 23-49.

Tinoca, L. (2012). *Promoting E-Assessment Quality in Higher Education: A Case Study in Online Professional Development*. International Conference on Information Communication Technologies in Education, pp. 213-223.

Tinoca, L.; A. Pereira & I. Oliveira (2014). A Conceptual Framework for E-Assessment in Higher Education: Authenticity, Consistency, Transparency, and Practicability. In S. Mukerji and P. Tripathi (Eds.) *Handbook of Research on Transnational Higher Education*, Hershey, PA: Information Science Reference, pp. 652-673.

Vonderwell, S.; X. Liang & K. Alderman (2007). Asynchronous Discussions and Assessment in Online Learning. *Journal of Research on Technology in Education*, Vol. 39, No. 3, pp. 309–328.

Western Interstate Commission for Higher Education (2002). *Best Practices for Electronically Offered Degree and Certificate Programs*. Boulder, CO: Western Cooperative for Educational Communications. Online Resource: http://www.niu.edu/assessment/manual/_docs/Best%20 Practices.pdf [Accessed on 2 January 2015].

Zingaro, D. (2012). Student Moderators in Asynchronous Online Discussion: A Question of Questions. *MERLOT Journal of Online Learning and Teaching*, Vol. 8, No. 3, pp. 159-173. Online Resource: http://jolt.merlot. org/vol8no3/zingaro_0912.pdf [Accessed on 20 March 2015].

Chapter 6

# Peer Assessment: A Learning Opportunity for Students in the Creative Arts

Katja Fleischmann

| Assessment Agency | Student-driven | * | Teacher-driven | |
|---|---|---|---|---|
| Assessment Outcomes | Flexible | | Fixed | * |
| Assessment Focus | Process | * | Outcome | |
| Assessment Context | Transferrable | * | Specific | |

## Introduction

This chapter shows how peer assessment helped first year creative arts students develop the ability to both critically assess the creative output of others and self-reflect – essential in the development of a creative practitioner. When reading this chapter, you will gain the following three insights:

1. peer assessment displays several benefits and potentials for creative arts education;

2. peer assessment can facilitate a powerful reflective practice for students in creative arts education;

3. peer assessment is a reliable and valid assessment strategy to add or replace the traditional studio critique.

Traditionally, education in the creative arts has embraced a master-apprenticeship model in which students develop their individual creativity, skills and critical thinking in small class environments (Lee, 2006; STP, 2009). The creative arts educator (master) guides each individual student (apprentice) on a journey of learning and exploration towards mastery as a designer, illustrator or digital artist in his or her own right. With small class sizes (twenty students or fewer) teaching and learning often assumes the form of one-on-one. This *"dialogical learning and teaching"* (Danvers, 2003:51) uses the studio critique – a formative assessment – in which feedback from the teacher functions as a catalyst to improve students' creative output, thinking processes and techniques (Lee, 2006; Ellmers, 2006).

The focus of a studio critique, commonly referred to as the 'crit' in studio-based creative arts education, is to trigger individual creative development through a circle of action and reflection (Oak, 2004; Ellmers, 2006). The crit attains a key goal of creative arts education, which is to foster the ability in each student to reflect on the quality of his/her creative output and that of others; students become reflective practitioners (Schön, 1987).

The crit, as a reflective practice, has always been central to the education of creative arts students (Uluoglu, 2000; Oak, 2004) but it has its critics. Some argue that the master-apprenticeship model generates a teacher-centred focus, encouraging students to try to please the teacher (Bose *et al.*, 2006; Ehmann, 2005) rather than attempt to explore and overcome creative barriers. Harpe and Peterson (2008) and Ehmann (2005) argue that it can lead to students becoming passive learners. Davies (2000) even suggests that the crit produces surface learning only.

Furthermore, increasing enrolment numbers in many Australian universities is shifting the focus away from the individual learner and his/her creative development (STP, 2009). In such context, some educators consider the crit, which provides individual and meaningful feedback to each student on progress and learning, no longer a viable assessment practice (Blythman *et al.*, 2007). However, the challenge to learning and teaching presented by the growth of student numbers also brings new opportunities. For example, peer interaction can encourage peer-led reflection (Capstick & Fleming, 2004) and peer assessment could flourish in creative arts education.

Based on the wide array of benefits of peer assessment described in the literature in other areas, this chapter explores the use of peer assessment in creative arts education, in particular as a learning opportunity to foster a vital reflective practice in creative arts students.

## Peer assessment, promoting active learning

Assessment is central to the learning process and according to Boud *et al.* (2001:117) *"the single most powerful influence on learning in formal courses"*. In recent years assessment practice has been reconceptualised, widening the repertoire to include strategies that *"not only measure learning as an end product"* but also act as *"crucial factor in enabling learning to take place"* (Cartney, 2010:551). One such strategy is peer assessment which can facilitate *"student cognitive development and active learning in various ways"* (Li, 2011:3).

Peer assessment breaks away from the notion that *"assessment is some-thing done to learners"* (Brown & Glasner, 1999:157) in that it engages students in the assessment process. Peer assessment provides students with an opportunity to evaluate, review and form a valid opinion about the quality of the work of their peers (Topping, 1998; Falchikov, 2001). Peer assessment challenges the notion of power and control associated with traditional assessment strategies that lie with the educator (Boud *et al.*, 2001; Cartney, 2010, see also Spiller and Peters & Bartholomew in this volume). Peer assessment gives students greater control and respon-sibility for their learning (Topping, 1998; Brew, 1999). It can be used for formative and summative assessments for a variety of outputs, e.g. oral presentations, writing, test performance, portfolios (Topping, 2010). In formative peer assessment activities students can take on *"roles of assessors (rating and commenting upon peers' work) and assessees (viewing and acting upon feedback)"* (Li, 2011:3).

The need to reduce the workload of teaching staff in large class environments was the initial driver in the growth in popularity of peer assessment (Vickerman, 2009; Mulder *et al.*, 2014). In particular, formative assessment, which requires educators to provide individual, timely and meaningful feedback to each student on progress and learning, can be laborious (Mosterta & Snowballb, 2013; Mulder *et al.*, 2014). Peer assessment can be time saving (Topping, 2010; Moore & Teather, 2013). Aside from such practical benefit for educa-tors, pedagogical research has shown that peer assessment practice can enhance student learning (see, e.g. Gibbs 1999; Li *et al.*, 2010; Mosterta & Snowballb, 2013).

The wide array of benefits of peer assessment are well documented in the literature and include, for example:

+ increasing learning (Falchikov, 1995; Li *et al.* , 2010);

+ increasing students' confidence (Falchikov, 1995; Cheng & Warren, 1999);

+ receiving more feedback; adequate and timely feedback (Gibbs, 1999);

+ developing evaluation skills (Cho *et al.*, 2006);

+ increasing sense of autonomy and motivation (Pope, 2001; Brown, 2004);

+ developing life-long learning skills such as critical thinking, high-order cognitive skills, and negotiation skills (Topping, 1998; Dochy *et al.*, 1999).

Despite its many benefits, peer assessment is still underutilised (Topping, 2010). Educators questioning reliability and validity of grades assigned by students might explain some hesitation to use peer assessment (Cho *et al.*, 2006). However, various studies on peer assessment found that grades given by students differ only slightly from those given by educators (Topping, 1998; Falchikov & Goldfinch, 2000; Cho *et al.*, 2006). Some studies concluded that when assessment criteria are explained to students or students are involved in developing the criteria, grades seem to be comparable (Brew, 1999). Furthermore, Cho *et al.* (2006) argue that when multiple reviewers are used in the peer assessment process high reliability is achieved.

## Assessment practice in creative arts education: the studio critique; an emotional roller coaster?

Traditional assessments, such as exams, have little importance in practice-based creative arts education. The small amount of published literature on assessment in creative arts education debates what should be assessed; outcome, process and/or personal development (Goldschmidt,

2003; Ehmann, 2005; Ellmers, 2006) and the use of assessment criteria in alignment with learning outcomes (Harland & Sawdon, 2011).

Giloi and Toit (2013:257) argued that creative arts educators *"have a deep-seated fear of over specifying and creating a rigid system for the assessment of creative work"*. This is because students develop creative solutions to open-ended problems, hence no single right answer exists (Blair, 2006).

Student work is largely assessed based on concepts of creativity, originality, vision or imagination (Jackson, 1995; Blair, 2006; Giloi & Toit, 2013) – what Gordon (2004) calls the *"wow-factor"* in creative work. However, these are *"notoriously slippery concepts"* (Jackson, 1995:9) which are hard to define and measure. Difficulties in defining these concepts as learning standards can also be noted in the quality assurance context in higher creative arts education.

Subject benchmark statements or national standards for creative arts education inform potential minimum acceptable levels that students must attain to be eligible for the award of a bachelor degree, rather than the optimum to be achieved (see, e.g. The Quality Assurance Agency for Higher Education, 2008; Australian Learning and Teaching Council, 2010). Nevertheless, progress has been made in recent years to define more clearly learning objectives and assessment criteria in creative arts education.

The critique or 'crit' is the central method of formative assessment in art and design education (Blythman *et al.*, 2007; The Quality Assurance Agency for Higher Education, 2008; Day, 2012). Crits occur frequently in formal and informal ways. At crits, students present their project in stages, from first ideas, work in progress and the final project, in front of student peers and educator (Lee, 2006). Students explain their thinking and receive feedback from the educator and sometimes from their student peers or creative arts professionals (Kuhn, 2001; Blair, 2006; Lee, 2006).

Crits provide a point of reflection which is anchored in Schön's (1983) concept of the *"reflective practitioner"*, in which students go through a cycle of action and reflection to improve their practice (Schön, 1987; Ellmers, 2006; Day, 2012). Hence, students learn from feedback and from their own experience.

In the report "Critiquing the Crit" (Blythman *et al.*, 2007:4), the crit was identified as having *"considerable strengths, many of which other disciplines envy and would like to emulate"*. These included support of peer learning and instant feedback, and this feedback can be a dialogic, fun element because it is communal and enables students to benchmark themselves against peers (Blythman *et al.*, 2007). However, the same report also revealed "*a deterioration in quality of many crit models through increasing student numbers and declining time resource*" (Blythman *et al.*, 2007:5) – a notion also noted by others (e.g. Blair, 2006). The report stated that due to increasing student numbers "*traditional ways of running crits were no longer viable*" (Blythman *et al.*, 2007:4).

Day (2012) explored the crit from the student perspective and discovered that students "*dislike the format and type of feedback received in the Crit*". Blair (2006:89) describes the crit as "*emotional roller coaster*" for students. Creative arts students often bring "*considerable personal experience into the subject matter of their work*" (McKillop, 2006:131) and can feel vulnerable when being exposed to constructive criticism.

They can experience the crit as stressful and the feedback sometimes as negative and subjective (Day, 2012; Blythman *et al.*, 2007). McKillop (2006:137) discovered in his study that students feel the crit as an assessment form is something "*done to you*", something "*uncomfortable or painful*".

To some extent, the discomfort comes from being critiqued in public with students feeling 'judged' based on their individuality instead of their artwork (McKillop, 2006). This feeling is reinforced "*because art and design has a hero culture which privileges the judgments and opinions of individual practitioners/teachers*" (Jackson, 1995:11). Although many creative arts educators have extensive professional experience and "*would be regarded as respectable judges of good or exceptional work in those areas*" (Gordon, 2004:70), increasing student numbers may limit the time for the educator to give considerate and constructive feedback. Blair (2006:91) also noted that the "*large crit inhibits the majority of students from giving feedback to their peers*" and hence the crit has become increasingly teacher-focused.

As a result, a unique characteristic of this assessment form in providing "*the multiple perspective is lost*" (Blythman *et al.*, 2007:7). Being presented with a singular teacher view in conjunction with the intense input of personal experience in generating creative work means that students "*can often find it difficult to step back and view their work objectively*" (McKillop, 2006:131). In addition, negative feelings can be a barrier to reflective thinking (Boud *et al.*, 1985 in McKillop, 2006).

The crit as the central assessment strategy in creative arts education, providing students with the opportunity to reflect on the quality of their creative practice and that of others, works well in small class environments. In the context of larger classes, running a crit in a traditional format can results in dubious student experiences. Hence, explorations in using alternative assessment strategies in creative arts education are needed (see for example Hager, this volume). Peer assessment as used in subjects of non-artistic nature has well-documented benefits which show great potential for its application in creative arts education.

## The potential of peer assessment in creative arts education

Pedagogical research has highlighted two general characteristics of peer assessment strategies that show a potential for its use in creative arts education. Firstly, various authors argue that assessing the work of peers promotes self-reflection (Topping, 1998; Brown & Glasner, 1999; Cheng & Warren, 1999; Pearce *et al.*, 2009).

Although the majority of studies on peer assessment focus on the feedback given to students, some studies explore the potential responses of students receiving peer feedback. For example, a study conducted by Mulder *et al.* (2014:671) found that *"students adopted almost two-thirds of reviewer suggestions overall"*. Cartney (2010) emphasises that students in general appreciated the feedback they received, and that students were going to utilise the feedback to adapt and improve the following assignment.

A student in her study explained: *"It wasn't just about giving feedback to other people it was also whilst I was giving the feedback I was questioning my own work and learning from other peoples' styles"* (Cartney, 2010:559). Price *et al.* (2010) made a similar discovery; students appreciate peer feedback because it helps them do better in the next assignment or improve the final product. However, action taken by students was dependent on the quality of the feedback.

The study from Mulder *et al.* (2014:671) confirms these findings; students *"tended to devalue criticism that did not justify the opinions expressed or that had poor grammar and spelling"*. Overall, students appreciate feedback that is detailed and constructive.

Secondly, peer assessment provides the opportunity to expose students to various perspectives and ways of approaching work (Dochy *et al.*, 1999). Peer assessment can introduce students to ambiguous feedback, a foretaste of the professional reality that they will encounter later in their careers. Multiple opinions enhance a student's capability to reflect and to act on that feedback. Presenting students with multiple views on their work also breaks away from the hero culture in creative arts education and hence the singular view approach to feedback often found in crits. In return, this might help students to benchmark themselves more realistically against their peers, which is essential for students to engage in a fruitful circle of action and reflection.

## Peer assessment supporting students' development as reflective practitioners: An Australian Case Study

Enrolment numbers have increased in the first year subject "*Introduction to Media Design*" (Bachelor of New Media Arts degree at James Cook University, Australia) from 50 students in 2007 to over 120 in 2011. Consequently, creative arts education at the School of Creative Arts has moved from small group education to educating students in large lecture theatres and in practical groups of 30-50 students. Although increasing enrolment numbers are generally a positive development, it clearly required rethinking the learning, teaching and assessment approaches. In smaller classes, the crit (informal and formal) involving individual and group conversations between educator and student(s), guided each student individually through an iterative work and learning process based on action and reflection.

The crit was the central assessment strategy for all learning activities. Given the need to look for alternative assessment strategies and the potential peer assessment holds for facilitating the development of students' critical reflection capabilities, peer assessment was introduced and trialled in a first year design subject.

The subject "*Introduction to Media Design*" has three assignments, one of which is a research assignment that requires students to explore historical and contemporary Australian graphic design. Students are given particular topics or can, with approval of the educator, self-select a topic that they will research and explore. They are required to share their findings and learning with their peers through an in-class creative presentation of 10 minutes.

This assignment underwent a major change over the years, with presentations delivered first by individual students in a small class environment and by groups in later years when student numbers started to increase. Feedback was usually given verbally directly to the individual students or groups after the presentation.

In addition, students received a written evaluation after all presentations were concluded. Although the use of rubrics, which outlined certain expectations, streamlined to some extent the written assessment component, the crit format as a tool for providing extensive verbal feedback became unsustainable due to the increasing student numbers. The educator felt that feedback was often rushed and too brief due to the higher number of presentations.

Furthermore, students were asked to present research findings to their peers to develop not only their presentation skills but also to present knowledge in a style and format that would engage their peers and create interest for the history of Australian graphic design. A re-occurring problem was that the majority of presentations tended to address only the educator as the person who would assess the work, instead of the whole class.

Facing enrolment numbers of 120 students, and therefore 30 group presentations, and considering the various benefits surrounding peer assessment, the decision was made to trial peer assessment in the subject *Introduction to Media Design*, a first semester first year subject.

Particularly in the first year, students need to be encouraged to develop their feedback beyond 'That's cool' or 'I don't like it'. Therefore, each student is asked to complete a marking rubric for each group presentation (see below Figure 1). The rubric requires students to give more comprehensive, constructive feedback. In addition to assessing various aspects of the quality of presentation (content knowledge, coherence and organisation, etc.), each student is asked to comment on two positive aspects of the presentation, giving reasons, and mention two aspects that would need improvement (if any), explaining why they need improvement and suggesting how they can be improved. The marking rubric is explained to students a week beforehand. Illustrations for each marking category enable students to understand, for example, the difference between being 'exceptional' and 'very good'. The explanation of the marking rubric also guides students in refining their own presentation according to these expectations. Depending on the class size, each student has to write fifteen constructive evaluations, and each group receives feedback and suggestions from approximately 30-65 peers. The educator sends out final results-based peer evaluation and comments to each group within a day or two of the assessment.

Group Name/number: _____ Total Points Earned: _____ / 100

| Content Knowledge | | | |
|---|---|---|---|
| Exceptional (25) | Very good (20) | Adequate (15) | Poor (10) |
| Group demonstrates full knowledge with explanations and elaboration. | Group is at ease with content, but fails to elaborate. | Group is uncomfortable with information and is able to answer only rudimentary questions. | Group does not have grasp of information and cannot answer questions about subject. |

| Coherence & Organization | | | |
|---|---|---|---|
| Exceptional (25) | Very good (20) | Adequate (15) | Poor (10) |
| Group presents information in logical, interesting sequence which audience can follow. | Group presents information in logical sequence which audience can follow. | Audience has difficulty following presentation. | Audience cannot understand presentation because there is no sequence of information. |

| Public Speaking | | | |
|---|---|---|---|
| **Exceptional (25)** | **Very good (20)** | **Adequate (15)** | **Poor (10)** |
| Poised, clear articulation; proper volume; steady rate; good posture and eye contact; enthusiasm; confidence. Presenter seldom returns to notes, maintains eye contact with audience throughout the presentation. | Clear articulation but not as polished; Presenter maintains eye contact with audience most of the time, but frequently returns to notes. | Some mumbling; little eye contact; uneven rate; Presenter reads most of report, but occasionally makes eye contact with audience. | Inaudible or too loud; rate too slow/fast; speaker seemed uninterested. Presenter reads entire report, making no eye contact with audience. |

| Quality of Presentation Slides & Handout | | | |
|---|---|---|---|
| **Exceptional (25)** | **Very good (20)** | **Adequate (15)** | **Poor (10)** |
| Presentation has a professional look with an overall graphical theme that appeals to the audience and compliments the topic. Information presented on each slide is understandable, readable and free of spelling errors. Presentation including all material and media is working properly. | The presentation has a professional look but is hard to understand at times; presentation has only 1-2 spelling errors. Presentation, including all material and media, is working properly. | Presentation does not follow visual guidelines and is hard to read or understand, but presentation, including all material and media, is working nearly without errors. | Presentation does not appear to be of any professional standard. Information on slides is hard to read and hard to understand. Presentation including all material and media is running with interruptions through technical errors. |

| Comments | |
|---|---|
| Point out at least **two things you thought were positive** and **two things that you thought need improvement** (if any). Give reasons **why** and suggest **how** they can be improved. | |

*Figure 1: Criteria for peer assessment of presentations*

*Methods*

During a period of two years, 240 undergraduate creative arts students participated in the peer assessment activity, 120 in each trial. Two sets of peer evaluations (30 groups in Trial 1 and 29 groups in Trial 2) are available for analysis to explore the research question: To what extent can peer assessment enhance student learning and reflective capabilities in creative arts education? First year student data was analysed for the following qualities of feedback:

+ Is it constructive and can it be helpful to students?

+ Can it initiate reflection; hence can students learn from it?

+ How diverse are the student views?

In addition to exploring the above questions, the final grades assigned through peer evaluations were compared with the educator's evaluation. This was to examine whether the peer assessment is reliable and valid in context of the cohort being first year, first semester students, whose perception on professionalism and expectations on assessment quality might not yet be fully developed. Therefore, the comparison of student and educator evaluation was used as check point in this study to establish whether peer assessment can be viable in a first-year creative arts learning environment.

To further validate this alternative assessment strategy, feedback from teaching and learning experts was invited which, combined with student feedback, will provide additional insight into the effectiveness of using peer assessment in creative arts education.

## Building reflective capabilities through peer assessment: Findings

The following explores two examples of completed peer assessments. These represent typical cases from the two-year trial, one evaluated by students as overall very good and another assessed as average. Table 1 shows the marking results for a presentation perceived by students as very good (score of 90, marked with a High Distinction).

| Presentation: History of Australian graphic design, 1970-1980 | | | | | | |
|---|---|---|---|---|---|---|
| | Number of students | | | | | |
| Category to be assessed | Exceptional | Very good | Adequate | Poor | Rating Average | Response Count |
| Content Knowledge | 39 | 22 | 4 | 1 | 22.50 | 66 |
| Coherence & Organization | 35 | 29 | 2 | 0 | 22.50 | 66 |
| Public Speaking | 45 | 20 | 1 | 0 | 23.33 | 66 |
| Quality of Presentation Slides | 32 | 30 | 4 | 0 | 22.12 | 66 |
| Point out at least two things you thought were positive and two things that you thought need improvement (if any). Give reasons why and suggest how they can be improved. | | | | | 56 | |
| Grade: High Distinction (HD) | | | | | | |

*Table 1: Peer assessment–marking sheet for a very good presentation*

Table 1 shows that nearly all students thought the presentation was 'exceptional' or 'very good' in all four categories. A few students (7% or less) evaluated the presentation as 'adequate' across the four categories and one student rated the presentation as 'poor' in content knowledge. The different number of students who selected 'exceptional' or 'very good' in the four categories (e.g. exceptional =39, 35, 45, 32) indicates that the assessment was a considered decision (opposed to students selecting 'exceptional' in all categories for the sake of ease).

Out of the 66 students who assessed the presentation, 56 students commented on positive aspects and things in need of improvement. Overall, the feedback contained 69 positive remarks and 18 remarks that noted the need for some improvement of the presentation.

The following themes emerged as positive aspects of the presentation, with the number of students noting it shown in brackets:

+ very good presentation skills, excellent public speaker (23)

+ very creative and well-designed slides (13)

+ engaging presentation through speaking free without notes (10)

Other positive aspects highlighted were:

+ questions at the end were well answered (4)

+ specific examples given were great (3)

+ first speaker introduced group members and projected his voice very well (3)

Typical comments included:

+ *"The speaking was very powerful and easy to understand, and the flow of the presentation was pretty good. The presenters managed to keep the presentation within the time limit too."*

+ *"Speaker spoke confidently, presentation was interesting, and slides were visually aesthetic, overall very well presented."*

+ *"Really well presented and the knowledge from the presenter was very good. There was almost constant eye contact and the presentation flowed nicely."*

+ *"Very impressive content knowledge. The speaker was extremely familiar with the information. It felt like the audience could trust what was said, and learn from it. The discussion was well formulated and the main speaker responded well to all questions asked."*

The comments above show that multiple comments highlight similar points enabling students receiving the feedback to identify particular strengths in their presentations.

Additionally, each comment offers positive reflection on a different aspect of the presentation. This made the feedback highly valuable for students, providing depth (affirmative pattern) and also breadth (various aspects).

The remarks which suggested enhancement of the presentation focused mainly on two aspects that could have been improved:

+ *"The main speaker was interactive and knew the content of the material however I would have liked to have seen the other person present more as well."* (5)

+ *"Only improvement I would see is staying better within time limit as the presentation was being cut short on the last topic."* (4)

The one student who evaluated the 'Content Knowledge' as 'Poor' commented: *"Best public speaking of the day. It was a decent deconstruction of the presented design pieces, but I'm not really sure they understood what the themes and general trends were behind them."* Although the comment starts out as somewhat considered evaluation, the critique at the end is presented as an opinion only with no further reasoning given. Therefore, the comment offers no value for reflection for the group receiving this feedback.

The second case introduces another typical example of peer assessment from the trials.

Table 2 shows the marking results for a presentation perceived by students as average (score of 70, marked with a Credit).

| Presentation: History of Australian graphic design, 1950-1960 | | | | | | |
|---|---|---|---|---|---|---|
| | Number of students | | | | | |
| Category to be assessed | Exceptional | Very good | Adequate | Poor | Rating Average | Response Count |
| Content Knowledge | 12 | 37 | 12 | 2 | 19.68 | 63 |
| Coherence & Organization | 4 | 20 | 34 | 5 | 16.83 | 63 |
| Public Speaking | 2 | 18 | 33 | 10 | 15.95 | 63 |
| Quality of Presentation Slides | 8 | 31 | 17 | 7 | 18.17 | 63 |
| Point out at least two things you thought were positive and two things that you thought need improvement (if any). Give reasons why and suggest how they can be improved. | | | | | 55 | |
| Grade: Credit (C) | | | | | | |

*Table 2: Peer assessment–marking sheet for an average presentation*

Table 2 shows that students had diverse views on the presentation. The assessment ranges from 'exceptional' to 'poor' in all four categories with 'very good' and 'adequate' being the highest populated. The qualitative feedback from students shows a similar split. From the 55 students who provided comments, 45 remarks focused on positive aspects and 41 remarks noted that some enhancement was needed.

The following themes were positive aspects of the presentation, with the number of students commenting on it shown in brackets:

+ effective and interesting video (16)

- good content knowledge (6)

- in-depth knowledge when answering questions (6)

Other positive aspects highlighted were:

- the music worked well and created a mood for listening (4)

- good introduction and conclusion (3)

- showed good examples and explanation of posters (2)

- the presentation was creative and different from everyone else who presented (2)

Aspects of the presentation that could have been improved were the following:

- use of video creates poor interaction with audience (15)

- there was little eye contact with camera (6)

- technical difficulties at the beginning (5)

- the music was a little too calming, distracted from the narrative (5)

Other points to enhance the presentation were:

- some more examples of pop art would have been good to see the idea behind that design style (2)

The following comments provide an insight into the disunity about the use of the video:

- *"I was very fond of the video presentation idea. It was a good way to pass through information on the subject without causing audience to get bored."*

- *"I don't think the videos were effective – it was just talking so it would have been more powerful to speak the content in person on the day. There was no emotion in the video so it was kind of boring."*

- *"The group presented through a video. It was a creative way to present it, however, there was no real interaction with the audience."*

Overall, these comments are reflective of a typical scenario students can encounter in creative arts education. While students are encouraged to take risks and 'think outside of the box' in order to push creative boundaries beyond the expected, attempts to do so do not always succeed. This can result in receiving contrasting feedback on the outcome.

## Discussion of key findings

Introducing peer assessment and hence shifting the power of assessment away from the educator gave first-year creative arts students the opportunity to evaluate creative presentations of their peers by using marking criteria and providing constructive qualitative feedback. The high number of students who took the opportunity to provide qualitative feedback (in the sample cases, 86% of students, which is a typical number across all cases) indicates that students take this shared control over assessment seriously. The quality of the feedback suggests that students are aware of the responsibility and engage earnestly in the peer assessment process.

The majority of feedback provided by students to their peers in this two-year trial was considerate and constructive. In order to provide such feedback students needed to view creative presentations, review and critically reflect on performances of their peers. Comments such as *the best of the day*" indicate evaluation across various presentations hence students benchmark the performances of their peers not only against marking criteria but also across presentations. It is fair to suggest that in this benchmarking process students also reflect on their own work. Hence, engaging first year creative arts students in peer assessment activity encourages self-reflection as is highlighted in the literature (e.g. Cartney, 2010; Li *et al.*, 2010).

The quality of the comments provided by students in both trials allows for students receiving the feedback to learn from it: students could identify the strengths and weaknesses of their work from the comments provided. In both cases there were only a few students who provided comments (10) that did not hold any learning value, such as "*Great job!*". The feedback that provided reasons for a particular evaluation and suggestions for improvement facilitates students to reflect more effectively. Some students, 14% in both trials, did not supply qualitative feedback.

Overall, the qualitative peer feedback provided the opportunity for reflection and learning for creative arts students. An external reviewer and peer learning expert of another Australian university who was invited to review the peer assessment strategy highlights: *"By getting students to engage with marking rubrics, ensuring that they understood what each of the criteria looked like and encouraging them to engage with judgment and analysis in this way ensures higher order learning outcomes as they can answer not only the 'what' but also the 'why' about what is a quality product or process".* (Director Teaching and Learning, 2014)

Given the large student numbers (120 creative arts students in each trial) the peer assessment worked well as a more efficient assessment strategy for the educator. The traditional crit would have involved giving individual verbal and written feedback to 30 groups in Trial 1 and 29 groups in Trial 2. Using peer assessment saved time from the educator's perspective.

Furthermore, the number of views supporting each theme of evaluation (positive/enhancement) may help students to step back from their work and engage with the feedback. Perhaps this is even more the case than if students had been presented with the singular educator's view because the feedback becomes less subjective, as is argued by Day (2012) and Blythman *et al.* (2007). Students might be more willing to take feedback on board and act upon it.

In addition, students received a wider variety of arguments, which gives them the opportunity to experience and think about the different ways in which their work can affect people. One of the faculty coordinators commented after reviewing the assessment approach: *"First year students often struggle to envision where their degree will take them and what their chosen profession actually requires of them as graduates. The engagement with professional approaches to creative practice, reflection on the experience, and engagement in constructive evaluation of peer work provides the students with an early and invaluable introduction to what it means being a professional".* (WIL Coordinator, 2014)

Introducing peer assessment in this large creative arts class environment is a good way for each student to learn that there is often not 'one right answer' to a problem in the creative arts. A student commented on the peer assessment experience that the best aspect was, *"that it stimulates the creativity, and makes the students understand that there isn't one way. Everyone sees an assignment differently, and that's what makes creativity cool."* (Student feedback on Subject, 2013)

The educator also noted a change in the way students presented their work by addressing everyone in the audience, not just the educator. This clearly shows a positive shift away from the teacher-centred focus of the assessment prevalent in previous years. Providing students with the power of assessment encourages them to stop trying to please the educator, as is sometimes the case in traditional crits (Ehmann, 2005; Bose *et al.*, 2006).

Overall, the grades determined by peer assessment in both trials (59 cases) coincided with grades the educator would have given, hence making the peer assessment reliable. This was also the case when peer evaluations ranged from 'exceptional' to 'poor' across categories (see Table 2); the resulting average grade still coincided with the educator's evaluation. This result confirms findings by Cho *et al.* (2006), who argue that multiple reviewers engaging in the peer assessment process ensure a high reliability.

## Conclusion

The ability to reflect is essential in the development of a creative practitioner. Creative arts students need to learn to critically assess the creative output of others and to self-reflect, in order to enable the circle of action and reflection innate to reflective practitioners (Schön, 1987). Introducing peer assessment in a first year creative arts subject proved to be a valid exercise in support of such goals.

Several benefits emerged through the introduction of peer assessment. Creative arts students critically engaged with the subject content and benchmarked peer performances and their own performance. Findings from the two-year trial suggest that peer assessment facilitates and provokes student reflection. Engaging students in thinking about the 'why' of their assessment and ensuring that they understand each assessment criteria promotes deep learning. Outcomes of and experiences made in this study align with Brown and Glasner's view on student learning (1999:158), which states, *"reflection on their own work and that of their peers is the learning".*

Introducing peer assessment in creative arts education is seen as not only beneficial for creative arts students giving the feedback but also for students receiving feedback. The breadth (variety of views) and depth (affirmative pattern) of comments presented introduces creative arts students to the realities of their future creative careers. Furthermore, the feedback from multiple reviewers does challenge the 'hero' status of the creative arts educator. Students might view their work more objectively when presented with more than the singular view of the educator.

Grades generated through the peer assessment, although in a first year class, were overall in line with the educator's evaluation, making this a valid and trusted exercise worth repeating. Future developments would make it mandatory for students to give qualitative feedback. However, the majority of students provided constructive feedback in addition to using the marking sheet. The high participation and quality of the feedback clearly suggests that students understood the value of this assessment strategy and embraced the responsibility in marking their peers. Giving creative arts students the power to evaluate their peers provides them with the opportunity to take greater responsibility for their learning. The notion that assessment in the creative arts education is something 'done to students' can be overcome by introducing peer assessment.

Overall, the introduction of a peer assessment strategy in the first semester of the creative arts degree at James Cook University has proven to be effective and hence is a viable alternative for the crit traditionally used. In the short term, peer assessment will not replace the crit completely in creative arts education but it can be used as a learning opportunity for students to develop reflective capabilities. This study suggests, against the background of the literature, that findings can inform assessment strategies in other disciplines of academic studies.

## About the author

Katja Fleischmann is Associate Professor in Media Design and Head of Design Discipline at College of Arts, Society and Education at James Cook University, Australia. She can be contacted at this email: katja.fleischmann@jcu.edu.au

## Bibliography

Australian Learning and Teaching Council. (2010). Learning and Teaching Academic Standards Project: Creative & Performing Arts. Strawberry Hills, Australia: Australian Government Department of Education, Employment and Workplace Relations.

Blair, B. (2006). 'At the end of a huge crit in the summer, it was "crap" – I'd worked really hard but all she said was "fine" and I was gutted.'. *Art, Design & Communication in Higher Education*, Vol. 5, No. 2, pp. 83-95.

Blythman, M.; S. Orr & B. Blair (2007). Critiquing the Crit. University of the Arts London.

Bose, M.; E. Pennypacker & T. Yahner (2006). Enhancing critical thinking through "independent design decision making" in the studio. Open House International, Vol. 31, No. 3, pp. 33-42.

Boud, D.; R. Cohen & J. Sampson (2001). Peer learning and assessment. In D. Boud, R. Cohen & J. Sampson (Eds.), *Peer learning in higher education: learning from & with each other*. London: Kogan Page, pp. 67-81.

Brew, A. (1999). Towards Autonomous Assessment: Using Self-Assessment and Peer Assessment. In S. Brown & A. Glasner (Eds.), *Assessment matters in higher education: choosing and using diverse approaches*. Buckingham Society for Research into Higher Education & Open University Press, pp. 159-171.

Brown, D. (2004). Language assessment: Principles and classroom practice. New York: Longman.

Brown, S. & A. Glasner (1999). Part 4 Towards Autonomous Assessment. In S. Brown & A. Glasner (Eds.), *Assessment matters in higher education: choosing and using diverse approaches*. Buckingham Society for Research into Higher Education & Open University Press, pp. 157-158.

Capstick, S. & H. Fleming (2004). The Learning Environment of Peer Assisted Learning.

Cartney, P. (2010). Exploring the use of peer assessment as a vehicle for closing the gap between feedback given and feedback used. *Assessment & Evaluation in Higher Education*, Vol. 35, No. 5, pp. 551-564.

Cheng, W. & M. Warren (1999).Peer and Teacher Assessment of the Oral and Written Tasks of a Group Project.*Assessment & Evaluation in Higher Education*, Vol. 24, No. 3, pp. 301-314.

Cho, K.; C. D. Schunn & R. W. Wilson (2006). Validity and Reliability of Scaffolded Peer Assessment of Writing From Instructor and Student Perspectives. *Journal of Educational Psychology*, Vol. 98, No. 4, pp. 891–901.

Danvers, J. (2003). Towards a Radical Pedagogy: Provisional Notes on Learning and Teaching in Art & Design. *International Journal of Art & Design Education*, Vol. 22, No. 1, pp. 47-57.

Davies, A. (2000) Using Assessment to Improve the Quality of Student Learning in Art and Design. Centre for Learning and Teaching in Art

& Design, University of the Arts London. Online resource: http://ualresearchonline.arts.ac.uk/626/ [Accessed 3 June 2015].

Day, P. (2012). The Art Group Crit. How do you make a Firing Squad Less Scary? . *Networks*. Online resource: http://arts.brighton.ac.uk/projects/networks/issue-18-july-2012/the-art-group-crit.-how-do-you-make-a-firing-squad-less-scary [Accessed 3 June 2015].

Ellmers, G. (2006). Reflection and Graphic Design Pedagogy: Developing a Reflective Framework to Enhance Learning in a Graphic Design Tertiary Environment. Paper presented at the *ACUADS 2006* conference, Monash University, School of Art, Victorian College of the Arts, Melbourne.

Ehmann, D. (2005). Using assessment to engage graphic design students in their learning experience. Paper presented at the 2005 Evaluations and Assessment Conference, 30 November – 1 December, Sydney.

Falchikov, N. (1995). Peer feedback marking: developing peer assessment. Innovations in Education and Training International, Vol. 32, No. 2, 175-187.

Falchikov, N. (2001). Learning together: Peer tutoring in higher education. London, Routledge Falmer.

Falchikov, N. & J. Goldfinch (2000). Student peer assessment in higher education: A meta-analysis comparing peer and teacher marks. Review of Educational Research, Vol. 70, pp. 287–322.

Freeman, M. & J. McKenzie (2001). Aligning peer assessment with peer learning for large classes: the case for an online self and peer assessment system. In D. R. Cohen & J. Sampson (Eds.), *Peer learning in higher education: learning from & with each other*. London: Kogan Page, pp. 156-189.

Giloi, S. & P. d. Toit (2013). Current Approaches to the Assessment of Graphic Design in a Higher Education Context. *International Journal of Art and Design Education*, Vol. 32, No. 2, pp. 256-268.

Gibbs, G. (1999). Using assessment strategically to change the way students learn. In Brown, S. & Glasner, A. (Eds.), Assessment matters in higher education: Choosing and using diverse approaches. Buckingham: Open University Press, pp. 41-53.

Goldschmidt, G. (2003). Expert knowledge or creative spark? Predicaments in design education. Paper presented at the Expertise in Design, Design Thinking Research Symposium 6, 17-19 November, University of Technology Sydney.

Gordon, J. (2004). The 'wow' factors: the assessment of practical media and creative arts subjects. *Art Design & Communication in Higher Education*, Vol. 3, No. 1, pp. 61–72.

Harland, R. & P. Sawdon (2011). From fail to first: Revising assessment criteria in art and design. *Art, Design & Communication in Higher Education*, Vol. 10, No. 1, pp. 67–88.

Haaga, D. A. F. (1993). Peer review of term papers in graduate psychology courses. Teaching of Psychology, Vol. 20, No. 1, pp. 28–32.

Harpe, B. d. l. & F. Peterson (2008). *A model for holistic studio assessment in the creative disciplines.* ATN Assessment 2008: Engaging Students with Assessment, 20-21 November, University of South Australia, Adelaide.

Jackson, B. (1995). Assessment practices in art and design: a contribution to student learning?

Kuhn, S. (2001). Learning from the Architecture Studio: Implications for Project-Based Pedagogy. *International Journal of Engineering Education*, Vol. 17, No. 4 and 5, pp. 349-352.

Lee, N. (2006). Design as a learning cycle: A conversational experience. *Studies in Learning, Evaluation Innovation and Development*, Vol. 3, No. 2, pp. 12-22.

Li, L. (2011). How Do Students of Diverse Achievement Levels Benefit from Peer Assessment? *International Journal for the Scholarship of Teaching and Learning*, Vol. 5, No. 2, Article 14, pp. 11-16.

Li, L.; X. Liu & A. L. Steckelberg (2010). Assessor or assesse: How student learning improves by giving and receiving peer feedback. *British Journal of Educational Technology*, Vol. 41, No. 3, pp. 525–536.

McKillop, C. (2006). Drawing on assessment: using visual representations to understand students' experiences of assessment in art and design. *Art, Design & Communication in Higher Education*, Vol. 5, No. 2, pp. 131-144.

Moore, C. & S. Teather (2013). Engaging students in peer review: Feedback as learning. *Issues in Educational Research, Vol. 23*, No. 2, pp. 196-211.

Mosterta, M. & J. D. Snowballb (2013). Where angels fear to tread: online peer-assessment in a large first-year class. *Assessment & Evaluation in Higher Education*, Vol. 38, No. 6, pp. 674–686.

Mulder, R.; C. Baik; C. Naylor & J. Pearce (2014). How does student peer review influence perceptions, engagement and academic outcomes? A case study. *Assessment & Evaluation in Higher Education*, Vol. 39, No. 6, pp. 657–677.

Oak, A. (2004). Conversation pieces: talking about artefacts in design education. *Working Papers in Art and Design journal*, 3.

Pearce, J.; R. A. Mulder & C. Baik (2009). Involving students in peer review: case studies and practical strategies for university teaching. *Centre for the Study of Higher Education, University of Melbourne.*

Pope, N. (2001). An examination of the use of peer rating for formative assessment in the context of the theory of consumption values. Assessment & Evaluation in Higher Education, Vol. 26, No. 3, pp. 235–246.

Schön, D. (1983). *The reflective practitioner: How professionals think in action.* New York: Basic Books.

Schön, D. (1987). *Educating the Reflective Practitioner,* Jossey-Bass, San Francisco.

Sober, R. G. (2009). Team working and peer assessment: The assessment process as an aid to effective learning in creative group project work. *The Higher Education Academy Art Design Media Subject Centre.*

STP (2009). Curriculum Development in Studio Teaching: Volume One, STP Final Report. *Studio Teaching Project.*

The Quality Assurance Agency for Higher Education (QAA). (2008). Subject benchmark statement: Art and design. Southgate Street, Gloucester, UK: The Quality Assurance Agency for Higher Education.

Topping, K. J. (1998). Peer assessment between students in college and university. Review of Educational Research, Vol. 68, pp. 249–276.

Topping, K. (2003). Self and peer assessment in school and university: Reliability, validity and utility. In Optimising new modes of assessment: In search of qualities and standards, ed. M. Segers, F. Dochy, and E. Cascallar, Dordrecht: Kluwer Academic, Vol. 1, pp. 55–87.

Topping, K. J. (2010). Peers as a Source of Formative Assessment. In H. L. Andrade & C. Gregory J (Eds.), *Handbook of Formative Assessment,* New York: Routledge, pp. 61-74.

Uluoglu, B. (2000). Design knowledge communicated in studio critiques. *Design Studies,* Vol. 21, No. 1, pp. 33-58.

UNSW. (2014). *Student Peer Assessment.* University of New South Wales, Online resource: https://teaching.unsw.edu.au/printpdf/544 [Accessed 3 June 2015].

Vickerman, P. (2009). Student perspectives on formative peer assessment: an attempt to deepen learning? *Assessment & Evaluation in Higher Education,* Vol. 34, No. 2, pp. 221-230.

Wands, B. (2001). A Philosophical Approach and Educational Options for the e-Designer. In Heller (Ed.). *The Education of an E-Designer,* New York: Allworth Press, pp. 20-23.

Chapter 7

# Student Self-assessment: ePortfolios and Learning in Higher Education

Lori L. Hager

| Assessment Agency | Student-driven | * | Teacher-driven | * |
| Assessment Outcomes | Fixed | | Flexible | * |
| Assessment Focus | Process | * | Outcome | |
| Assessment Context | Specific | | Transferrable | * |

## Introduction

This chapter presents findings from a long-term project integrating ePortfolios into graduate education, where it describes a process of supporting students' self-assessment. Reading this chapter you will gain the following insights:

1. knowledge of how students value ePortfolios as a way to integrate, apply, and make learning visible across courses and in complementary learning activities;

2. reflection on the values and goals of student self-assessment in contemporary and future learning in higher education;

3. how one comprehensive learning environment, organised around a digital commons, fostered and harnessed student centred learning and assessment, and how this might inform own practices;

4. thinking "outside the box" about ePortfolios as process and product in 21st century learning spaces.

Jenkins (2006:37) discusses the need to harness the learner as co-creator in knowledge generation in a "distributed cognition" approach. Through applying a distributed cognition approach to the student ePortfolio process, readers will gain insight into ePortfolios as a learning assessment strategy.

Universities and colleges employ ePortfolios for a variety of purposes, including to support students in professional and career advancements (professional portfolios), for student-centred assessment and reflection (academic portfolios that represent a student's "body of work,") and for the purposes of institutional accreditation (provide a means to archive and represent student achievement across schools). Effective ePortfolios are integrated into coursework and student learning (Tosh:3): "*With ePortfolios the pedagogy shifts from a course-driven focus to a student-centred approach placing emphasis for learning firmly on the student.*" Students document and legitimize their learning choices through a record in their ePortfolios.

Participation in ePortfolio learning enhances student engagement, critical reflection and analysis, and collaborative teaching-learning environments (Cambridge, 2010; Cambridge *et al.*, 2009; Rhodes, 2011; Light et al., 2011). Effective ePortfolios foster communities of learning and of practice, extending classroom learning into the community through both formal and informal pathways (Barrett, 2011; Batson, 2002; Cambridge, 2010; Cambridge *et al.*, 2009; Hager & Ugoretz, 2013). ePortfolios capitalize on the social networking behaviours of students and support and enhancememeaning making, communication and collaboration, harnessing skill sets necessary for the next generation of meaning makers. They make learning (and knowledge generation) visible to students, peers, faculty, and professionals. ePortfolios *can be* a means for students to demonstrate how transformations in thinking and learning occurred – transformations that document and demonstrate what they learned from each iteration and their problem-solving process. These qualities of formative ePortfolios, with a focus on assessment through learning, can foster innovation and other 21st century learning outcomes necessary for learning and employability.

## Integrative and Applied Learning

The American Association of Colleges and Universities (AAC&U) document integrative and applied learning as an essential learning outcome for 21st century students. Integrative and applied learning according to the AAC&U (*The Essential Learning Outcomes*) refers to "*Synthesis and advanced accomplishment across general and specialized studies*" as "*demonstrated through the application of knowledge, skills, and responsibilities to new settings and complex problems.*" The ability to synthesize across a range of learning experiences and environments, and then to apply the results through innovative practices, is a hallmark of 21st century education and an outcome of effective ePortfolio practices.

In *Confronting the Challenges of Participatory Culture*, Jenkins *et al* (2006) identifies the particular challenge of embracing new medias in 21st century learning as one of fostering participation. Jenkins applies the concept of distributed cognition to integrative learning with technology. Distributed cognition is a learning theory that has been widely applied to computer science and, more recently, to cooperative education, or what is commonly referred to as *experiential learning*. In conjunction with participatory culture, distributed cognition may be a useful approach to ePortfolio learning for 21st century education frameworks that involve integrative and applied learning.

The hallmark of distributed cognition is learning as a social act involving activities and technologies (Rogers 1997:2): "*The distributed cognition approach aims to show how intelligent processes in human activity transcend the boundaries of the individual actor. Hence, instead of focusing on human activity in terms of processes acting upon representations inside an individual actor's head, the method seeks to apply the same cognitive concepts, but this time, to the interactions among a number of human actors and technological devices for a given activity.*"

Furthermore, Kolb (1984:41) defines learning as "*the process whereby knowledge is created through the transformation of experience. Knowledge results from the combination of grasping and transforming experience.*" Grounded in Dewey's theories of learning, Kolb's theory shares basic tenets with experiential education theories that require learning to be transmitted through active reflection and application.

Kolb describes the four stages of the experiential learning cycle as "adaptive learning modes", which include:

+ Concrete Experience (Experiencing): what did I do?

+ Reflective Observation (Reflecting): what did I learn?

+ Abstract Conceptualization (Thinking): what does it mean?

+ Active Experimentation (Acting): how does it apply?

Kolb (1984:42) describes the implications of the model as follows: "*The central idea here is that learning, and therefore knowing, requires both a grasp or figurative representation of experience and some transformation of that representation. Either the figurative grasp or operative transformation alone is not sufficient. The simple perception of experience is not sufficient for learning; something must be done with it.*"

ePortfolios can be an effective pedagogical approach that supports students in the adaptive learning cycle through the effective use of prompts and encouragement of careful student reflection and selection of work that illustrates and highlights progress through the learning cycle. With pedagogy and learning at their core, ePortfolios leverage and harness familiar technologies integrated into the process and products of learning, in an approach that Jenkins (2004:8) refers to as an "*ecological approach*" to learning with technology: "*Rather than dealing with each technology in isolation, we would do better to take an ecological approach, thinking about the interrelationship among all of these different communication technologies, the cultural communities that grow up around them, and the activities they support.*"

In ePortfolio learning communities, students create and maintain learning ePortfolios, connecting curricular and co-curricular learning and achievements, providing evidence of the development of skills, critically reflecting about and analyzing their progress, and embedding technology strategies in their approach to research and professional practice.

The ability to synthesize, communicate, collaborate, and create something new are part of the range of so-called "soft skills" which both employers and education policy makers are now focusing on in identifying future education needs. However, U.S. employers complain that today's young adults are not equipped with the skills they need to succeed in the 21st century workforce.

In 2006 (Casner), the Conference Board and three other organizations issued a report, *Are They Really Ready to Work?* Based on a survey of several hundred employers, the report concluded by calling for more focus on the development of such "21st century skills" as critical thinking, problem solving, creativity and communication. Silverman (2010:np) reports that firms are increasingly asking to see evidence of job candidates' web presence, rather than a resume: "*Companies are increasingly relying on social networks such as LinkedIn, video profiles and online quizzes to gauge candidates' suitability for a job. While most still request a résumé as part of the application package, some are bypassing the staid requirement altogether.*"

As reported in *Documenting learning with ePortfolios: A guide for college instructors* (Light *et al.*, 2011:Kindle Location 471-476), central to ePortfolios is "*the process of reflecting on the growth of one's knowledge and capabilities over time with an emphasis on metacognition by intentionally providing structured time and space for learners to consider and document the process of their learning and not just the product (assignments, tests, and so on).*" The value of assessment for learning, rather than assessment of learning, is well documented in this anthology (Stupans; Fleischmann; Hunter, this volume). Light *et al.* (2011:Kindle Location 471-476) further assert that "*This process highlights the affordances of ePortfolios as not only potentially transformational with respect to individual learning and development, but also the effectiveness of ePortfolios as assessment tools*" because they "*enable students to authentically represent their own learning in a way that makes sense to them and encourages them, ultimately, to take responsibility for their own learning.*"

Findings from the ePortfolio Project presented in this chapter suggest that "ePortfolio learning" fosters habits of mind conducive to the kinds of 21st century skills that creative business leaders are clamouring for, and that are useful for addressing the challenges that higher education is facing, as alternative, technology rich educational structures compete with traditional educational institutions. This ePortfolio Project took place within, and was supported by, the cultural community that grew up around it and that allowed innovation in learning and the applications of learning to occur and be made visible.

This chapter examines the efficacy of applying learning ePortfolios as a means to foster student self-assessment in support of 21st century learning outcomes. A survey that illustrates student perceptions of the value of learning ePortfolios is presented and discussed. Findings from the survey, and lessons learned from the ePortfolio Project relative to assessment, are considered.

## Project Description

ePortfolios began at the University of Oregon in the Arts and Administration Program in order to connect the professional development and technology components of the curriculum. Students developed showcase ePortfolios that highlighted their growing proficiencies in the application of advanced technological tools through a professional website that they created, and which allowed them to showcase their work, particularly in internships, research, and technology design. From this small course-based project in one professional program, the ePortfolio Project grew to encompass faculty and students in other professional programs on campus including Business and Architecture, stimulating innovation in applying web 2.0/3.0 tools for higher education, and involving hundreds of faculty and students in developing course, program, and professional ePortfolios (Bramhall *et al.*, 2011).

Throughout the development of the project, assessment and evaluations were conducted for the purposes of continual program improvement and in order to understand factors in student and faculty engagement. The case study presented in this chapter is one assessment that was conducted in order to determine the effectiveness of ePortfolios, related specifically to student perceptions of the value of ePortfolios for the development of 21st century skills. Findings suggest that students learned "habits of mind" related to critical reflection through participation in ePortfolios, while learning the value of documenting transformations that occurred in thinking and learning. These "habits of mind" transferred to the workplace as students applied the toolsets in a distributed cognition approach to learning.

In the ePortfolio Project, students post their two-year academic plan and are encouraged to document their growth and provide evidence of achievements, in this way embedding habits of reflection, evaluation, and documentation. Student ePortfolio requirements include setting and connecting learning objectives between courses, posting relevant projects and reflections that document and make visible learning transformations and progress toward academic and professional objectives and skills. Using a WordPress platform, faculty syndicate student learning ePortfolios to instructional blogs, thus fostering a community learning environment conducive to collaboration and student-centred learning. Course and student ePortfolios are linked and connected on a virtual hub, or digital commons. The results of utilising a shared learning commons include:

- greater degree of student participation in curriculum;

- increases in the quality of assignments as students are able to access and build upon previous students' work;

- greater alignment across the curriculum as faculty are able to view other courses' content, and build upon student work.

An in-depth discussion of related findings from the cross-interdisciplinary implementation of the project are available from the Inter/National Coalition for Electronic Portfolio Research (Bramhall, *et al.*, 2012). The importance of curricular co-creation between faculty and students is also well documented in this anthology (Cygman; Fleischmann; Stupans; all in this volume).

Students post their academic plan and are encouraged to utilize the system in order to provide evidence of achievements and document their growth over time. In this way, habits of reflection, evaluation, and documentation are embedded in the learning process. Students are also encouraged to document and provide evidence of their professional growth through their internships, practicums and other professional activities, and are encouraged to engage as thoughtful digital citizens. At the end of the term, students reflect on their course learning objectives and analyse how they participated in working towards their objectives, identifying transformative moments and discussing and providing evidence of how their thinking has changed, relevant to their future growth. These artefacts and reflections are posted on the student learning ePortfolios, where all curricular and co-curricular learning can be managed in an environment where students have the greatest degree of control over privacy settings, and are also able to copy and migrate their materials to external hosting when they graduate.

## *Presentation of Survey Findings*

The author conducted a survey to assess how students use their ePortfolios and to discover what they value about learning in and through ePortfolios in an open source environment. The survey was sent to current graduate students and alumnus via Qualtrics, an open source online survey platform. Of the thirty-two respondents, eighteen were current students and fourteen were alumnus. Though the sample size is too small to generalize, the survey, combined with examples from the student learning ePortfolios, reveal both anticipated as well unanticipated outcomes, and may be useful in demonstrating how ePortfolios are valuable for learning assessment.

Students use their learning ePortfolios in support of curriculum goals, but they also extend and innovate the ways they use and apply the product and process in unanticipated ways. The survey found that respondents use their ePortfolio for a variety of purposes, including posting assignments and reflections on readings and class discussions. Students also use it for aggregating their academic resources and materials, documenting their internships and practicum, as well as their graduate research. Many students use their learning ePortfolio for career advancement, offering it as a link to prospective employers.

Respondents noted that learning to present themselves online through utilizing current web 2.0/3.0 tools was a significant benefit to their participation, as was the ability to aggregate all their materials and resources and to track their academic progress through graduate school.

| # | Answer | | Response | % |
|---|--------|---|----------|---|
| 1 | Posting written assignments | | 30 | 94% |
| 2 | Posting media/design assignments | | 32 | 100% |
| 3 | Posting course learning objectives | | 32 | 100% |
| 4 | Posting additional/optional blog posts | | 17 | 53% |
| 5 | Aggregating academic resources | | 13 | 41% |
| 6 | Documenting internship | | 22 | 69% |
| 7 | Documenting practicum | | 17 | 53% |
| 8 | Documenting graduate research | | 14 | 44% |
| 9 | Communication with professors | | 19 | 59% |
| 10 | Communications with students | | 4 | 13% |
| 11 | Sharing with Family/Friends | | 8 | 25% |
| 12 | Other | | 5 | 16% |

*Figure 1: Use of ePortfolios for classes and coursework.*

Respondents also reported that their use of ePortfolios extended beyond their graduate program to applied practices. Students appreciated the skills they learned through using ePortfolios for their relevance to their current jobs and internships. One respondent noted, "I ended up using the same blog software to create a program blog, and we now have high school student teachers blogging to document their experience in learning to teach art." Others note that they use what they learned to set up websites for internship sites and to manage blogs at their current places of work. Students have also been invited to review professional web resources and to serve as guest bloggers on national professional platforms.

| # | Answer | | Response | % |
|---|--------|---|----------|---|
| 1 | Learning how to present myself professionally | | 21 | 70% |
| 2 | Sending out to potential internship sites | | 5 | 17% |
| 3 | Sending out to potential job opportunities | | 8 | 27% |
| 4 | Becoming familiar with website development software | | 29 | 97% |
| 5 | Becoming proficient with website development software | | 17 | 57% |
| 6 | Other | | 2 | 7% |

*Figure 2: Benefits of showcase ePortfolios.*

When asked if they used their ePortfolio beyond the minimum course requirements, students replied that they use it to aggregate resource materials and to document co-curricular projects that they are working on, and that they often use these skills at work. Many students make use of their proficiencies to create and document community based projects they are developing, or demonstrate how they are connecting their research and professional practices through research blog sites. The extension of skills and tools learned through ePortfolios were unanticipated and driven by student innovation, as they began to freely experiment with using ePortfolio processes for other applications, such as communication and dissemination of course projects, internships, research and community-based projects.

Regarding collaboration as one of the critical 21st century skills, one student noted that "I have created sites for three other courses to share that coursework and facilitate group projects." Another respondent acknowledged that participation in ePortfolios helped to "facilitate more meaningful and valuable group projects." Students were able to view each other's process and reflections as they moved through the collaborative process.They also benefited from being able to access previous students' approaches to problem-solving and build from these. The quality of student work improved, both from student and faculty perspectives.

When asked about the benefit of using ePortfolios in addition to increasing their digital literacy, 29% of the respondents valued making learning visible and demonstrations of achievement, and 36% of respondents valued developing habits of mind, such as critical reflection and self-evaluation. Though at first these percentages seem rather low, critical reflection and self-evaluation were not initially an overt focus or goal of the project – they became part of the intentional objectives as students reflected on how ePortfolios were being used, and their value over time.

| # | Answer | | Response | % |
|---|--------|---|----------|---|
| 1 | Habits of Mind: Critical Reflection, Self-evaluation, etc | | 16 | 50% |
| 2 | Learning how to use wordpress | | 25 | 78% |
| 3 | Using social media | | 7 | 22% |
| 4 | Making learning visible - demonstrations of achievement | | 16 | 50% |
| 5 | Having a visible record of my work over time | | 15 | 47% |
| 6 | Blogging and digital citizenship | | 7 | 22% |
| 7 | Other | | 2 | 6% |

*Figure 3: What would you consider to be the most important benefits of using ePortfolios?*

Respondents noted that participation in learning ePortfolios helped them increase skills in integrating technology into program development and documentation – an essential skill for today's workforce – and found the skills they learned to be highly relevant to their job preparation and growth.

The robust reflection required of ePortfolios when used as a learning and assessment strategy reveal benchmark, or "aha," moments in learning, which are not otherwise captured. When students post their demonstrations of learning, they critically reflect on the process of conceptualization, of iteration, what worked and what didn't work, in both the process and the final outcome of the learning process. The student's learning and self-assessment is then made tangible and visible and, in the process of reflecting, students deepen their own assessment. For faculty, the student ePortfolios can be a meaningful way of capturing benchmarks in peda-gogy and strengthening the connections between learning outcomes, course content and course assessments.

One of the most immediate and unexpected results of the implementation was the widespread adoption of the platform across an array of applications. Graduate students apply what they are learning from utilizing their learning ePortfolios in the WordPress environment to create project blogs to:

+ demonstrate co-curricular work;

+ collaborate and represent projects in class;

+ share field journals when they are away on their internships;

+ create project and research sites to help enrich and inform engage-ment with the material;

+ develop websites for professional organizations and associations for communication, documentation, and evaluation.

Implications for lifelong learning are also suggested in such student self-reporting as perception of the value of engaging in learning ePortfolios in a WordPress environment: importance of its use as a marketing tool and branding, personal expression, information collection, communica-tion and distribution of work, and for job advancement. Said one student:

+ *"I blog for other organizations already, and the entries can serve as writing samples for potential jobs. I use a variety of social media for research and making professional connections."*

In the distributed cognition approach, this student engaged in the fourth tier of the learning cycle, as she began to actively experiment with the application of learning and knowledge. Students report that their learning has changed as a result of their use of learning ePortfolios, providing evidence of the development of critical reflection for self-assessment. For example, students report that:

+ *"I am forced to look back on my work and reflect on how it informed my understanding of the course topics. I am also more organized in my documentation of work."*

+ *"Having a centralized place for all of my work and thoughts (learning goals/reflections) has helped me track my overall learning and draw conclusions/see themes over the quarters."*

Students post their overall two-year learning objectives, their academic plans, and connect each class to these objectives. Students then post their course learning objectives, reflections and critical analyses of the readings, collaboration with other students, and artefacts that demonstrate how their learning has changed during the course. Students report that this assists them to self-assess their own learning process for the course:

+ *"Classes that utilize the ePortfolio typically ask for pre and post reflections on the class, so it helps to identify how I learn and grow throughout the course."*

Participating course faculty ask students to create learning objectives and to connect these to their overall learning objectives, and then to reflect and articulate how their learning and thinking is changing as a result of their curricular and co-curricular activities. How students reflect on their objectives also *makes learning visible* for the professors and for classmates as students articulate transformative moments in learning that are not captured in course evaluations:

+ *"By developing our ePortfolios in AAD, and sharing our learning, resources, and research with a broad audience in an accessible and open fashion, we are putting social capital development into practice through a transmedia platform."*

Students are innovating with the system, and adapting and modifying it for unanticipated purposes. One student created a robust research site, which aggregates her research inquiry, reflections, readings, and resources for her terminal research.

*Figure 4: Student research portfolio created for terminal research project on community-driven urban design.*

Students also use what they learn in ePortfolios to create professional networking and development opportunities. They report:

+ *"I used it to document my graduate experience beyond coursework, and used it to compile links and resources of interest to me."*

+ *"I used it to document special topics and practicum coursework as well as extra-curricular projects."*

+ *"I used WordPress syndication to communicate with my peers and colleagues. I am also able to implement RSS and Twitter feed displaying the most recent updates from local arts organizations not necessarily affiliated with AAD."*

One student's innovative application led to professional opportunities and demonstrates how active experimentation leads to integrative learning: "I used the blog as a way to post my participation in conferences, extra-curricular activities, and personal projects." One recent graduate student's final reflection points to the importance of a distributed cognition approach to learning:

+ *"This learning ePortfolio has been an evolving process and a major part of my growth and development here at UO. My hope is that site serves not only as a tool for me (both as a process and product), but also as a reference for other students working their way through the AAD program. As an incoming student, I learned a great deal from examining second-year students' ePortfolios, discovering what I did and didn't like regarding content layout and design, and gaining direction on assignments that seemed vague and ambiguous. I value being a part of a learning community, and AAD ePortfolios make for a great addition into our personal learning network."*

## Conclusion and Discussion

In the *ePortfolio Project*, we sought a way to make what was happening in classes visible and to:

+ generate a forum for students and faculty to share how they were extending their thinking and applied practices to outside the classroom;

+ create a virtual community where students articulate value, and where students, faculty, and professional partners foster connections between curricular and co-curricular work;

+ make evident how students transfer skills and knowledge across a range of experiences.

For our project, the research led us to anticipate that an effective ePortfolio project can assist students to learn and apply critical 21$^{st}$ century skills in "active reflection and application," as described in Kolb's distributed cognition approach with students at the centre of the learning cycle. Data suggests that ePortfolios help create a structure for students to move through the learning cycle of *experiencing, reflecting, thinking, and acting* in a self-reflective act that transforms learning into a co-constructed creative enterprise.

The graduate student learning ePortfolios connects curricular and co-curricular learning and achievements and provides evidence of the development of professional skills and a means to critically reflect about and analyze the learning process, while embedding technology-rich strategies in research and professional practice. Results of the project suggest that "ePortfolio learning" fosters habits of mind conducive to 21st century skills and is fundamental to addressing challenges in education as alternative, technology-rich educational structures replace traditional classroom learning environments.

Self-reports such as those reflected here demonstrate how students transferred ePortfolio learning into skills that they apply in their schooling and workplace. When ePortfolios were integrated into the curriculum, faculty noted an increase in student agency toward their own learning and education, increased critical reflection and collaboration, and significant benefits to student employability. As well, the ways in which students began to integrate, apply, and innovate with their ePortfolios for their research, experiential and cooperative education, and their team-based projects, point to the importance of supporting a participatory learning culture, such as Jenkins (2006) describes.

Furthermore, as we began to build a community learning space where students and faculty could view student work and course content across a range of student cohorts, faculty were provided a means for robust feedback about the effectiveness and outcome of assignments that was previously impossible in the university formal quantitative course evaluations. Consequently, faculty were able to adjust and focus course assignment and syllabi based on the student learning and participation: *"Aggregate instructional blogs allow professors to tailor their teaching by monitoring and documenting overall progress through a living syllabus. A robust class blog that reveals multiple perspectives and invites comments can facilitate cross-exposure to new ideas, stimulating collaborative thinking. As a public mechanism, the blog format allows for external discourse, opening the door to professional networks and the broader academic community."* (INCEPR final report).

As well, students began to build on the work of previous cohorts of students, using earlier approaches as a foundation on which to extend knowledge and improve the quality of response to the assignments, particularly in the project-based learning assignments. Consequently, faculty and students became co-creators in curriculum improvement. This suggests that ePortfolios, when effective, have the capacity to provide a format for learning that addresses and engages 21$^{st}$ century learning skills such as creativity, collaboration, and communication.

This project extended individual, stand-alone ePortfolios to encompass a community-based approach so that, rather than individual demonstrations of learning through single-authored ePortfolios, it is the connections discovered between courses and extended in co-curricular learning that students rate as highly valuable for their ability to integrate, apply, and extend their formal learning into professional applications. The inclusion of open source social media ePortfolio approaches to learning are valued by students for their support of making learning visible across the curriculum and in connecting co-curricular learning and professional development. The critical self-reflection that ePortfolios support is a valued mechanism for making learning visible in a tangible and practical way for students, employers, and faculty.

ePortfolios support a student centred pedagogy that thrives in experiential, and experimental, education. The proliferation of education technologies liberates education from traditional pedagogical and classroom structures, and the use of ePortfolios across the curriculum supports the development of skill sets necessary for the next generation of meaning makers, such as critical thinking and collaboration. ePortfolios can provide a means to both practice and demonstrate transformations in thinking and learning, and to make the applications of learning (and knowledge generation) visible to students, peers, faculty and professionals. The ability of students to document and demonstrate what they learned, and their problem-solving process, can lead to transformations in learning and outcomes. As educators, fostering learning in this way not only has the potential of preparing students for the new 21$^{st}$ century workplace, but of opening up the learning landscape to fuel global education rich in international connectivity.

In an age of standardized testing, it can be difficult to argue for and advocate for making learning visible, because of inherent risks to the learner and the institution. However, as a distributed cognition approach to learning, ePortfolios' strength is in fostering a collaborative learning environment where risk and innovation are a product of visible learning and robust self-assessment. The support of learning in a participatory environment fosters habits of reflection and assessment that connect and make visible the learning modes Kolb describes. Where a leading design company has the motto "Fail Often and Succeed Sooner", (as cited in Rocco), it may be in everyone's best interest to foster an environment where the ability to reflect, iterate, and revise is part of the assessment and learning cycle, and subsequently evidence for capability and success in the 21$^{st}$ century workplace.

## About the Author

Lori L. Hager is Assistant Professor at University of Oregon. She can be contacted at this email: drlorihager@gmail.com

## Bibliography

American Association of Colleges and Universities. (n.d.). *The Essential Learning Outcomes*. Online Resource: http://www.aacu.org/leap/essential-learning-outcomes [Accessed 10 April 2015].

Bramhall, R.; N. Cheng & L. Hager (2011). Inter/National Coalition of Electronic Portfolio Research Cohort V Final Report – University of Oregon. http://ncepr.org/finalreports/cohort5/UO%20Final%20Report.pdf. [Accessed 10 January 2015]

Brown, G.; N. Peterson; A. Wilson & J. Ptaszynski (2008). Out of the classroom and beyond. *Innovate* Vol 4., No. 5.

Cambridge, B. L.; S. Kahn; D. P. Tompkins & K. B. Yancey (Eds.) (2001). *Electronic portfolios: Emerging practices in student, faculty, and institutional learning*. Washington, DC: American Association for Higher Education.

Cambridge, D.; B. Cambridge & K. Yancey (Eds.) (2009). *Electronic portfolios 2.0: Emergent research on implementation and impact*. Sterling, VA: Stylus Publishing, LLC.

Casner-Lotto, J. (2006). Are they really ready to work: Employers perspectives on the basic knowledge and applied skills of new entrants to the 21$^{st}$ century workforce. *The Conference Board*. Online Resource: http://www.p21.org/storage/documents/FINAL_REPORT_PDF09-29-06.pdf [Accessed on 16 February 2015].

Hager, L. & J. Ugoretz (2013). Learning from the Open: Web 3.0 ePortfolios. ePIC Proceedings: London, England, 2013.

Hunter, M. (2015). *Transformative Power of Assessment: Implementing a Student-Centred Methodology in a Culturally Constraining Context*.

Jenkins, H. (2006). *Confronting the challenges of participatory culture: Media education for the 21ˢᵗcentury*. Cambridge, MIT Press. Online Resource: http://mitpress.mit.edu/sites/default/files/titles/free_download/9780262513623_Confronting_the_Challenges.pdf [Accessed on 16 February 2015].

Light, T. P.; H. L. Chen & J. C. Ittelson (2011-11-18). *Documenting learning with ePortfolios: A guide for college instructors*. John Wiley and Sons. Kindle Edition.

Office of Education Technology. (2010). *Transforming American education: Learning powered by technology*. Washington DC: U.S. Department of Education. Online Resource: http://www.ed.gov/sites/default/files/NETP-2010-final-report.pdf [Accessed on 16 February 2015].

Rhodes, T. (2011). Making Learning Visible and Meaningful Through Electronic Portfolios. Change. January-February. http://www.changemag.org/Archives/Back%20Issues/2011/January-February%202011/making-learning-visible-full.html [Accessed 17 March 2015].

Rocco Landesman comments at the Arts Education Partnership's opening plenary. (2010). Washington DC: National Endowment for the Arts. Online Resource: http://www.arts.gov/news/news10/ELI-Rocco.html [Accessed on 16 February 2015].

Rogers, Y. (1997). *A Brief Introduction to Distributed Cognition*. Interact Lab, School of Cognitive and Computing Sciences, University of Sussex.

Silverman, R. E. (2010). No more resumes, say some firms. *The Wall Street Journal*. Online Resource: http://online.wsj.com/article/SB10001424052970203750404577173031991814896.html [Accessed on 15 February 2015].

Tosh, D.; B. Werdmuller; H. Chen; T. Light & J. Haywood. (2006). The Learning Landscape: A Conceptual Framework for ePortfolios. In A. Jafari & C. Kaufman (Eds.), *Handbook of Research on ePortfolios*. Hershey Penn: The Idea Group, pp. 24-43.

Chapter 8

# Transformative Power of Assessment: Implementing a Student-centred Methodology in a Culturally Constraining Context

Maja Hunter

| Assessment Agency | Student-driven | * | Teacher-driven | |
|---|---|---|---|---|
| Assessment Outcomes | Fixed | | Flexible | * |
| Assessment Focus | Process | * | Outcome | |
| Assessment Context | Specific | * | Transferrable | * |

## Introduction

This chapter describes a process of implementing an innovative – within the local Omani cultural context – teaching and learning methodology with emphasis on the embedded transformative assessment.

Even though we are quite well into it, the 21$^{st}$ century with its political, economic, technological, social and other changes constitutes an enormous challenge for higher education institutions and educators. Many questions arise, such as:

  +  how do we prepare students for the fast changing world with its professional demands?;

+ how do we equip them with the necessary knowledge, skills and abilities in order to make sure they succeed in the world of the 21$^{st}$ century?;

+ what is it that the students should learn?; and

+ how do we evaluate what the students have learned?

Assessment that enhances student learning and is innovative and effective still seems to be a rare phenomenon within higher education institutions. It has become commonplace that assessment is most often reduced to various measurements of achievement, generally imposed by university assessment policy that varies little from one department to another. Grade fever and/or obsession with the grade point average obscure the fundamental role of assessment in learning.

There is a strongly felt need to move beyond the current forms of formative and summative assessment to develop innovative models that demonstrably enhance learning. Grounded in contemporary theories of learning, such as Mezirow's (1978, 1991, 2000) theory of transformative learning, assessment can contribute to enhancing student learning and developing skills and abilities that are essential in the modern world, such as critical thinking, autonomous and lifelong learning, teamwork and adaptability, to name just a few. This chapter presents the case of empowering student learning through the development and implementation of an innovative approach to assessment as embedded within Problem Based Learning (PBL) in the culturally specific context of Sultan Qaboos University, Oman.

When Problem Based Learning was being shaped and implemented as an innovative teaching and learning approach at McMaster University Medical School in Canada, Oman's present statehood was only beginning to take form. There was no university there in the 1960s. Sultan Qaboos University, the first and only state university in the Sultanate of Oman, was established in the 1980s, 20 years after implementing PBL at McMaster University. Certain higher education practices, considered as quite well established in many parts of the world, at SQU often constitute a groundbreaking innovation, which illustrates that, when considering innovation, one must place it within the given cultural and historical context (see Cifuentes-Goodbody and Karatsolis, this volume).

Reading this chapter there are at least three insights to be gained, both for teacher practitioners and for educational researchers:

1. the knowledge that a culturally constrained environment plays a significant role and might even act as a brake on the introduction of innovative approaches to the classroom and, more particularly, to assessment;

2. the introduction of such innovations as Problem Based Learning and transformative learning, which entail specific approaches to assessment in order to be successful, require considerable sensitivity and cultural awareness on the part of the teacher, regarding issues such as gender in approaches to teamwork which entail young men and women working alongside each other; and

3. assessment has the power to be one of the means of enhancing student learning only under the condition of being an integral part of the learning process, aligned with the learning objectives, and in itself serving as a pedagogical tool.

## Contextual constraints of the study: the case of Sultan Qaboos University

Sultan Qaboos University lies on the outskirts of Oman's capital city, Muscat, on a plain between a high range of rough, jutting mountains and just miles from the very blue waters of the Bay of Oman. Founded in the 1980s by the current Sultan Qaboos Bin Said, the campus is dominated by a high bell tower, which leads the gaze to the large, elegant mosque at the institution's heart. With an overall enrolment of over fifteen thousand students drawn from high schools around the country, SQU offers both undergraduate and graduate programmes, with instruction principally in English and a teaching staff drawn from many parts of the world.

Hired within the College of Economics and Political Science, I joined a staff of more than 50 professors and quickly started coming to terms with the many different features that became part of my cultural context. As a Western woman, my first tasks included dressing in a culturally appropriate manner and observing a policy of discretion in regard to the political and religious nature of the country. I welcomed my female students, who entered from one side of the classroom from the hallways and stairways that were specifically reserved for them, along with the male students from their designated entrances. In the spacious classrooms, my students would observe a culturally-imposed seating arrangement, with the female students grouped on one side, and the male students on the other. This separation was made more visibly obvious as the female students wore black 'abbayas' and the male students wore white 'dishdashas' and the traditional 'kumma' on their heads.

The College of Economics' assessment policy was well established and focused on teacher-driven summative assessment, based on 2 mid-term tests and a final exam. A distinguishing feature of the assessment policy resided in the requirement that fifty percent of the students were expected to achieve in the A and B grade range, with the other fifty percent below this cutoff mark.

Students did not need to engage in critical thinking nor did they experience collaborative learning. I was not alone in finding that such approaches to assessment, which conditioned the type of teaching and learning the students experienced, were not effective in promoting learning as understood through Sadler's (1998) conditions for effective feedback.

A practitioner of Problem Based Learning and a user of various forms of assessment including self- and peer-assessment, along with collaborative approaches to classroom learning, I immediately found myself at odds with the system. As the then-head of department shared my views and had found himself facing the same dilemmas, he supported and encouraged integrating Problem Based Learning as a teaching and learning methodology for courses offered within the area of business communication.

We were also successful in designing and implementing courses that were offered as university electives to a wider population of students. The courses included a wide range of approaches to teaching and learning: collaborative and project based learning, portfolios, self- and peer-assessment, team-based work, community-based projects, etc. This eventually led to the development of an innovative approach to assessment, described herein, that enhanced learning principally by empowering our students to learn for themselves rather than simply for the grade. Such assessment would play an integral role in the transformation of students' perspectives and help them make a step on their way to becoming autonomous, reflective, lifelong learners capable of critical and creative thinking.

As argued by Mezirow (2000), it is of crucial importance that learning focuses and develops contextual understanding, critical reflection and the ability to assess and negotiate meanings. Mezirow claims that our knowledge, beliefs, values and our feelings depend on the biographical, historical and cultural context. The importance of the aforementioned context became even more apparent to me as I began my work at SQU.

The notions that shape the specific contours of this context can be briefly summarised as follows. Foremost among these was gender. Oman, as a Muslim country, has undertaken to move in the direction of empowering women in society: women can seek education to the highest level, drive and move about freely, have the right to own property and to hold bank accounts, run for political office and hold executive positions in companies. However, there is still a very constraining general approach to gender relations and the roles of each gender within society.

Many of my students, both men and women, when asked, claimed that the woman's role was to take care of the family, to raise the children and that her place was at home in the kitchen. The man's role was to go out and to take care of all of the external business: earn the living, do the shopping, so that the woman is not seen nor exposed.

As an illustration of the current situation, although an Omani woman is supposedly free to travel, she nonetheless is obliged to travel with her closest male relative (father, brother or an uncle, but not with a cousin, given that they can legally marry). Even though the university is open to both genders, there is no real encouragement of genders mixing or of even working together. My first hours in the classroom at SQU caused me a considerable disturbance, which I later came to think of as my first 'disorienting dilemma', that took some time to work out: I would have to develop strategies to bring the teaching methodologies I believed in into the classroom and I realised this would be a challenging and complex process that would lead me to question my own set of assumptions about learning and teaching.

The second contextual constraint was language: the medium of instruction at SQU is English, which often happens to be the student's second or even third language. Despite the fact that 99% of my students were Omanis, the Omani society is not as homogeneous as it could initially appear. Given Oman's history of trade along the spice and silk routes, its reach extended from eastern Africa to the Indian subcontinent. Consequently, most of my students spoke Arabic as their first language, while a non-negligible number spoke Swahili or Urdu as their first language and Arabic as their second. Many students struggled with English, which had an impeding influence on the learning process.

Another contextual constraint that merits mention is the prominent role of religion within the society. Daily religious practice includes five calls to prayer and each entailed a preparatory phase followed by the prayer itself. It is easy to imagine the disruption this could cause to class attendance and the overall functioning of the university.

Within the SQU classroom, such topics as Omani politics and Islamic religion were not to be discussed. This would clearly constitute a serious constraint on my ability to lead my students to reflect critically on vital areas sustaining their understanding, or in Mezirow's terms (2009), their meaning perspectives or frames of reference, of their place in society and of the social and interpersonal relations between them.

## Theoretical underpinnings of the approach

*"A defining condition of being human is our urgent need to understand and order the meaning sof our experience. To integrate it with what we know, to avoid the threat of chaos. If we are unable to understand, we often turn to tradition, thoughtlessly seize explanations by authority figures, or resort to various psychological mechanisms, such as projection and rationalization, to create imaginary meanings"*, Mezirow (2000:4).

This quote from Mezirow brilliantly summarises the importance of learning as understanding and creating meaning. In order to avoid chaos and conflict, people must constantly evaluate and challenge their beliefs, question the ways of 'what' and 'how' they know. In today's globalising world, it is of crucial importance for people to acquire and develop a number of qualities that would enable them not only to do business and cooperate together, but also to respect one another, to value human life – the greatest gift of all – and, no matter how pompous it sounds, to preserve peace on earth. Achieving that often requires transforming many of people's beliefs and assumptions.

Transformative learning has the potential to constitute an integral part of higher education. It would seem that universities offer students numerous *"opportunities to challenge assumptions, question ways of knowing, and examine critically alternative perspectives with the anticipated outcome of developing a broader, more inclusive, more critical worldview"*, Herbers & Nelson (2009:6).

According to Mezirow (1991:167), perspective transformation, a key outcome of transformative learning, is a process of becoming critically aware of *"our underlying assumptions and how and why they come to constrain the way we perceive, understand and feel about our world."* Mezirow (2000:22) believes that transformative learning involves critical reflection on premises about oneself and he identifies the following phases of perspective transformation:

+ *a disorienting dilemma;*

+ *self-examination with feelings of fear, anger, guilt, or shame;*

+ *a critical assessment of assumptions;*

+ *recognition that one's discontent and the process of transformation are shared;*

+ *exploration of options for new roles, relationships, and actions;*

+ *planning a course of action;*

+ *acquiring knowledge and skills for implementing one's plans;*

+ *provisional trying of new roles;*

+ *building of competence and self-confidence in new roles and relationships;*

+ *a reintegration into one's life on the basis of conditions dictated by one's new perspective".*

In his research Mezirow (1991:168) writes that at the onset of perspective transformation there is a disorienting dilemma, which he describes as an *"externally imposed epochal dilemma."* However, it does not necessarily have to be a grave, calamitous event, as long as it creates an internal imbalance. It is in this moment of experiencing imbalance and stepping out of one's comfort zone that the most significant and transformative learning may take place.

Mezirow (1991:168) claims that an *"eye-opening discussion, book, poem, or painting or efforts to understand a different culture with customs that contradict our own previously accepted presuppositions"* may constitute a disorienting dilemma that leads to a transformation of perspective.

## Transformative assessment: an innovative component

According to Taylor (2006), there are four integral elements of transformative learning: the transformative educator, the transformative classroom environment, the transformative text, and the transformative student. Given that Mezirow's theory of transformative learning originated through his work with adult education, there was no need for him to be concerned with assessment as it is commonly understood, i.e., in the form of grades or certificates. Consequently, transformative learning as a field has been largely studied within the area of adult education.

As transformative learning, however, penetrates tertiary education (Herbers and Nelson, 2009), I would add another component, namely, transformative assessment. During the process of transformative learning, it is also essential that both the transformative educator and the transformative student be willingly confronted with internal conflicts, dilemmas and with intense feelings triggered by the process of learning in a safe environment. The means of assessing transformative learning require an innovative approach that draws on available theory while opening the door to new research. This approach to assessment will also be necessarily bound by the constraints specific to each cultural setting, as in this case, to those I found at SQU.

## Self- and peer-assessment

There is a general agreement among tertiary educators that students should be able to reflect on their own progress, through the means of self-assessment and that of their classmates through peer-assessment (see Peters and Bartholomew, this volume). By involving students in self-and peer-assessment activities, which provide students with the opportunity to develop metacognitive and higher-order thinking skills, teachers empower their students to take responsibility for their own learning, thus partly drawing out the authority from the teachers (Hendry, 1996).

In terms of student empowerment, Stefani (1994) observes that many teachers seem troubled by the idea of passing any portion of assessment over to students. According to Stefani, this fear is generated by the possibility that the student grades will not be in correspondence with the teachers' grades. In a paper reporting the results of a study of students self-assessing and peer-assessing a biochemistry laboratory practical report, however, Stefani dismisses such a possibility. Her study has shown that student assessment can be as reliable as that of teachers and as such it can be helpful in dispelling fears related to empowering students in the area of assessment.

Cranton (1994) identified increased learner's decision-making and empowerment as essential for transformative learning. Most university teachers would agree that students, in general, do not devote any time and effort to producing assignments that are not going to be assessed. Students rarely do any 'extra work' in order to generate knowledge, advance learning or for the pure pleasure of it. It appears that while all the assignments must be assessed, however, they do not have to be marked to generate the necessary learning (Gibbs & Simpson, 2004). In a study conducted by Forbes & Spence (1991), the researchers demonstrate that the lack of teachers' assessment of an assigned task did indeed lower students' exam marks.

The introduction of periodic peer-assessment without grades, however, significantly contributed to the increase in students' exam marks. This is a powerful example of how students' engagement and taking responsibility for their own learning can enhance learning.

Boud (2003) identified eight major goals of the process of self-assessment: individual self-monitoring and measuring progress, promoting how-to-learn skills, diagnosis and remediation, as a substitute for other forms of assessment, to improve academic practice, to consolidate learning, to recognise prior learning, and to deepen self knowledge and self understanding. He also noted that all assessment should involve establishing criteria and evaluate work based on these criteria.

## Feedback

In his paper on formative assessment, Sadler (1998) postulates that it is the quality of feedback that enhances student learning, not just its quantity. What matters is not only *"the technical structure of the feedback (such as its accuracy, comprehensiveness and appropriateness) but also its accessibility to the learner (as a communication), its catalytic and coaching value, and its ability to inspire confidence and hope"* (Sadler, 1998:84).

According to Forbes and Spence (1991), it is not so much the quality of the feedback, but rather the level of students' engagement with the feedback that plays a crucial role in enhancing students' learning. In a study of innovation in assessment conducted in an engineering course, they have observed that peer assessment provided instantly during classes, even if of low quality, resulted in a significant increase in student performance. This was opposed to high-quality teacher feedback provided much later and to which students as a consequence had not attended. In order to effectively impact student learning, teacher feedback, among others, must be regular, quick and detailed; emphasise the learning rather than the grade; be understandable; give students a leveraging point to improve their work and ensure positive self-esteem along with a sense of personal engagement in the learning process (Gibbs, 2006).

## Embedding transformative assessment within PBL

Students learning in order to achieve a 'good grade' seems to be a common phenomenon at universities all over the globe. The situation at SQU was not an exception. Upon my arrival at the College of Economics and Political Sciences, I learned from colleagues (and students) that students were used to what they called 'spoon feeding' and 'negotiating' grades with teachers was not a rare situation.

Students were accustomed to lecture-style classes and to learning material by heart from American textbooks which were hardly suitable for their cultural, economic and political context in order to pass the two midterm and one final exam and receive a very summative, letter grade at the end of their course. Teachers had little input in the preparation of the final exam. The retention of knowledge was minimal and so were the critical thinking abilities of the students.

Such assessment clearly did not support learning as understood through the prism of Mezirow's theory of transformative learning. In his research Mezirow (2009:103) writes: *"Transformative learning is a rational, metacognitive process of reassessing reasons that support problematic meaning perspectives or frames of references, including those representing such contextual cultural factors as ideology, religion, politics, class, race, gender and others. It is a process by which adults learn how to think critically for themselves rather than take assumption supporting a point of view for granted."*

PBL, while not new, remains a relatively underused teaching and learning method. More traditional and widespread methods of learning, such as lecturing, are teacher-centred, and cast the teacher as guru-authority; the learning is based on some kind of transmission of 'knowledge', as in facts or content that is being passed from the teacher to students.

Upon entering a PBL classroom, however, students hear a very different message: the student is responsible for conducting the learning process and may even be responsible for determining the learning content. No longer a passive recipient of knowledge nor an onlooker or an auditor attending a lecture, the student is encouraged and even expected to take responsibility for their own learning. Together with the teacher, the student determines what will be learnt and the manner in which this will be accomplished.

For students experiencing the PBL classroom for the first time, this can constitute quite a shock. Approaches to PBL differ from the traditional in which the teacher will deliver the problem as a task to be solved to the less structured in which the student(s) will determine the problem to be solved according to a set of criteria given by the teacher. In both approaches, the first step involves brainstorming and sharing ideas.

Giving voice to one's ideas is a significant opportunity for empowerment in the learning process but presupposes a stage upon which the student is able to speak as an equal among his/her peers. As one female student stated in her reflections on the learning process: *"I also have learned to stand for what I believe in, even though sometimes I would have to start a fight with Mohammad. I have learned to deal with boys and to have respect from people around me."*

In order to ensure students' engagement with learning, it was necessary to construct the syllabus in a fashion that would allow the students to assume responsibility for their learning. Therefore, within the prescribed course material and learning outcomes, the students, in the process of brainstorming followed by negotiations, would come up with the theme for the course, which would then serve as the vehicle for knowledge. For example, within the context of the course on business communication, students might select the topic of volunteerism and community service as the main theme. Upon selecting the topic, they would split into gender-blended teams of five or six, and decide on the subtopics they would work on, as well as the role division within the group. Each team was composed of a team leader, scribe, researchers; each person was account-able for their share of the work. The teams were negotiating, discussing and recognising prior knowledge while identifying the learning objec-tives and planning the course work for the weeks to come. Each member would then work on their own, conducting research or other appropriate learning steps, which they reported on during the following class session. The learning outcomes were incorporated into their project work and presented periodically to other teams for immediate peer feedback.

The assessment of their work was composed of several elements (as described in Fig. 1) and each of the phases of the assessment process contained critical reflection, often facilitated by the instructor. This included:

+ self-assessment: each student had to fill in their self-assessment review sheet;

+ peer assessment: each student had to fill in a form assessing each of their team members based on the quality and quantity of conducted work as defined in the course objectives and desired learning outcomes;

+ peer and teacher generated immediate feedback arising from the class sessions and periodical presentations constituting 'progress reports', as well as more formal presentations related to the 'final product';

+ a final element of student assessment composed of reflective diaries which each student was obliged to keep, in order to record their observations and thoughts related to class discussions, teamwork, and the observed progress of the group.

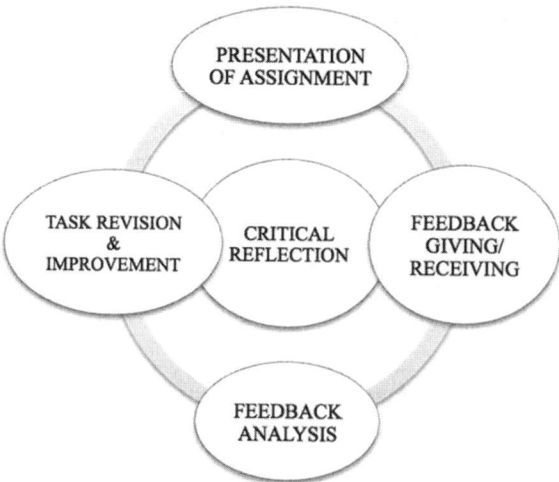

*Figure 1. Feedback analysis loop.*

The last formative element of assessment was reserved for the teacher who, on the basis of the student's written reflection, took into consideration the student's measurable and observable progress. This final element of assessment also incorporated evaluating the final product, which could include a portfolio, presentation, exhibition, video, etc. Activities students conducted during the course work might include: conducting discussions, debates, interviews, writing formal business letters, proposals, progress report, etc. All of the activities arose from the students' teamwork relating to the topic they had selected at the beginning of the course. As students assumed responsibility for their own learning and progress, they were consequently much more emotionally invested in accomplishing the various activities.

Within the SQU context, the teacher was still bound by university policy regarding grading, including the distribution of the final grade, which also had to be a letter grade. This came to be a major inhibiting factor to the innovative process described above and later acted as a brake on the transformation of the department.

# Outcomes: perspective change and critical reflection

Mezirow (2009), in his theory of transformative learning, postulates that the disorienting dilemma acts as the trigger for a learning process that can result in perspective change. Herbers and Nelson (2009) suggest that the disorienting dilemma may serve as a catalyst for students to examine long-held assumptions about themselves and others that impede them from developing a more inclusive world view or resolving important issues in their lives.

The disorienting dilemma, or quandary, may arise in the course of a PBL classroom for several reasons: the necessity for students to negotiate their learning among themselves; the sudden blending of genders in team-based learning; the sense of empowerment in being asked to lead their own learning and assessment.

Finding oneself quite abruptly in a context that allows the student the freedom to express himself/herself can be disorienting. To quote one student:

> "But it's the traditions that control our life and sometimes it's difficult to change it. I don't think that SQU is in a real co-educational system. It seems like a mixed university but actually it is not. Between the two genders there is no communication, as they are really from different planets, it's as you can say forbidden, not a good thing and sometimes when man talk to a woman many people will start to tell rumors about these two."

PBL is an intellectual exercise that requires that the learners come together throughout the entire process. Although some stages are conducted independently, such as information gathering, the goal is for each individual to return to the group with the relevant material. It presupposes that the students work together as equals in a climate of mutual respect, that the teacher act as facilitator rather than as authority, and that the learning process will welcome uncertainty and discovery. Another central component of PBL is the reflective diary which again acts as an agent of empowerment but also as a source of questioning and intellectual disruption. It is in this manner, and in the context of these cultural constraints specific to the SQU classroom, that the disorienting dilemma became a feature of the PBL learning process.

Within the confines of traditional assessment, both formative and summative, an act of learning must be parcelled out for evaluation. While formative assessment seeks to inform both the learner and the teacher of how best to adapt the learning process in order for the student to successfully execute the assigned tasks, assessment within the transformative learning process is a shifting notion of understanding between teacher and learner.

It requires that the learner arrive at a point of self-awareness and self-examination that can be expressed through various channels, for example, through the reflective diary or in class discussion, and that the teacher be able to highlight or capture the student's perceived change in meaning or perspective. Assessment in this sense is perhaps better understood through the metaphor of the climber ascending the cliff face and setting the piton in the stone to support the next step and to ensure safety in the event of a fall, both for himself and for those to follow.

Challenging one's long-held beliefs and assumptions can be perilous and unbalancing until one has reached the next level. The teacher often acts as a belayer to the learner-climber and observes the learner in his/her ascent of the unknown. Thus assessment within transformative learning becomes a fluid notion that acts in harmony with the learner's own experience yet empowers the learner to press further in his/her search for understanding.

Through my experience implementing PBL, I have developed a learning spiral comprising 6 stages:

1) brainstorming;

2) task (product) and topic selection;

3) identifying existing knowledge and deciding what to learn;

4) individual research;

5) presentation;

6) final product.

Transformative assessment within the PBL learning spiral is a three-part mechanism involving:

1) feedback;

2) reflection;

3) means for improvement.

Embedded throughout each stage of the learning spiral, and as stated previously, it is conducted by a number of sources: the learner, peers and teacher.

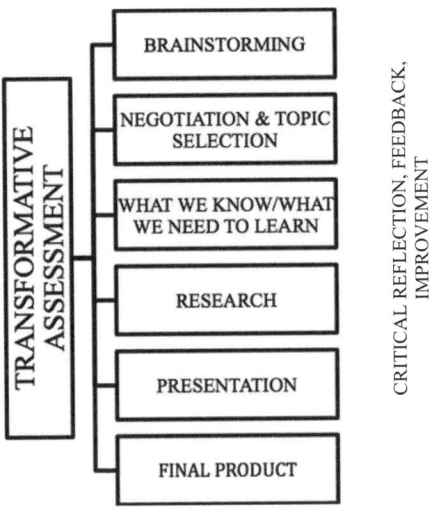

*Figure 2. Transformative assessment within the PBL learning process.*

Assessment conducted within the transformative PBL context will seek to be sensitive to the changes in perspective as they evolve in the learner's symbolic production. It is thus important that all parties engaged in the assessment process share in the key values that allow it to happen: empathy, mutual respect and tolerance. The process of perspective change as described by Mezirow (2000) entails the confrontation of commonly held views and assumptions between those involved in the process, most often through group discussion. Assessment is therefore a process of exchange and negotiated understanding which relates back to an individual's own sense of achievement or increased ability to cope or overcome a challenging situation. In this way, the student may *"acquire the skills and resources (internal and external) to resolve the impasse between new challenges and ineffective responses"*, Herbers & Nelson (2009:6).

One student's diary reflections illustrate this perspective change:

> *"I knew I was on the right side from the beginning: against restrictions. I think that citizens should have democracy and freedom of choice. It was an interesting discussion and I learned quite a few things. There were some ideas from others that I had never considered."*

Critical reflection and discourse, that question the assumptions, beliefs and thinking habits that construct one's viewpoint, constitute key aspects of Mezirow's (1997) theory of transformative learning. Transforming one's ethnocentric mindset, for example, passes through the critical reflection on one's own bias in the way one views others.

Mezirow (1997) indicates that transformative learning is constructed on two major planes: on the first, through increased awareness and critical examination of one's own assumptions and those of the people around oneself, and through redefining problems imaginatively from another perspective. On a second plane, discourse is needed in order for a student to validate his/her understanding of the problem and to adjust his/her beliefs accordingly. Mezirow (1997:10) reminds us that learning is a social process and that discourse is central to making meaning: *"Effective discourse depends on how well the educator can create a situation in which those participating have full information; are free from coercion; have equal opportunity to assume the various roles of discourse (to advance beliefs, challenge, defend, explain, assess evidence, and judge arguments); become critically reflective of assumptions, are empathic and open to other perspectives, are willing to listen and to search for common ground or a synthesis of different points of view; and can make a tentative best judgment to guide action."*

The teacher's ability to create the above conditions will have an enormous impact on the quality of learning taking place in the transformative context. New information acts as a resource in the transformative learning process and, consequently, the traditional assessment practice of evaluating the transmission of knowledge as information would contradict the transformative learning process. Students must then be coaxed away from the desire to be assessed traditionally on rote learning and become confident in the process that allows them to reach new understanding about their beliefs and assumptions. Assessing their critical thinking skills and ability to think creatively in a process that entails group deliberation and problem solving is challenging in a traditional educational context. Assessing student progress in the context of transformative PBL classroom necessitates building confidence in students' capacity to evaluate their own learning. At the same time, as the teacher leaves the role of authority figure to accompany the students in their journey, the students progressively take on a leadership role in directing their own learning. This, too, can be part of the assessment criteria that can be reflected in non-traditional or innovative methods such as student portfolios that demonstrate critical reflection and awareness, self and peer review, reflective diaries, and student-initiated final product.

## Conclusion

Most educators would agree that a "one size fits all" approach towards assessment must be avoided. While designing assessment that promotes students' learning, one should take into consideration that such assessment must be student-centred, reflect student-centred curriculum, and be aligned with learning objectives. Assessment should ideally be oriented to the learning needs of the individual student and take into consideration the culture-specific context, as well as the diversity commonly found today in universities around the globe. Only then can it play a truly supporting role in the learning process. Assessment itself should allow students opportunities for improvement and growth.

There seems to be very little doubt as to the efficacy of students' empowerment within their own learning process. Innovative teaching and learning methods that are combined with student-centred, transformative assessment have the power to enhance students' learning significantly. This can transform learning into life-long attitudes that promote greater self-awareness, critical thinking abilities as well as independence in gaining knowledge. However, the true success of innovative teaching and assessment of learning can be achieved only with the recognition and support of the university's administration and policy makers.

During my five-year period of work at SQU, I became a witness to transformative change in my students. The transformative assessment described herein led to the change of perspective in my students, but also in myself. Since the process of transformative learning is sustained by critical thinking, Mezirow (1990) places assessment within the critical thinking process as a going back to one's initial premises or presuppositions and assessing their validity or reliability or pertinence even to the problem needing to be solved or the meaning needing to be adjusted.

The teacher's assessment, expressed as a grade required by the university, must flesh out, validate and render visible the student's learning process. The cultural constraints specific to each university setting will enable or inhibit the teacher/facilitator's ability to express that transformative learning process.

## About the Author

Maja Hunter is the Head of Curriculum Development and Research at Ermitage International School of France. Previously, she was the Head of Business Communication Area at the College of Economics and Political Science at Sultan Qaboos University, Muscat, Oman. She can be contacted at this email: mahunter@ermitage.fr

## Bibliography

Astin, A. W. & A. L. Antonio (2012). *Assessment for Excellence: The Philosophy and Practice of Assessment and Evaluation in Higher Education.* Rowman Littlefield Publishing.

Biggs, J. (2003). *Teaching for quality learning at university.* Buckingham: Society for Research into Higher Education, Open University Press.

Boud, D. (2003). *Enhancing learning through self assessment,* Routledge Falmer.

Cranton, P. (1994). Self-directed and transformative instructional development. *The Journal of Higher Education,* Vol. 65, No.6, pp. 726-744.

Forbes, D. & J. Spence (1991). An experiment in assessment for a large class. In R. Smith (Ed.) *Innovations in engineering education.* London: Ellis Horwood. Gibbs, G. (2006). How assessment frames student learning. In C. Bryan & K.

Clegg (Eds.) *Innovative Assessment in Higher Education.* London: Routledge.

Gibbs G. & C. Simpson (2004). Conditions under which assessment supports students' learning. *Learning and Teaching in Higher Education,* Vol. 1, pp. 3–31.

Hendry, G. D. (1996). Constructivism and educational practice. *Australian Journal of Education,* Vol. 40, No. 1, pp. 19-45.

Herbers, M. S. & B. Mullins Nelson. (2009). Using the disorienting dilemma to promote transformative learning. *Journal on Excellence in College Teaching,* Vol. 20, No. 1, pp. 5-34.

Mezirow, J. (1978). Perspective transformation. *Adult Education,* Vol. 28, No. 2, pp. 100-110.

Mezirow, J. (1990). *Fostering critical reflection in adulthood : a guide to transformative and emancipatory learning,* Jossey-Bass.

Mezirow, J. (1991). *Transformative dimensions of adult learning.* San Francisco: Jossey-Bass.

Mezirow, J. (1997). Transformative learning: from theory to practice. *New Directions for Adult and Continuing Education,* Vol. 97, No. 74, pp. 5-12.

Mezirow, J. (2000). Learning to think like an adult – core concepts of transformation theory. In J. Mezirow and Associates. *Learning as transformation: critical perspectives on a theory in progress.* San Francisco: Jossey-Bass, pp. 3-33.

Mezirow, J. (2009). An overview on transformative learning. In K. Illeris *Contemporary Theories of Learning. Learning theorists…in their own words.* Routledge, London.

Sadler, D. R. (1998). Formative assessment: revisiting the territory. *Assessment in Education,* Vol. 5, No. 1, pp. 77–84.

Stefani, L. A. J. (1994). Peer, self, and tutor assessment: relative reliabilities, *Studies in Higher Education,* Vol. 19, No. 1, pp. 69-75.

Taylor, E. W. (2006). The challenge of teaching for change. In E. Taylor (Ed.), *Teaching for change: Fostering transformative learning in the classroom.* New Directions for Adult and Continuing Education, No. 109. San Francisco: Jossey-Bass, pp. 91-96.

Chapter 9

# The Trust Issue: Implementing Peer-Assessment in an Undergraduate Professional Development Context

Michael Peters and Paul Bartholomew

| Assessment Agency | Student-driven | * | Teacher-driven | * |
|---|---|---|---|---|
| Assessment Outcomes | Fixed | | Flexible | * |
| Assessment Focus | Process | * | Outcome | |
| Assessment Context | Specific | | Transferrable | * |

## Introduction

This chapter shows how, in a specific UK context, student-focused and student-led assessment practice contributed to the empowerment of students as autonomous learners. It also complements the chapter (in this volume) by Fleischmann in which peer assessment is used as a vehicle to foster critical thinking in creative arts students in Australia.

The drastic changes enforced upon the UK's university sector within the past few years and, in particular, the political agenda to make higher education accessible to a wider section of the population has meant that universities have had to reconsider how they construct their programmes.

Through this chapter, we discuss how a module within a Foundation Year programme of study was developed to follow the constructive alignment model as proposed by Biggs and Tang (2007). This model proposes that teaching and learning activities and assessment should align with the intended learning outcomes of the programme via a process of knowledge construction.

Through the presentation of a case study (rather than case study research – Bartholomew, 2015) in engineering education in the United Kingdom, we discuss how peer-assessment and reflective essays, within one module of an Engineering and Applied Science Foundation Year programme, have contributed to developing learner autonomy within the wider programme and for the students' ongoing experience. By reading this chapter we anticipate you will:

1. gain an insight into the design of preparatory programmes in higher education;

2. learn of a structured technology-supported approach to the deployment of peer-assessment and the introduction of reflective writing to students who have never experienced it before; and

3. receive a narrative evaluation as to the efficacy of the approach.

The chapter starts by discussing some assessment literature, looks at the development of a student-led assessment regime applicable to the module, continues by outlining the context of the module, the development of the assessment artefacts and student feedback and, finally, offers conclusions and recommendations. First, we offer some definitions to clarify our language use for an international readership:

| Term | Definition |
| --- | --- |
| Foundation Programme | A preparatory programme run by universities designed to furnish prospective undergraduate students with the skills and knowledge necessary to prepare them for successful undergraduate study. Such programmes are typically taken by students who have 'just missed' the grades to enter their chosen programme or are making a switch of domain focus away from elective subjects taken in the final years of their secondary education |
| Module | A structured deliverable component of a programme of study; often referred to as a 'course' in a non-UK context |
| Assessment regime | The totality of the assessment activities/tasks required of a student through the study of a module |
| Assessment artefact | A discrete piece of work that is submitted by the student for the purposes of being assessed |

*Table 1: Definitions of terms used within this chapter that may be new to some readers.*

In order to provide a framework for discussion, two broad paradigms of learning are proposed and used within this chapter: Teacher-centred learning and Student-centred learning, with consideration given to the role of assessment in those two paradigms. It would be naïve to think that these paradigms are mutually exclusive; in reality they lie on a continuum, as shown in Figure 1. The majority of programmes would probably include aspects of teacher-centred learning and student-centred learning.

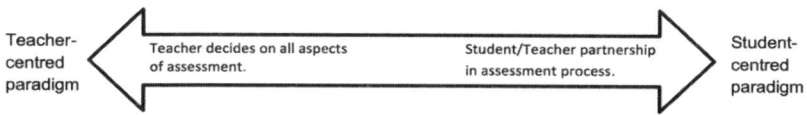

*Figure 1: Assessment Continuum.*

In relation to assessment design, we contend that these paradigms of *learning* correlate well with certain *assessment* paradigms – namely, assessment *of* learning and assessment *for* learning (Black & Wiliam, 1998; Earl, 2003; Bloxham & Boyd, 2007). In a teacher-centred model, assessment is mainly used to as a way to ensure students 'prove' they have acquired a number of facts deemed to be essential for their development. The teacher makes a judgement as to what is deemed important enough to be examined (or indeed to earn a mark!) by taking into account any accrediting body requirements and their own personal viewpoint. This process does not necessarily contribute to students' learning, as the act of being assessed does not offer an opportunity for further development – it merely provides the opportunity for the demonstration of some aspects of what has been learnt prior to engaging in the assessment opportunity.

This stance of end-point summative assessment of what has been learnt is transmitted to the students, who then may expect to be taught to the assessment. Savin-Baden (2000:61) suggested that this type of scenario could be described as a 'reproductive pedagogy'. By this she means the students in this type of learning mode adopt methods of learning that encourage them to be surface learners with a propensity for valuing (or least accepting) declarative knowledge.

Challenges emerge when students adopt a stance in which they view their teachers as the suppliers of legitimate knowledge and thus, fearful of the implications of a deviance from perceived doctrine, avoid taking 'risks' with their learning. Allied to this stance is the notion of *"strategic learning"* (Entwhistle, 1981:102) where the student seeks out cues in order to pass the assessment for the module. Laurillard (2002) made the important point that there is a difference between assessing what students know and what they can do. She goes on to say that traditional forms of assessment are seen to be inadequate since they fail to assess students' capabilities in the authentic activities of their particular disciplines.

This correlates well with the notion of assessment of learning: *"Assessment of learning characterises how we may traditionally view assessment. It involves making judgements about students' summative achievement for purposes of selection and certification."* Bloxham & Boyd (2007:15). In the case of coursework for example, this paradigm is manifested as a summative assessment regime where the form of the assessment is decided exclusively by the teacher, is then marked by the teacher using pre-determined criteria (by the teacher) to award a grade and, once marked, is returned to the student with some form of feedback that reflects the thoughts of the teacher as they relate to the teacher's concept of what is important.

In a student-centred paradigm, the assessment takes on more of a formative character. The main aim of the assessment is not purely to quantify a student's performance in a post-hoc way, but to help them draw learning value from the process of engaging with assessment tasks – not just as a consumer of the assessment regime but as a designer of it too. In this paradigm, the students work with their teachers to define the performance criteria and the form the assessment should take, with an emphasis on encouraging the student to develop self- and peer-assessment skills. Savin-Badin (2000:63) refers to this domain as *"a reflective pedagogy"* encompassing the notion that learning and knowledge are flexible entities. A typical characteristic of this domain is the critical evaluation of personal knowledge and of propositional knowledge on the student's terms. The student is able to engage with the knowledge and at the same time not just accept it as fact, but question it. In relation to assessment paradigms, this correlates with the notion of assessment *for* learning.

In describing the term 'assessment *as* learning' as a sub-set of assessment *for* learning, Bloxham & Boyd (2007) citing Black & Wiliam

(1998:15) state that *"assessment as learning is a subset of assessment for learning and sees student involvement in assessment, using feedback, participating in peer assessment, and self-monitoring of progress as moments of learning in themselves... ...Students come to have a better understanding of the subject matter and their own learning through their close involvement with assessment."*

## Engagement and empowerment

Mayes (2006) refers to how 'engagement' relates to a student's attitudes and commitment to their studies and how 'empowerment' relates to their capability and competency to do so effectively. In order for students to be successful, they need to be engaged and empowered – meaning that, in terms of the learning experience, they must be encouraged to be committed to their studies and encouraged to take responsibility for their own learning (Tinto, 2005). In addition to academic engagement, the student also needs to be socially empowered, which involves offering opportunities for students to engage dialogically with both peers and staff to become acculturated to university life (QAA Scotland, 2009).

The process of learning inevitably involves the tacit monitoring, reflection and self-assessment of any work performed by the student. One of the purposes of introducing the portfolio, reflective essay and peer-assessment dimensions to the module being discussed in this chapter was to strengthen these internal processes by making them explicit. Students can only achieve the intended learning outcomes of a module or programme if they have a clear idea of what they are supposed to achieve. Allied to this is the notion of ownership of the goal and assessing their progress towards achieving the goal. Unfortunately, there is sometimes a mismatch between the intended learning outcome and the student's perception of it. Nicol and Macfarlane-Dick (2004) suggest that strategies to clarify criteria, standards and goals include discussion and reflection about criteria and standards by involving students in peer-assessment.

The introduction of peer-assessment within this reported context afforded the opportunity to explore the issues around assessment. Although initially the explorations were focused on the peer-assessment process, they soon expanded to incorporate the purpose of the portfolio and the reflective essay assessment items. These explorations revealed how the students perceived their roles within the learning environment. The impression received was that they saw themselves as passive recipients and were accustomed to the 'terms and conditions' of learning and teaching being set by an authority figure – namely, the teacher. They did not have a 'voice' in any aspect of the process and considered the only motivational factor to be the achievement of high grades in the assessment. Indeed, the impression received was more the avoidance of low grades and the ignominy of not being on a par with their peers. In education parlance, they felt disempowered and absorbing knowledge and developing new skills were simply a means of passing assessments with the hope of getting a good qualification, which would lead to a good job.

Our intentions behind getting students to set the assessment criteria and assess their peers' work, was to involve them in the learning process with the aim of increasing their motivation and thus their engagement. As Yorke (2005) pointed out, a major component of academic motivation is how students perceive their role within the learning process. If they are to gain a sense of control of their learning, assessment practices need to be designed in order for them to develop skills in monitoring, judging and managing their own learning; i.e. empowerment. However, it is important to appreciate that engagement is seen as a necessary but insufficient condition for empowerment; i.e. students can be engaged without much sense of empowerment (QAA Scotland, 2009). An important aspect of students commenting on and judging the work of their peers against criteria is that it can be transferred to their own work. Through this means, the student takes on a teacher role and, as such, they help develop their skills in monitoring, judging and managing their own learning. This development of the skill of assessment can be a transformative process for the students; the notion of assessment, as a transformative learning process, is explored further by Hunter (in this volume).

## Developing a Student-centred approach to Assessment

In order to develop a more student-centred learning paradigm within the module, the three-stage model proposed by Biggs & Tang (2007) was adopted: 1) setting the criteria, 2) selecting the evidence and 3) making a judgement. Traditionally, the teacher deals with all three stages, but in a more student-centred paradigm, the student is more actively involved. Table 2 compares these two models.

| Stage | Teacher driven | Student driven |
|---|---|---|
| Setting the criteria | Teacher sets the criteria based on own judgement, criteria imposed by professional bodies. Language used tends to be technical. Learning outcomes are quantified. | Students actively involved in setting the criteria. Helps them to know what the criteria means. Language used tends to be meaningful to the cohort. Encourages them to apply the criteria to themselves and others. |
| Selecting the evidence | Teacher decides on the evidence to be used in deciding whether students have acquired sufficient knowledge and/or skills to be awarded an appropriate grade. | Students make judgements on what constitutes good and bad evidence. Students decide on grade boundaries. |
| Making a judgement | Teacher makes a judgement as to how much of the module content has been learned correctly and assigns a mark. The overall mark is normally an aggregate of marks assigned to the different criteria attributed to subsections of the work. | Students encouraged to undertake self-assessment and to assess their peers' work. Must be able to defend their judgements if challenged by the assessee. |
| Outcome | Encourages students to 'work to the grade'. Feedback given by teacher used by students to meet the next set of criteria. | Assessment becomes a meaningful learning activity. Students gain an insight into the assessment process and can use this knowledge to develop as learners. |

*Table 2: Comparison of teacher- and student-driven models.*

# The Context of the Module

To clarify, the programme of study that forms the context of this chapter is situated at Level 3 in the National Qualifications Framework (NQF). It is classed as a pre-undergraduate programme and is designed to furnish prospective undergraduate students with the skills and knowledge necessary to prepare them for undergraduate study. In a university context, these types of programmes are known as Foundation Years or Year 0 programmes. The programme is an important aspect of the widening participation agenda – for some prospective students it affords the opportunity to study at university when they might otherwise not have the opportunity to do so. Typical profiles of students enrolling in these programmes are overseas students whose home education systems have 12 years of compulsory education compared to the UK's 13 years, students who have studied subjects not relevant to their chosen undergraduate programme, or students who have not achieved the required entry criteria to enrol in their chosen undergraduate programme.

Prior to the developments reported in this chapter, the programme had been running for many years with little development. A new Programme Director was appointed and, along with the programme team, decided to introduce a new module. The rationale behind the introduction of this module emerged from evidence that suggested that many teachers and school children did not appreciate what engineering entails (Engineering, 2007). In addition to ameliorating this position, factors such as student engagement, validity of assessment, curriculum alignment and assessment for learning were key in the design and implementation of the module and its assessment – and so, the opportunity was taken to introduce a more student-centred approach to learning.

This new module was designed to give the students the opportunity to have a 'taste' of the different engineering disciplines offered by Aston University. The cohort were subdivided into four groups. Each group in turn spent two weeks experiencing an introduction to a particular discipline, and the students were taught as a single cohort for the module reported in this chapter.

# Development of the Assessment Method

Since the aim of this particular module was not primarily about enhancing engineering knowledge and skills but about empowering students to make an informed choice in relation to the branch of engineering they wished to study, the question of how to most legitimately assess them was raised. After exploring options with the University's Centre for Learning Innovation and Professional Practice, a peer-assessed portfolio leading to a reflective essay – a regime (scheme) designed to motivate reflection by the student – was selected. We define peer assessment as "student engagement in a process of mutual assessment and feedback". We argue that there are two crucial design imperatives that underpin successful peer assessment:

1. an acknowledgement that students do not know how to engage with peer assessment, either as an assessor or an 'assessee', and will need to be trained;

2. student learning emerges primarily from their role as assessor, not 'assessee'.

With this in mind, the first session of the module comprised a briefing on peer assessment that included:

+ a definition of peer assessment;

+ the pedagogic rationale for deploying peer assessment:

    + student ownership of the assessment process;

    + the value of negotiating assessment criteria with students;

    + the assessment for/as learning approach – how peer assessment asks students to make critical judgements;

    + the need to negotiate with peers, leading to the development of negotiation skills;

    + the emergent learning dialogues that come about as a result of peer engagement in the giving and receiving of feedback.

+ an honest addressing of students' concerns relating to peer assessment:

+ perceptions of additional workload;

+ the perceived lack of legitimacy of peer feedback;

+ the perception of undertaking work that the 'lecturer is already paid to do';

+ the intra-group social dynamics that might be seen to inhibit fair and robust assessment;

  + the introduction to the concept of a portfolio as an assessment artefact;

  + the introduction to the concept and structure of marking rubrics;

  + the facilitated student-production of potential assessment criteria.

The portfolio (one of the assessment artefacts within the assessment regime) was designed to be the means by which students would be able to record significant events and critically reflect upon how their personal attributes came into play. In order to assist them in the documenting process, the portfolio was divided into six skill sections: independent enquirer, creative thinker, reflective learner, team worker, self-manager and effective participator. Each skill section was then given a number of sub-headings in order to guide the students in identifying events that would help them to articulate a particular skill.

The ethos of the portfolio was that students should be encouraged to take ownership of their learning (McCombs, 2015) through being involved in the decision-making process. In order to make informed choices in relation to their to-be-chosen branch of engineering, they had to be aware of their personal attributes and how these attributes affect their learning (Savin-Baden, 2000). For example, to be able to learn within a group (such as groups promoted by problem-based learning) the student must know how to work effectively as a team member. If they are unaware of the skill set required and whether they possess such a skill, they would find group work challenging.

A less well-supported portfolio (without a reflective essay) was used with the previous cohort with less than satisfactory results; the pilot year revealed that students, first of all, did not like having to complete a portfolio, did not understand the purpose of a portfolio and did not appreciate the value of being aware of one's personal attributes and how these impacted on their learning. Reflecting back on the implementation of the portfolio it was realised that the students, in their previous educational experiences, were not given the opportunity to think about how their personal attributes impacted on their learning. In addition to this, they were accustomed to being taught with little opportunity to demonstrate autonomy in their learning.

In the second iteration of introducing the portfolio, a more student-centred approach was adopted in order to encourage the students to engage in all aspects of the assessment regime. Rather than impose a set of what students sometimes perceive as arbitrary assessment criteria, the students were given the opportunity to set the criteria themselves. This was done by using a piece of software called *Padlet* (see Figure 2). The six skill sections were listed down the left hand side and titles for the assessment criteria across the top. The titles were deliberately framed in everyday language ie. 'criteria for an excellent portfolio', 'criteria for a good portfolio' and so on. It was then left for the students to specify a more precise set of criteria, which they would have to use to assess their peers' work. Prior to asking them to set the criteria, a class discussion was held on what constituted meaningful criteria.

The purpose of the discussion was to highlight the need to set criteria against which meaningful judgements could be made. It is interesting to note that some students used criteria that they had encountered in previous academic work. For example, in the reflective learning skill section, one student proposed *"Reviews progress towards achieving set goals"*, which is the sort of criterion a teacher would set. This implies the strong influence of criteria they have encountered in the past whereas statements such as *"Reviewing what you've done well and less well"* is typical of the language you would expect students to use. In other instances, criteria were set that would be extremely difficult to judge in terms of meeting them. For example, *"Works confidently in a team and discusses issues to solve problems"* would be extremely difficult to judge without direct observation of the episode where teamwork was undertaken.

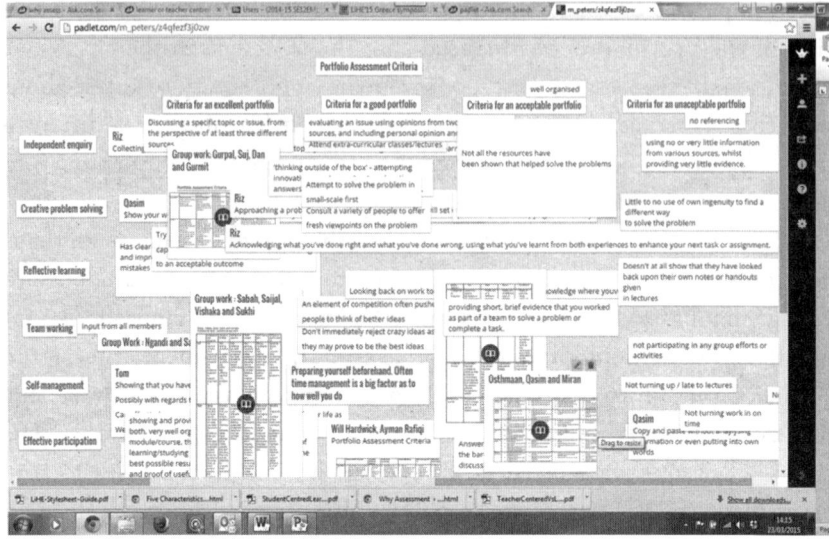

*Figure 2: Padlet with student responses.*

## A note about 'Padlet'

In simple terms, *Padlet* is an electronic 'comment wall' where the students could 'stick' their contribution to the assessment criteria. The benefit of using such a system is that it is transparent and open so the students could see the contributions made by their peers. For any (perhaps shy) student who was reticent to become involved, this software provided the opportunity for them to get an idea of what was expected and make their own contribution. This process was started in the first introductory session of the module and continued into the second, keeping the *Padlet* 'wall' open in the intervening period. Once the wall was closed, the students were given the opportunity to decide if they wanted the tutor to finalise the assessment criteria, or if their suggestions were to be used as is. The cohort decided they wanted to leave the assessment criteria as they had posted it.

To complete the three stages of assessment discussed, the students would use the criteria they had created to assess the work of their peers. In addition to setting the criteria, the students were given the freedom to present their portfolios in whatever form they thought was appropriate; since presenting information in an appropriate way to a particular audience is a skill in itself. The only guidance given was that their portfolio had to be structured in such a way that the assessor would be able to find any evidence to back up any claims they made. For example, some students ordered their portfolios under the skill sections, others by subject and some by key episodes. They were also advised that the skills were not necessarily independent of one another and therefore a key episode could encompass more than one skill. For instance, if they were working in a group on an experiment, they would employ group working skills, creative problem solving, independent enquiry and reflective learning. The challenge for them was to make clear which particular skill was utilised within the resolution of the experiment. It was also emphasised they should include any unsuccessful attempts and any strategies they adopted to overcome any challenges in performing the task; i.e. they should reflect upon their experience and how it enhanced their learning.

In order to give some reassurance to the students who were not comfortable with having their work assessed by their peers, they were informed that once they received their work back with the grade and associated feedback, they could challenge it. The constraint they were given was they had to engage in a dialectic or, in other words, provide a reasoned argument as to why they disagreed with the grade and convince the programme director to change the grade (for a fuller discussion of the use of dialectics in assessment see Rasmussen and Heldbjerg, in this volume).

The final assessment artefact to be submitted by the students was a reflective essay. This was chosen since reflection is *"a process through which social beings examine themselves within a cultural context"* (Savin-Baden, 2000); the cultural context in this instance being a university learning environment. The students were advised to use evidence from their portfolios to qualify any statements they made. They were also encouraged to incorporate evidence from other sources such as professional body websites. To assist them in gathering their evidence, a series of talks was organised where internal and external staff discussed their careers and what it meant to be an Engineer or Applied Scientist. By attending these talks, the students were able to develop a sense of contextualising their studies in terms of the 'real world' of employment. All of the speakers willingly engaged with the students and were only too pleased to continue discussions after the allotted time and to give contact details so the students could request further information or explore possibilities of employment.

The reflective essay provided the students with the opportunity to articulate reasons why they had chosen a particular engineering discipline. In the process of articulating their reasons, they would have to identify the engineering discipline they were interested in, find out the skills and knowledge required and critically examine why they found this particular discipline attractive. The only restriction imposed upon them was that the essay should be no longer than 1,000 words. The purpose of this restriction was to help them to think hard about their decision and only present what they considered to be the most important aspects of their choice.

The prospect of writing a reflective essay posed particular challenges for this pre-undergraduate student group, since the vast majority did not know about reflection – in particular, they didn't know how to link their reflections to their personal attributes. A number of sessions had to be organised in which the process of reflection and how it related to their personal attributes was discussed. In these sessions, the students tended to identify the areas they found challenging but were reticent to recognise and articulate what they were good at. It quickly became evident that the educational use of the word 'reflection' was the main problem. This is a word that is often used within an educational context with little consideration given to how students interpret it.

The experience of discussing the term with the students highlighted the fact they considered it to be analogous with feedback in the sense that it was about improving. This interpretation is understandable, since in most cases it is used within the context of thinking about when things have gone wrong. For example, people are often told if their behaviour has been unacceptable, to reflect upon the experience and articulate what they have learned from it. This 'everyday' use of the word all too easily becomes the accepted definition and so, when they are confronted with the more precise, educational use of the word, they apply it through the lens of their colloquial definition. The outcome from this is that students interpret the whole process of reflection as one where the situation to be reflected upon is a negative one. To overcome this imbalance, the students were asked to reflect upon what they thought they were good at.

A striking example of the difficulty they had with saying 'good' things about themselves was in relation to group work. In all groups someone usually takes on the role as the leader, making decisions for the group, organising the work and so on. This could be done explicitly or, more usually, someone assumes the role. When the group were asked *"who likes to be a leader?"* no one would 'admit' to it. It took a considerable amount of persuasion to convince the students that it was acceptable to identify their strengths and to articulate them to other people.

Another term that proved to be problematic was 'creativity'. As was the case with the discussion around reflection, time was allocated to discuss this term. When the cohort was asked what creativity meant and who were classed as creative people, the discipline of engineering was not mentioned. They considered creative people to be artists, musicians and fiction writers. When asked if they considered engineers to be creative people, a stunned silence ensued. It was apparent they had never considered engineers as creative people. Once they had accepted that engineers were creative, they were able to give examples that demonstrated creativity and hence formed a notion of what it meant to be creative.

The informal discussions with the students after they had submitted their essays revealed they found this form of assessment particularly difficult and challenging. It is something they did not expect to be involved in on an engineering programme and also something they had not experienced before, so they did not know what was expected. In other words, they did not have any episodic memories that they could use to formulate a coherent response. The combination of the reflective essay and the portfolio led some students to say how the experience has given them an insight into the assessment process, and how it made them realise the importance of recognising, acknowledging and being able to articulate their personal attributes.

## Student perceptions of this implementation of peer assessment

In order to gain a sense of how the students felt about assessing the work of others and having their work assessed by a peer, a simple analysis was performed. The students were asked to comment upon the following two questions: (1) How do you feel about marking someone else's work? and, (2) How do you feel about one of your colleagues marking your work?

In total there were 80 responses (approximately 60% of the cohort). In answer to question (1), 45% reported they enjoyed and/or found the experience beneficial, 36% did not express a strong opinion either way, and 19% would have preferred not to have done it.

Comments in support of the peer assessment included "*I felt confident in my abilities to mark someone else's work. It also gave us the chance to see other people's work and also an insight into what a marker looks at when reading work*" and "*It helped in terms of seeing how we could go further and improve.*" On the negative side, some students commented "*Pointless; I am not a person getting paid to professionally mark somebody's work*" and "*Uncomfortable as I feel that I am being unfair on the student*".

In response to the second question, 42% did not like having their worked marked by a peer, 25% did not express an opinion either way, and 33% thought it was a good idea. Comments made by the students in support of their peers marking their work included "*That's ok since I know teachers won't give high marks, although it could be considered perfect*" and "*I feel comfortable with colleagues marking my work because they will mark it fairly*". Those that did not think having their work marked by a peer was a good idea included "*I don't think people will really bother to read my hard work and will dismiss my efforts all because my portfolio is bigger than others*" and "*I wouldn't want that because I have done my work for the profs and not for students. Getting it checked by a friend is ok, but not someone I don't know*".

Figure 3 is a screenshot of one student's comments with regards to the portfolios he marked. Prior to the overall comments, the students commented on the individual skill sections with regard to the amount and quality of evidence provided in support of claims made by the author of the portfolio.

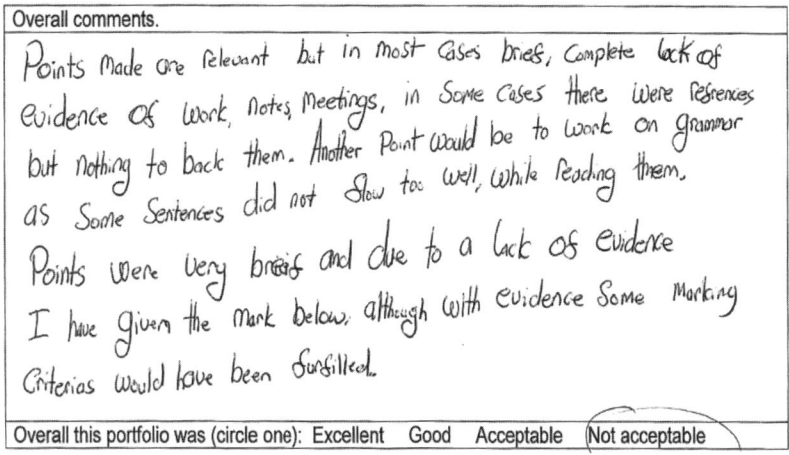

Figure 3: Example of comments for a portfolio deemed to be not acceptable.

In order to aid readability (for this chapter), transcripts of student comments for a 'not acceptable portfolio', an 'acceptable portfolio', a 'good portfolio' and, finally, an 'excellent portfolio' have been included below:

Not Acceptable:

> "Points made are relevant but in most cases brief, complete lack of evidence of work, notes, meetings, in some cases there were references but nothing to back them. Another point would be to work on grammar as some sentences did not flow well, while reading them. Points were very brief and due to lack of evidence I have given the mark below although with evidence some marking criteria would have been fulfilled".

Acceptable:

> "He starts the portfolio off well and the case study showed a lot of skills. However the portfolio was incomplete as he hasn't written about half the points and if he has he didn't show evidence."

Good Portfolio:

> "Well written from their point of view and shows where they showed each of these skills throughout the year in their work. The evidence provided, only linked back to the ideas briefly, but at other times linked well. Evidence was provided in detail for a number of points but lacking in some areas yet still covered the criteria."

Excellent Portfolio:

> "The whole layout of the portfolio is really good from start to finish. I like the way at the start they cover all the work they have been involved with up until this point. Then at the end they cover each of the six skill sections required in detail. They have provided evidence for each point they make and the whole portfolio is written in detail and is easy to read. Punctuation and spelling are good. Overall this is a very good portfolio."

## Tutor Reflections on the Implementation and Administering of the Assessment

From a tutor perspective, the implementation of the new module and the associated model of assessment were challenging, to say the least. The pilot (previous) year, when the portfolio was introduced for the first time, highlighted the anxiety experienced by many of the students. Their main anxiety centred on what was expected of them. It was assumed they would be familiar with portfolios based on their experiences prior to coming to university. This assumption was based on anecdotal evidence from discussions with secondary school teachers and, therefore, any instruction about the portfolio was minimal. The lessons learned from this experience resulted in (for the second iteration) lesson time being timetabled to discuss issues such as the purpose of the portfolio, reasons for using it as an instrument of assessment, and how they would benefit from using one. These lessons were concentrated at the start of the academic year, but students in their meetings with personal tutors still expressed concerns about the layout and what should be recorded.

The reflective essays revealed that many of the students valued the opportunity to have a 'taste' of the different engineering disciplines offered by Aston University. As one student wrote, "*I am grateful for the opportunity* to taste the different engineering subjects as it helped me to decide what I wanted to do in the future". Another student wrote, "even though I knew that I wanted to study chemical engineering, the chance to try electronics etc reinforced my desire to be a chemical engineer because I think my personal strengths are more like the ones required to be a Chemical Engineer". It was interesting to read within a good proportion of the reflective essays that one of the main motivational factors for choosing a particular discipline was salary.

At the time of writing, the highest paid engineers worked within the Chemical Engineering industry, but this may, and probably will, change in the future. Some students linked their decision to their 'love' of a particular subject at school. The students who enjoyed Physics and Mathematics, tended to choose Mechanical Engineering whereas those who enjoyed ICT (Information Communications Technology) chose Computer Science or Electronics. If Chemistry was enjoyed at school or college, the students chose Chemical Engineering.

The peer assessment aspect of the module did not seem to concern the students in the initial stages. This may be because, at that time, assessment was a long way away and they felt they would deal with it at a later time. This, in some respects, is typical human behaviour; the belief is that clarity will come with time and, therefore, there is no need to plan or be concerned for now. The logistics of implementing and administering this form of assessment were considerable. In the first instance, timetabling the taster sessions, for approximately 160 students divided into four groups on a rotational basis, proved challenging regarding allocation of laboratories and lecture rooms. The marking of the reflective essays took a considerable amount of time but it was felt to be a worthwhile investment; feedback could be obtained on how the students viewed the 'taster' sessions, and insight could be gained into some of the factors that motivated their choice of engineering discipline. It also afforded the opportunity to judge which aspects of the whole programme the students found valuable, compared to what the tutor thought would be valuable.

The majority of students valued the sessions in which staff and people external to the University talked about their research, their careers or their company. From these talks, the students were able to see how important personal attributes – like being able to work as part of a team, being creative, being capable of independent enquiry and importantly and having belief in oneself – were valued and essential ingredients for being successful. The students used these talks as evidence in their reflective essays and in their portfolios.

From a learning development perspective, the experience of introducing these students to peer assessment was interesting and rewarding. Peer assessment 'scales' really well, meaning that as programmes grow, so do the resources that are required to administer and manage the assessment. This is one of the reasons why I (Paul) find myself suggesting peer assessment as a potential viable candidate for assessment regimes. Despite the affordance of scalability, it's seldom an easy sell – all too often academics need persuading that it is OK to let go of the teacher-centred reins. The very same briefing on peer assessment that I gave to the students in the first session of the module is derived from the one I use on the academic staff development programmes. I would suggest there is no less of a need for it there. Of course, I note with resigned dismay that, despite the comprehensive briefing I gave to students, some students still don't 'get it' and miss (or perhaps simply don't value) the learning that can cascade from making judgements on the work of others.

## Conclusions

It is our opinion that the UK's compulsory (secondary) education system does not necessarily prepare students to become autonomous learners. The anxiety experienced by many of the students seemed to indicate they were not comfortable with working with tutors on determining some aspects of their learning journey. They were accustomed to a regimented way of studying in which they were told what to learn, how to learn and what was important, and were assured that they would be assessed in a particular way. The students viewed the tutors as the suppliers of knowledge and assumed this knowledge was not contestable. This position made them feel 'comfortable' and therefore they could mitigate responsibility for their learning to an authority figure – and if they did not learn it was due to 'bad teaching' or being taught the wrong topics.

When dealing with assessment, the students were accustomed to being 'coached' in how to approach summative assessments by means of continually attempting previous examination papers. This approach to learning had become ingrained to such a point the students assumed this was the purpose of learning.

When they were faced with the prospect of having to decide what constituted legitimate knowledge, what evidence demonstrated, what they could *do* rather than what they *knew* and how to assemble this information in a coherent, systematic form, they felt overwhelmed.

It is easy to blame schools and colleges for a lack of diligence in preparing students for university education but, as with all academic institutions, they have to work within guidelines and regulations that at times may be adjunct to sound educational philosophy as informed by research. The portfolio and reflective essay also demonstrated how the conceptions of students' personal attributes influenced their choice of future engineering discipline. In some cases, they perceived engineers working within Chemical Engineering or Mechanical Engineering as engineers who had to be creative, good at working in teams and good problem solvers, whereas they felt Computer Scientists and Electronics Engineers did not necessarily have to possess these attributes.

Overall, we believe the assessment for this module achieved its intended outcome; the students had to think critically about the reasons they wanted to be a particular kind of engineer and provide evidence to support their choice. From an educational perspective, the students were taken outside of their 'comfort zone' and experienced uncertainty in assessment, in terms of not being given a prescriptive formula for how to achieve high grades. They also gained an insight as assessors of other people's work, thus having the opportunity to nurture and reinforce the activity of critically analysing information against a set of criteria they were partly responsible for creating. We contend that through their immersion in a process that demanded their active engagement in an assessment process designed to stretch their criticality, to question and even empower themselves, their opportunity to learn was enhanced.

## About the Authors

Professor Dr. Paul Bartholomew is Director of Learning Innovation and Professional Practice at Aston University, Birmingham, England. He can be contacted at this email: p.bartholomew@aston.ac.uk

Dr. Michael Peters is Director of Engineering and Science Foundation Programmes at Aston University, Birmingham, England. He can be contacted at this email: m.peters@aston.ac.uk

# Bibliography

Bartholomew, P. (2015). Learning Through Auto-Ethnographic Case Study Research in C. Guerin; P. Bartholomew & C. Nygaard (Eds) (2015). *Learning to Research, Researching to Learn.* Oxfordshire, Libri Publishing.

Biggs, J. & C. Tang (2007). *Teaching for Quality Learning at University* (3rd ed.). Maidenhead: McGraw Hill.

Black, P. & D. Wiliam (1998). *Inside the Black Box: Raising Standards through Classroom Assessment.* London: NFER/Nelson.

Bloxham, S. & P. Boyd (2007). *Developing Effective Assessment in Higher Education: A Practical Guide.* Maidenhead: McGraw Hill.

Earle, L. M. (2003). *Assessment as Learning.* Thousand Oaks, CA: Corwin Press.

Entwhistle, J. (1981). *Styles of Learning and Teaching.* New York: John Wiley and Sons.

Laurillard, D. (2002). *Rethinking University Teaching, a framework for the effective use of learning technologies* (2nd ed.). Abingdon: RoutledgeFalmer.

Mayes, T. (2006). *QAA Scotland: Enhancement themes briefing note.* Online Resource. http://www.enhancementthemes.ac.uk/themes/FirstYear/overieew.asp [Accessed 20 April 2015].

McCombs, B. (2015). *American Psychological Association.* Retrieved January 6, 2015, from http://www.apa.org/education/k12/learners.aspx

Nicol, D. & D. Macfarlene-Dick (2004). *Rethinking formative assessment in HE:a theoretical model and seven principles of good feedback practice.* Higher Education Academy, UK.

QAA Scotland. (2009). *Quality enhancement themes:The first year experience.* Mansfield: Linney Direct.

Royal Academy of Engineering. (2007). *New survey finds deep misconceptions of engineering among young people that could worsen shortfall in engineers.* London: Royal Academy of Engineering.

Savin-Baden, M. (2000). *Problem-based learning in Higher Education: Untold stories.* Milton Keynes: Open University press.

Tinto, V. (2005). Epilogue: Moving from theory to action. In A. Seidman (Ed.), *College student retention:formula for student success* (pp. 317-333). Westport: American Council on Education and Praeger Publishers.

Yorke, M. (2005). Increasing the chances of student success. In C. Rust (Ed.), *Improving student learning 12. Diversity and inclusivity* (pp. 35-52). Oxford: Oxford Centre for Staff and Learning Development.

# Using Assessment Couplings to Engage Stakeholders in Co-curricular Activities

Jesper Piihl and Kristin Balslev Munksgaard

| Assessment Agency | Student-driven | | Teacher-driven | * |
|---|---|---|---|---|
| Assessment Outcomes | Flexible | * | Fixed | * |
| Assessment Focus | Process | * | Outcome | |
| Assessment Context | Transferrable | * | Specific | |

## Introduction

This chapter develops a framework for coupling learning activities with indeterminate learning outcomes to curriculum through assessment. Thus, the framework will be of interest to readers who are seeking stronger stakeholder engagement (students, faculty, business, external bodies, etc.) in co-curricular activities.

Developing students' abilities to connect academic learning to real-life problem solving, and thereby their "employability", is given a high priority on the political agenda around higher education (Knight & Yorke, 2004). A primary means to accomplish this is to raise relevance in/of learning activities.

This priority raises at least two interesting challenges for designing learning activities, since real-life situations and related problem solving often:

1.  involve cross-disciplinary issues to be addressed, which are not easily incorporated in single courses focusing on particular subject matters;

2. involve many stakeholders – often external to the university – with many different interests and perspectives.

Seeking to design learning activities that incorporate these challenges of real-life situations often leads to a complexity that entails learning activities for which we cannot easily set up pre-determined learning goals. In other words, a consequence of the challenges of simulating real-life problem solving in higher education learning activities is that it opens the way for important and relevant but indeterminate learning outcomes that are difficult to assess.

A way to approach this dilemma is to develop co-curricular activities that make it possible to meet these challenges and thus supplement curricular activities. This approach, however, raises the additional challenge of how to couple these activities. As a way to discuss these couplings, we draw on the notion of loosely coupled systems (Weick, 1976).

Based on a case study of a particular learning event – Camp GetCloser at University of Southern Denmark – a framework is developed suggesting how assessment can be used as a device to couple together co-curricular activities, simulating real-life situations and the heterogeneous interests of the many stakeholders, to curricular learning activities.

The chapter contributes to the literature on assessment by supplanting the focus from the traditional role of assessment of students in individual courses to a new role of assessment as a tactical tool for coupling co-curricular learning activities involving many stakeholders into curriculum within different disciplines. Reading the chapter you will gain three important insights:

1. knowledge of how to integrate learning activities at camps into curriculum while bridging interests of many stakeholders (such as faculty, firms, and students);

2. how to design assessment activities that links camp activities with curriculum through purposes of feeding forward, out and back – to make camp activities closely or loosely coupled to existing courses; and

3. inspiration for ways to discuss how assessment and learning activities can be linked to development of students' competencies in metacognition.

# Relevance and indeterminate learning outcomes

To develop curriculum and learning experience to enhance students' employability, Knight and Yorke (2004) describe what they term the USEM framework. They argue that the traditional focus on understanding content and developing skills needs to be supplemented by a focus on the development of students' efficacy beliefs and metacognition. Students' efficacy beliefs refer to students' confidence in their ability to impact situations and events, whereas metacognition refers to an *"awareness of what one knows and can do, and how one learns more"* (Knight & Yorke, 2004:39).

Furthermore, they question the ability to transfer learning between contexts and argue that, to enhance employability, the student must be faced with many different types of contexts of learning and reflection: *"If there is to be any hope of complex learning transferring from one context to another, then there is agreement that the learner needs to use that learning in different situations, to be aware of using it, and to reflect on the sorts of situations in which it would be good to use it in future"* (Knight & Yorke, 2004:183). This fundamental perspective of learning is related to a definition of quality in higher education that focuses on the transformation of the student through the learning processes (Harvey & Green, 1993) (See Hunter, this volume, for a discussion of transformational learning, and Hager, this volume, for a discussion of learning outcomes for the 21st century).

Knight (2002), argues that active engagement by the student is vital in learning; especially when learning involves engagement with communities of practice, involvement in a variety of networks, and to the amount and quality of interchanges with others. However, in these open networks, learning is indeterminate, because learning emerges within ongoing interactions. Therefore, it is very difficult to plan the learning outcomes in advance. Knight (2002:276) forwards the perspective that *"it is best to provide the conditions for good learning and then to trust the process: generally, good learning engagements will have good outcomes"*.

Based on this perspective of learning, Knight (2002) further discusses problems with summative assessment. Summative assessments are widely used as 'feed-out' mechanisms to communicate performance to external stakeholders. Therefore, validity and reliability in these assessments are crucial, whereas acknowledgement of indeterminate aspects of learning makes it difficult to make assessments fulfilling these requirements of validity and reliability. The literature on assessment suggests that students *"are strategic in their use of time and 'selectively negligent' in avoiding content that they believe is not likely to be assessed"* (Gibbs & Simpson, 2004:6). So, if we want:

+ to integrate learning activities with many stakeholders to enhance relevance and hence indeterminate learning outcomes into curriculum; and

+ to make the broader learning outcomes of co-curricular activities an integrated part of a standard learning experience for all students,

then we need to consider the issue of assessment, even though the learning outcomes are difficult to specify and hence to assess.

## Camps as a learning activity addressing relevance

One learning activity that can address the learning outcomes, described above, is the camp model. In a camp, students work in groups on real-life problems during one or more intensive days. Camps are often acknowledged as a means for students to develop innovative solutions to real-life problems (Lassen & Nielsen, 2008). Further, camps are diffusing in the educational landscape as a way to let students develop their skills in linking theoretical learning to practical issues (Bager, 2011).

Bager (2011) argues that camps can change the learning situation from being occupied with the transfer of existing knowledge to future-oriented knowledge creation situations, in which the role of the teacher changes into the role of the facilitator. The facilitating process can be very tightly directed by teachers (Lassen & Nielsen, 2008) or more student-directed. Bager (2011) states that, for students, the primary learning outcomes of camps are improved understanding of other disciplines, improved understanding of application of disciplinary knowledge to real-life problems and getting to know personal attributes. In this way, camps address the E and the M in the USEM model presented above.

In general, camps are often organised either as voluntary extra-curricular activities or as courses with their own ECTS decoupled from the rest of curriculum (e.g. Hansen & Byrge, 2008). However, if such activities are organised as extra-curricular activities, we risk that the students who decide to participate are the students who already have a focus on relevance in their education, or even feel they are skilled and want to practice further. The limitation of a camp as a course with own ECTS, is that it risks being seen as an event that students may attend simply to earn credits, without further consideration as to how it links to the overall curriculum and academic learning.

Important as these learning outcomes might be to promote relevance and employability, Bager (2011) notes that camps challenge established ideas in academia, and that they sometimes are regarded as relevant extra-curricular activities that should not qualify to earn study points. Therefore, organising camps as a (co-)curricular activity needs to take the perspective of faculty into account, since many interests and perspectives on learning, quality and relevance potentially collide.

Since camps explicitly work with real-life problems, the perspective from external stakeholders must be included. This entails a potential increase in complexity, since the criteria for evaluating quality and relevance are potentially different when seen from the perspective of companies, as compared to faculty.

The complex challenges of setting up appropriate learning and assessment in co-curricular activities can be illustrated as in figure 1 below. This figure shows the potential conflicting goals of indeterminate learning outcomes, students' focus assessment, priorities of faculty members and external stakeholders as it addresses issues of:

1. organising learning activities that are open for students' engagements in various networks and communities, resulting in important but indeterminate learning outcomes;

2. finding ways to include assessment in these activities, since many students plan their engagement strategically from this perspective; and

3. finding ways to make this sufficiently acceptable amongst faculty members;

even though the criteria for defining value by external stakeholders potentially challenge established ways of thinking in academia.

Figure 1 illustrates these elements, and the gaps between the elements illustrate potential conflicts inherent in the camp idea.

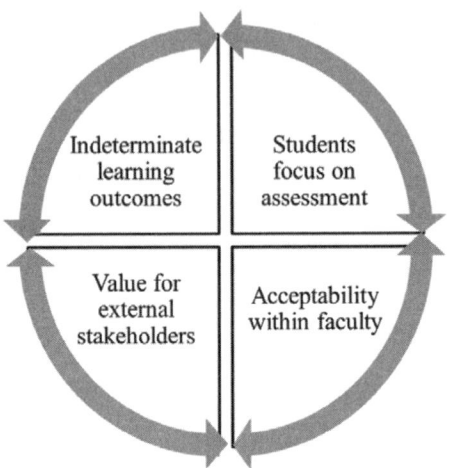

*Figure 1: Potential conflicting interests to couple when enhancing relevance through a camp as co-curricular activity.*

## Loose coupling as a framework for rethinking assessment

This section presents the theoretical basis for developing a general framework for the way in which assessment can play a role in coupling the potentially conflicting goals issued in the previous section. Since these goals involve the relationship between different entities, learning activity, students, faculty, and others, we build our theoretical framework with the idea of loosely coupled systems.

Weick (1976) discusses the idea of loose coupling as a concept for understanding how elements in an organisational system are linked by the example of educational organisations. Weick (1976:3) notes that the concept of loose coupling "*intends to convey the image that coupled events are responsive, but that each event also preserves its own identity and some evidence of its physical or logical separateness*". A key to understanding the coupling between two entities is the number of variables they share and the strengths/weaknesses of these variables. Furthermore, the concept of loose coupling suggests that an organisational system consists of building blocks, where new elements can be attached and existing ones can be severed with relatively little disturbance in the overall system (Weick, 1976).

Relating this concept to a learning activity, like a co-curricular camp event, sensitises us to view it as a network of events and stakeholders related to each other, while at the same time each event and stakeholder maintains its own identity, interests etc. This means that changes in one element do not simply diffuse through the system, but each stakeholder can create some leeway to translate changes according to their own interests (Latour, 1986). In this way, such a learning activity may be attachable to an existing curriculum with relatively little disturbance in the existing activities.

Figure 2 summarises the framework for understanding how assessments can be organised to link co-curricular activities (such as a camp event) to curriculum and is discussed in more detail below.

| | | Coupling between co-curricular and curricular activities | | |
| --- | --- | --- | --- | --- |
| | | Tight | Loose | De-coupled |
| Purpose of assessment | Feed out | Types of links: Structural links and/or Processual links | | No links |
| | Feed back | | | |
| | Feed forward | | | |

*Figure 2: Framework for designing assessments as a device for coupling co-curricular activities to curriculum.*

In the previous section, two concerns were highlighted. One concern was that the perspective of learning focused on indeterminate learning outcomes and therefore the unsuitability of summative assessment and feed-out. The other concern was that students wanted to focus their engagement on activities that are clearly linked to assessments.

Biggs (2012) turns the idea that students read the curriculum backwards from assessment into a principle for designing courses, where objectives, assessment, and learning activities are aligned to address the same agenda and support each other. In this way *"the students are "entrapped" in [a] web of consistency, optimising the likelihood that they will engage in the appropriate learning activities"* (Biggs, 2012:45).

Biggs' idea of alignment suggests building couplings between elements to entrap the student, whereas Knight's (2002) argument can be read as suggesting avoiding too tight links to assure that important but indeterminate learning outcomes are not neglected as a consequence of attempts to assure validity and reliability.

Within the framework of couplings, this can be seen as a question regarding looseness/tightness of couplings, which is depicted at the horizontal axis in the framework. The concept of loose coupling turns this controversy into an issue that can be dealt with strategically in connecting elements. Instead of considering the links as either existing or not, the links can be considered as something that can be designed purposely along a continuum ranging from loosely to tightly coupled.

Another discussion on assessment concerns the use of assessment as feed-out, feed-back or feed-forward mechanism – the vertical dimension in the framework. Knight (2002) argues that summative assessment has the purpose of feeding information regarding the students out to stakeholders external to the learning situation itself. Formative assessments have the purpose of giving feedback to the students regarding their progress compared to the learning outcomes of the course. Furthermore, Higgins *et al.* (2001) suggest that assessment can also be reframed to feed forward into a piece of future work.

Tightness of coupling can be created by various means. Tightness can be created structurally by formally connecting activities to curriculum, or processually by the way in which the activities are integrated into the learning activities and other activities within curriculum. This is illustrated in the centre of the framework.

To investigate how these potentially conflicting goals between relevance, stakeholder interests, indeterminate learning outcomes and students focus on assessment, the next sections present a specific co-curricular camp activity and discuss the role of assessment in the camp, in order to develop insights for future activities with important but indeterminate learning outcomes.

# Presenting Camp GetCloser

Camp GetCloser is an initiative at the University of Southern Denmark involving more than 500 students from social sciences (business students) and humanities (design students). Students from all years of study participate; from first year bachelor students to last year masters students. At the camp, companies are invited to present real-life problems to be solved by the students. All activities during the camp are related to a common theme – in 2014: 'China in Business' and in 2015: 'Sustainability'. In this section, we describe the intended learning outcomes of this specific co-curricular camp event, the planned activities for organising the camp and the related assessment of the students' work.

The empirical basis consists of qualitative data from the camp. Interviews and evaluations among participating students, faculty and companies have been completed and data are also drawn from student assessment reports.

The camp is coupled to curriculum through assessment activities in a range of courses. To discuss issues related to assessment, four selected courses related to the camp are presented, covering different stages of student education ranging from bachelor to master level. Furthermore, these are selected to show variance in types of assessments.

## Intended learning outcomes

The main aim of camp GetCloser is to create room for real-life working processes for the students, involving managerial and group dynamic issues to be solved, as well as project uncertainties and ambiguities to be taken into consideration. Categorised as a variation of case-based learning, the prime objective is to create a space for the students to engage in and direct their own learning process which, in the categorisation of Branch *et al.* (2014), will qualify as student-directed and process-oriented. At GetCloser, activities are planned to consider a threefold broad learning outcome to develop students' competences by training their ability to:

1. apply academic theory and methodology;

2. create value; and

3. do so in collaboration with others.

Additionally, learning activities are organised to contribute to student learnings on the chosen theme of the camp.

## Camp activities and elements

Camp GetCloser is held during one week in the middle of the semester, in which other teaching activities are temporarily suspended. Therefore, students are able to engage in the camp without worrying about missing curricular activities. Every student enters camp activities as part of a 'regular' curricular course. This means that a least one course per semester is chosen as camp-related. The faculty at these courses introduce and discuss the camp theme prior to the event. The degree of particularity and meticulousness in discussions in each course depends in part on the relatedness between the camp theme and the course subject and in part on each faculty member's engagement and interest in the camp.

Prior to the camp, students are divided into groups with an appointed student project manager. This is intended to facilitate space for the real-life group dynamics that students are likely to experience in their subsequent working careers. To commence the role as project manager, the appointed students are invited to participate in seminars prior to the camp. These seminars introduce methods and tools for project teamwork.

During the camp, each group of students plan their own activities. Presentations by experts, discussions with the participating companies, idea generation workshops and meetings with business mentors are among the camp activities planned for the students to choose among. Each group is assigned a facilitator or supervisor (PhD students and junior faculty) with whom they can consult on subject matters or when experiencing teamwork dysfunctions. During the camp, a few deliverables are to be handed in (i.e. a group photo or a tweet from an expert presentation). These deliverables are planned simply for the organisers to have some sense of student progress and engagement.

## Two-step assessment in courses related to Camp GetCloser

The camp activities and the students' work are assessed in two steps. The first step of assessment commences on the last day of the camp when student groups present their solutions to the companies. The solutions are assessed by external stakeholders, i.e. company representatives and local business people, to include their interpretation of the assessment criteria. This assessment is decoupled from formal curricular activities, and the assessment criteria used are developed with inspiration from similar camp events (facilitated by Venture Cup and Connect Denmark). In broad terms, the assessment criteria relate to the quality of solution, the quality of communicating the solution and the motivation of the students. Each criterion is judged on a scale and weighted. This assessment is organised with semi-finals and a final announcing a camp winner awarded a prize.

The second step of assessment initiates after the camp, when activities and learnings are discussed in the specific curricular courses coupled to the camp. Here we present four different examples selected to show the range of variations.

The first example is an introductory course on 'Entrepreneurship' for 1st semester bachelor students, which, in short, aims at giving the students a basic knowledge and understanding of relevant concepts and theories on entrepreneurship. The exam condition of this course is a two-page student assignment stating learning needs and participation in camp GetCloser. In the assignment the student is to reflect on two questions:

1.  how do significant entrepreneurial terms relate to activities of the camp?

2.  what did you learn?

Part of this course is thus an assessment that directs attention towards learning styles and application of theory at an initial level.

The second example is a 3rd semester bachelor course on 'Relationship and Service Marketing'. This is an advanced course in the sense that it aims at broadening students' knowledge of basic marketing by introducing different marketing disciplines. The exam condition of this course is that the student formulates a research question related to the theme of camp GetCloser as prescribed by the course teacher. Here the relatedness between the research questions and the camp theme varies from student to student and is dependent on approval by the teacher. As such, the assessment is linked to the course by providing real-life cases and/or relevant subject matters.

The course 'International Business Analysis' is the third example, aimed at providing 5ᵗʰ semester bachelor students with knowledge on theory and methods to understand company challenges in an international business context. The exam in this course is in two parts. One is a short report including reflections on the theme of camp GetCloser related to the course subject. This report accounts for 25% of a student's final grade in the course. The other is a written assignment based on a research question approved by the course teacher. This assignment accounts for 75% of the grade. Thus, the assessment coupled to camp activities influences the grade directly in the course.

The final example is a master course on 'Leadership' aimed at providing students with knowledge and capabilities to lead organisational processes. The students selected for a project leader role at camp GetCloser follow this particular course. In a reflection report, each student is assigned to explain two issues with reference to the field of leadership and organisational change:

1. which considerations did you have regarding your leadership role in your group during Camp GetCloser?

2. what specific experience did your leadership role give you for future reference?

In this course, the assessment is thus intended to direct the students' attention towards their role as leaders and towards the application of theoretical knowledge in this role. Thereby, the intention is not only to provide the basis for reflections after the camp but, by giving the assignment to the students prior to the camp, it also to directs their attention towards the role they are going to perform within the camp. Thus the assessment also feeds forward into the camp itself by directing the students' attention to their academic knowledge that can underpin their role.

## Analysing Camp GetCloser: Emerging learning, stakeholders' reactions and assessments

This section presents some of the issues emerging during the processes of designing and implementing the camp. In the actual progress of the week-long camp, experiences of indeterminate learning outcomes emerged, just as reactions from stakeholders brought additional insights.

## Indeterminate learning outcomes

In the corridors of campus, intense interactions evolve within and across the different groups of stakeholders during the week and, in this way, students are actively involved in a variety of networks and communities of practice. Students come in earlier than normal and are found in intense discussions with CEOs from the different companies, in debates with faculty, and in intense work within their groups. It is impossible to account for the amount of learning emerging in these networks.

A vital issue is how problems encountered by the students during the camp are approached. From a perspective in which learning is considered to be an effect of *"what the teacher does"* (Biggs, 2012), mistakes and inconsistencies leading to problems for the students can be interpreted as a fallacy in the design of the camp activities. However, within the perspective where learning is considered to be an effect of *"what the student does"* (Biggs, 2012), problems, mistakes, and inconsistencies can be regarded as elements that "infuse realism" into the activities. Apart from planned course activities at universities, events are often unpredictable, and the competent practitioner must be able to act with others under such circumstances. Here we present two examples of indeterminate learning occurring during GetCloser, illustrating the diversity of learning outcomes, which cannot be planned in advance.

In one group, students experienced an unanticipated outcome in relation to learning about leadership. The most senior of the students who was appointed project leader did not show up for the camp; the remaining students were in their first and second year of study. They approached one of the organisers with their frustrations: the leader of the group did not show up, and now they did not know how to carry on with the assignment since there was no one to direct them. This led to a discussion on the role of leadership in groups. The students learned what the absence of leadership or direction could feel like. Not from reading about it but from their own experience. Furthermore, a discussion of perspectives of leadership emerged. Is leadership attached to a specific role or a specific person? Or could leadership emerge relationally within a group? The group of students could have this discussion based on their specific experience – and not just with reference to specific sections in a text book. On the last day of the camp it turned out that this group reached the final. One of the students explained that suddenly they found a sense of direction in their work and started to share ideas, perspectives and tasks without a specific person taking leadership. Leadership emerged in the relations among the members of the group!

As another example, some students complained that the company problems should have been screened and delimited in a better way to make sure that is was possible to apply theory from their disciplines to solve them. This could have been regarded as a fallacy in the design of the camp from a "what the teacher does" perspective. However, it formed the basis for discussions regarding the rigour-relevance dilemma described by Schön (1995). As practitioners, we cannot expect problems to be framed to fit disciplinary theories and methodologies. Again, this could be discussed based on current experience by the students and not just as an abstract idea.

## Relevance as perceived by stakeholders

Setting up a camp is dependent on the contribution from many stakeholders, and this section discusses the relevance as perceived by stakeholders to the camp. The interests for participation and perception of relevance are likely to vary among different stakeholders. The design of a camp must take the different interests of these stakeholders into account by selecting an appropriate theme, designing appropriate activities and designing appropriate assessments. The most immediate stakeholders of GetCloser are discussed in more detail below.

First of all, we need commitment from students. Students are not a homogeneous group, but represent different disciplines and academic levels. Some illustrative comments from students reflect their various interests in and perception of relevance of the camp:

+ *"I would rather have spent the week preparing for exams – activities such as the camp should never replace real teaching."*

+ *"It was great meeting some of the older students. Knowing what they can, their competencies, I am more determined to be an active student. I want to be able to do what they do!"*

+ *"Cool to have to plan our own activities."*

- ✦ *"Should I stay away from my job in order to solve a real problem for a company, without getting paid?"*

So, some students worry how the camp may influence their learning: Does this activity improve their chances of passing exams – or would they be better off with traditional teaching? How does engagement in this learning activity balance other commitments in their lives? Others find inspiration in meeting and working with students at other levels.

A vital group of stakeholders is the faculty. Two groups of stakeholders at the university are taken into consideration here. First, the Head of Department is responsible for allocating and prioritising resources. Students' employability is one main concern for this stakeholder. The second group is course directors and faculty – whether directly involved in the camp or "disturbed" by the event. One interest among course directors and faculty in the specific courses is the discretion to run the course in a way which is optimal for the specific subject and curriculum activities. The following quotes illustrate the different perceptions of relevance of the camp event among faculty:

- ✦ *"I find it really difficult to relate the camp theme to my course!"*

- ✦ *"I really appreciate being able to use the cases [the participating companies, eds.] in my course – then I do not need to spend time finding and preparing cases myself."*

- ✦ *"Reading the students' reflection report after the camp, I realised how I needed to discuss study technics with my students."*

- ✦ *"I can't help thinking of the students' reflection reports assessing their learnings from the camp as something extra we impose on the students. Besides it will take me h… of a time to read and mark them."*

- ✦ *"I was positively surprised how the students were able to reflect on their learnings during the camp – and how they could relate discussion from the course to the camp. And they are only 1st semester students."*

An evolving discussion among this group of stakeholders concerned whether this learning activity could substitute learning activities in existing courses and thereby reduce the number of lectures during the semester. Or, if the lectures missed in the camp week should be replaced by extra lectures in other weeks. Some course directors acknowledged the relevance of the learning during the camp, while others insisted that it could not be at the expense of the content in their specific course.

Related to this, some course directors and faculty had doubts about the relevance and quality of the camp event. Besides being a "disruption" in the flow of lessons in specific courses, they questioned the implication from the camp on students' learning and competencies. This was especially a concern among humanities teachers. One concern related to whether their students would feel left out and not able to contribute on equal terms with students from social science. Another concern was whether a camp event would actually underpin the specific humanity competences to be developed for these students. The following quote illustrates how a faculty member changed his opinion during the camp:

+ *"I admit that I was really sceptical when introduced to the camp. But now I really acknowledge the learning potential. Especially we had great discussions with the students after the camp on how their academic competences can unfold in relation to real-life contexts and in relation to students from social science."*

The last group of stakeholders is the companies involved in the camp. The motivation of the companies to participate is primarily to attain a solution to their specific problem or, at least, get some new inspiration. Examples of companies participating in camp GetCloser in 2014 are Sourzing.com, seeking innovative solutions to handle quality issues with Chinese suppliers, and BioTrans Nordic, developing green solutions to minimise food waste and therefore seeking guidance on how to enter the Chinese market. Some reflections on relevance from the participating companies are captured in the following illustrative quotes:

+ *"They [the students, eds.] were very dedicated and very interested in coming up with the best possible solution to our problem."*

+ *"We have made some good contacts to some students, and we plan to assign them for solving specific projects."*

As appears from the above, companies are interested in meeting engaged students and also, to some extent, in taking responsibility for educating a future workforce. In general, the companies argue that events like GetCloser enhance students 'employability', whereas they have no interests in the curricular assessment in courses related to the camp.

## Camp GetCloser interpreted through the framework

Reading the theoretical issues on camps and assessments and the design and experience of Camp GetCloser through the lens of the framework in Figure 2, we see that the use of assessment created different types of couplings between the different stakeholders.

The dilemma between different assessment criteria among stakeholders from business, and faculty from a variety of different courses, was handled through creating and decoupling two assessments: one assessment within the camp week by external stakeholders focusing on the productions in the groups; and another faculty assessment of each student within a specific course.

Some courses were linked to the camp through an assessment allowing this as an activity within curriculum, whereas other courses were completely de-coupled. It is therefore possible, from an organising perspective, to approach the course directors within the curriculum openly and negotiate which courses to couple and which to de-couple, based on the engagement possible to foster from course directors.

Looking at the specific courses, they also distinguish by type of tightness of coupling and purpose:

1. Entrepreneurship: medium to loose coupling, feed-back (reflection report) (also some element of feed-forward by letting the students discuss in class how theory and concepts can be applied);

2. Relationship and Service Marketing: loose coupling, feed-back (cases used for exam);

3. International Business Analysis: medium to tight coupling, feed-back (part of grade for exam);

4. Leadership: tight coupling, feed-forward (preparing students to act as project leaders), feed-out (letting others know how these student are going to act as project leaders), feed-back (reflection report).

Together these assessments illustrate a variety of couplings as shown in Figure 3, and the framework suggests directions for developing these further in the future.

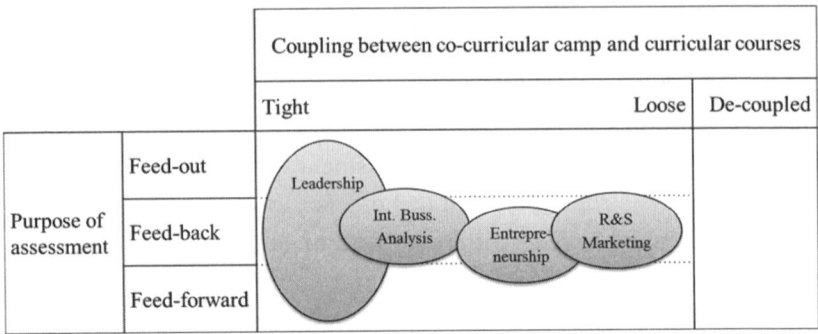

*Figure 3: Examples of courses' use of assessments to link camp to curriculum.*

Furthermore, these assessments – whether tight or loose – show how assessment can function as a link between camp event and curriculum and encourage students, as well as faculty, within curriculum to purposely reflect on the use of learning in various situations, which was suggested by Knight and Yorke (2004) as an element in enhancing employability, as previously discussed.

In our data, we also reported a faculty member from the humanities who at the outset was sceptical concerning the camp, but afterwards found that the camp provided unique opportunities for discussing how academic competences can unfold in real-life contexts. This example shows that, even if courses are structurally de-coupled from the camp, couplings can be created by integrating the activities into the reflective discussions performed within courses.

## Conclusions: Linking co-curricular activities within determinate learning outcomes to curriculum

Building relevance into higher education requires development of students' abilities for dealing with the complexity of real-life situations. In this chapter we have argued for student 'employability' as abilities for:

+ understanding the gaps between the tidiness of theory and the uncertainty of practice;

+ reflecting on ways to apply theory to practice;

+ networking, negotiating and collaborating with peers and inter-acting with different stakeholders.

Broad learning outcomes like these can only be partly planned for and will more often emerge indeterminately. This chapter develops a frame-work using assessment as a device for coupling co-curricular activities with indeterminate learning outcomes with curricular activities. To enhance students' employability, the theory of learning proposed in this chapter suggests that it is important that understanding of academic content and development of specific skills is supplemented by a focus on development of students' efficacy and metacognition. In addition, it is considered important that this is organised within different contexts and in networks with external stakeholders.

In ordinary course activities, students develop understanding of content and eventually of skills within the USEM framework (Knight & Yorke, 2004). Co-curricular activities can create arenas for developing students' personal competences to engage in problem-solving and interactions with many stakeholders (efficacy) and their abilities to apply and transfer academic theories and procedures in new contexts (metacognition).

A camp as described in this chapter provides such an arena. Here students from different academic disciplines and semesters come together with businesses to develop and suggest solutions to real-life problems. Students from later semesters experience that they have advanced competences compared to younger students and younger students can learn from more experienced students, thereby seeing what compe-tences they are developing which, in turn, contributes to develop the students' efficacy beliefs. By experiencing a camp in different phases of the students' development (one each year of study), every student prac-tices their competences to engage with their understandings and skills in diverse professional contexts, which improves their ability to develop and transfer knowledge and hence develop their metacognition.

The learning outcomes from camps are, however, hard to define and measure and hence to assess with reliability and validity. Therefore, participation in camps is often a co-curricular activity. This chapter developed a framework for discussing how/when/why assessment can create loose and tight coupling between camp activities and curricular activities, and how these translate into specific types of assessments. The design of assessments can be applied tactically to create tight and/or loose couplings between stakeholders and activities, i.e. couplings between courses within existing curricula and special learning ambitions within the co-curricular activities.

The presented framework also provides insights for organising co-curricular activities, exemplified through the design of a camp, and trying to couple it to curriculum. We suggest the following steps:

Structurally:

1. negotiate with course directors and teachers in specific courses to decide which courses to couple to the co-curricular activity and which to de-couple;

2. evaluate how tightly the intended learning outcomes of each course can be tied to the potential learning outcomes of the activity;

3. decide the tightness of structural coupling in each course.

Processually:

1. consider the purpose of assessment in each course: feed-out, feed-back or feed-forward;

2. consider how assessment and learning can be linked to the development of self-efficacy in each course;

3. consider how assessment and learning activities can be linked to the development of competences in metacognition.

## About the Authors

Jesper Piihl is Associate Professor at the Faculty of Business and Social Sciences, Department of Entrepreneurship and Relationship management, University of Southern Denmark. He can be contacted at this email: jpi@sam.sdu.dk

Kristin Balslev Munksgaard is Associate Professor at the Faculty of Business and Social Sciences, Department of Entrepreneurship and Relationship management, University of Southern Denmark. She can be contacted at this email: kbm@sam.sdu.dk

# Bibliography

Bager, T. (2011). The camp model for entrepreneurship teaching. *International Entrepreneurship and Management Journal*, Vol. 7, No. 2, pp. 279-296.

Biggs, J. (2012). What the student does: teaching for enhanced learning. *Higher Education Research & Development*, Vol. 31, No. 1, pp. 39-55.

Branch, J.; P. Bartholomew & C. Nygaard (2014). An Introduction to Case-based Learning. In J. Branch; P. Bartholomew & C. Nygaard (Eds.), *Case-Based Learning in Higher Education*, Oxfordshire: Libri Publishing Ltd., pp. 1-16.

Gibbs, G. & C. Simpson (2004). Conditions under which assessment supports students' learning. *Learning and teaching in higher education*, Vol. 1, No. 1, pp. 3-31.

Hansen, S. & C. Byrge (2008). WOFIE – Fire dages workshop for 450 studerende i entreprenørskab. In T. Bager & S. L. Nielsen (Eds.), *Entreprenørskab og Kompetencer*, København: Børsens Forlag, pp. 197-207.

Harvey, L. & D. Green (1993). Defining Quality. *Assessment & Evaluation in Higher Education*, Vol. 18, No. 1, pp. 9-34.

Higgins, R.; P. Hartley & A. Skelton (2001). Getting the Message Across: The problem of communicating assessment feedback. *Teaching in Higher Education*, Vol. 6, No. 2, pp. 269-274.

Knight, P. T. (2002). Summative Assessment in Higher Education: Practices in disarray. *Studies in Higher Education*, Vol. 27, No. 3, pp. 275-286.

Knight, P. T. & M. Yorke (2004). *Learning, Curriculum and Employability in Higher Education*. London: RoutledgeFalmer.

Lassen, H. A. & S. L. Nielsen (2008). VisionCamp: Om innovativ faglighed som omdrejningspunkt for entreprenant kompetenceudvikling. In T. Bager, & S. L. Nielsen (Eds.), *Entreprenørskab og Kompetencer*, København: Børsens Forlag, pp. 179-195.

Latour, B. (1986). The powers of association. In J. Law (Ed.), *Power, Action and Belief*, London: Routledge & Kegan Paul, pp. 264-280.

Schön, D. A. (1995). The New Scholarship Requires a New Epistemology. *Change*, Vol., No. November/December, pp. 27-34.

Weick, K. E. (1976). Educational Organizations as Loosely Coupled Systems. *Administrative Science Quarterly*, Vol. 21, No. 1, pp. 1-19.

# Assuring Achievement of Learning Outcomes Through Assessment: A Case Study in Pharmacy

Ieva Stupans

| Assessment Agency | Student-driven | Teacher-driven | * |
| Assessment Outcomes | Fixed | Flexible | * |
| Assessment Focus | Process | Outcome | * |
| Assessment Context | Specific | Transferrable | * |

## Introduction

This chapter illustrates a case in which learning outcomes are not assured through a single non-invigilated online test. In the chapter, I argue that multiple iterations of assessments which integrate a number of learning outcomes may be required in order to assure a non-negotiable learning outcome. This chapter begins by briefly discussing curriculum design and learning outcomes, particularly in the context of Australian higher education. I consider:

1. a number of assessment approaches and their alignment with learning and learning outcomes; and

2. assuring learning outcomes.

The potential for serious medication errors in healthcare is a reality. *"(a United States (US) pharmacist) … failed to recognize that a pharmacy technician he was supervising had made a chemotherapy solution with far too much sodium chloride in it. The final solution was supposed to contain 0.9% sodium chloride but it was over 20%"* (Institute for Safe Medication Practices, 2014, webpage). Prevention of such incidents relies heavily on the knowledge and abilities of individual healthcare professionals, such as pharmacists, who are required to have absolute accuracy in medication prescription processing. The question for those teaching pharmacy programmes is how to assure that graduating students have the knowledge and abilities required to ensure that they can demonstrate the required attention to detail and complete error-free calculations. Assuring achievement of learning outcomes, in the case of pharmacy students around calculations, is critical. The question of how achievement can be demonstrated deserves consideration, particularly for some "non-negotiable" learning outcomes. What we need to achieve in this case is *"designing our courses such that students could not exit …without necessarily having met the learning outcomes"* (Lawson, nd:np).

The case is then presented of assessment of the ability to complete error-free calculations, in online non-invigilated short form tests and in invigilated examinations, in an Australian pharmacy programme. Other professional discipline academics may also need to confront the teaching and assessment of non-negotiable learning outcomes; thus the chapter provides coherent, pragmatic guidance for those who may be considering assessment of non-negotiable learning outcomes. Reading this chapter you will gain the following four insights:

1. online test does not assure learning;

2. programs need iterative integrated assessments to assure learning;

3. student view of assessment is not the same as staff's; and

4. we haven't really started to think about "compensation" in terms of assessing learning outcomes in examinations.

## Aligning learning outcomes, learning and assessment

Spady's (1994:1) work on outcomes-based curriculum design referred specifically to primary and high school education: *"Outcome-Based*

*Education means clearly focusing and organizing everything in an educational system around what is essential for all students to be able to do successfully at the end of their learning experiences. This means starting with a clear picture of what is important for students to be able to do, then organizing the curriculum, instruction, and assessment to make sure this learning ultimately happens".*

However, curriculum design based around achievement of learning outcomes has been adopted widely across higher education (Markle *et al.,* 2013). Unit (subject) and programme learning outcomes describe what learners are supposed to be able to do at the completion of a unit or the programme. Once it is determined what outcomes are *"essential for all students to be able to do",* appropriate organisation of learning opportunities means that all students can learn and succeed, but not all at the same time, or in the same way (Spady, 1994). Thus, good curriculum design relies on alignment between outcomes, learning opportunities and assessment. Individual units which make up a programme of study have learning outcomes, as do the individual assessment items for a particular unit. A programme map links the different components of the curriculum: learning outcomes to learning opportunities and to assessment. A programme map presents the organisation of learning opportunities and assessment of knowledge and skills in a way that eliminates redundancy; however, it also indicates where they occur. Using a 50% pass mark in a unit permits some students to progress through a programme of study without requiring them to demonstrate that they have achieved all of the learning outcomes of that unit. For some learning outcomes, this may not be contentious; however, in the case of non-negotiable learning outcomes, it raises a serious question about whether some of the learning outcomes should be essential requirements, which students should be required to demonstrate before they can progress.

In Australia, a funded nationwide pharmacy discipline network has developed learning outcomes and exemplar standards for programmes preparing pharmacy professionals (Stupans *et al*, in press). The University of New England has adopted these learning outcomes so that graduates are required to be able to *"formulate, prepare and also supply medications and therapeutic products"* (Stupans *et al.,* in press). Of relevance to the case study presented in this paper is one of the exemplar standards for this learning outcome: *"Clarify medication orders, assess appropriateness of prescribed medicines, use pharmaceutical calculations to verify the safety of doses and administration rates and follow systematic dispensing procedures"* (Stupans *et al.*, in press).

The requirement for pharmacists to be able to complete error-free calculations is not restricted to Australia. For example, in the US, the NAPLEX Competency Statements provide a blueprint of the topics covered on the examination used to determine entry-level US pharmacist competency, including the ability to perform calculations (Newton *et al.*, 2008).

## Assessment Practice – an overview

Good assessment practice is widely discussed in the literature; the focus in this section is to provide a very brief overview of the principles related to the case study presented in this chapter. In Australia, a large national project has focused on defining the role of assessment as having the central focus in teaching and curriculum (Boud, 2010), as well as crucially aligning learning outcomes and assessment. Assessment is thus not an "add on" to curriculum design. This is irrespective of whether assessment is described as formative (i.e. assessment is to support learning) or summative (i.e. provides a summary of extent or degree of student learning) (Boud, 2010; Bennett, 2011).The central role of assessment is eloquently captured in the following: *"By aligning assessment with the expected learning outcomes of students and the teaching and learning activities, and by choosing proper assessment methods and tasks, teachers can effectively guide students' study practices and enhance deep, meaning-oriented learning"* (Postareff *et al.*, 2012:84).

Effective teaching practice is much more than focusing on assessment; however, several principles of effective teaching are directly relevant to good assessment practice; first, good teaching provides students with prompt feedback and second, good teaching emphasizes time-on-task (Chickering & Gamson, 1987). Teachers' feedback on assessed work is a consistent source of students' dissatisfaction as reported in surveys and reports, prompting extensive discussion in the literature around principles of good feedback practice (Nicol & Draper, 2009). It is important to recognise that prompt feedback may include that of fellow students and teachers as well as online interactive programmes. Time-on-task, both quality and quantity, has significant influence on learning performance, with researchers identifying that students need *"time to talk, write, reflect, and otherwise engage in activities"* (Cross, 1999:10).

Assessment methods are also widely discussed in the literature. In contemporary education, practice marks achieved through assessment undertaken during semester, in or away from class, also contribute to, or indeed make up, unit grades. Assessment tasks falling into this category include an ever increasing array of possibilities including peer and self-assessed tasks, contributions to online discussions, presentations, essays, portfolios, collaborative team tasks and practical performances.

Of relevance to this chapter, short form tests and examinations are widely used in higher education. They include short constructed response and selected response questions such as true/false and multiple choice questions. Short form tests may be used in both formative and summative assessment as they can sample a wide range of content and are easy and quick to score with high marker reliability. In a constructed response question, students have to create their own answers and reveal some of their thinking. Constructed responses include essays, short answer responses and the solution of mathematical problems (Kastner & Stangla, 2011).

What is not widely acknowledged (Eisenkraemer *et al.*, 2013) is that tests as an assessment approach can also act as a recovery practice that evokes the memory. Tests may thus be used as a learning tool and produce knowledge that can be retrieved flexibly and transferred to other situations. A substantial body of work recommends that teachers use quizzing, both formal and informal, as a tool to help students remember (Roediger & Karpicke, 2006) and thus the distinction between assessment *of* and assessment *for* learning is blurred. The success of this approach has also been demonstrated recently in a US pharmacy programme, albeit not in pharmaceutical calculations (Stewart *et al.*, 2014). Students study and learn more when given assignments and tests, as opposed to their passive reading of materials. The findings of this body of work align with the emphasis in good teaching on time-on-task.

Globally, the paradigm shift in curriculum development to the articulation of learning outcomes has aligned with increased adoption by teachers of authentic assessment. Authentic learning and assessment emphasizes students' need to learn and subsequently demonstrate the ability to *apply* the knowledge and skills in real-world or authentic contexts. Students may be asked to perform real-world tasks that are either replicas of, or analogous to, the kinds of problems faced by professionals (Mueller, 2005). Economic realities as regards teaching mean that authentic assessment is used selectively and application of knowledge is also assessed through problem-solving questions, short form constructed response or selected response in examinations and tests.

Although timed unseen closed-book invigilated examinations are a frequently used form of assessment, particularly in health disciplines and sciences, the literature is mostly silent on the attributes of high quality examination papers. There are some discussions on the types of questions which focus students on higher levels of learning (Crossley *et al.*, 2002) and general advice on aspects such as the time period to complete the examination, the target student group, the nature of questions and their layout in the sections of the paper and the scoring of each question (Azzopardi *et al.*, 2007).

## Online formative and summative tests and examinations

The relative simplicity of short form tests means that these questions are very easily adapted for automated online testing for either summative or formative assessment (Cygman, this volume). In formative assessments, online automated short form assessment may be used to provide instantaneous computer-generated feedback allowing students to discover gaps in their knowledge. Current software capability means that constructed and selected response type questions can be included in online tests, although there may be some restrictions in answer format.

For teachers, the provision of feedback and grading is relatively simple in an online test as compared to a paper-based test. With appropriate data capture, automated online short form tests are also able to provide analytics on questions, thus facilitating identification of those questions posing difficulty for students through question-by-question profiles and allowing opportunities for teachers to make informed, targeted and timely interventions. Analytics regarding the engagement of students in reviewing resources and undertaking test activities are also relatively easy to obtain from the learning management system (LMS).

We know that open book tests and examinations have the potential to measure students' ability to organize and use or apply information, rather than simply memorizing it, so these tests and examinations offer the possibility of assessing higher order learning. Non-invigilated online examinations and tests, even if timed, can be presumed to be open book; students' use of reference materials is not regulated. Non-invigilated online examinations and tests may also present significant perceived challenges regarding academic integrity. Student-to-student sharing of responses to questions through a number of different devices and approaches, such as recording of screens which are subsequently distributed, are unregulated (Tao & Li, 2012).

It is important to note, however, that other within unit assessments are also frequently non-invigilated and, therefore, there may also be unregulated sharing in these circumstances. There is suggestion that differential learning may occur when students know they will have invigilated examinations, as opposed to non-invigilated examinations, with findings of increased learning by invigilated students (Wellman, 2005), presumably as an outcome of potential for sharing of responses to questions and less self-reliance in the non-invigilated group.

Questions and answers from non-invigilated online examinations and tests may also readily surface into the public domain, thus integrity of their future use is potentially compromised. More importantly, the use of these answers by students to achieve completion of online tests and the awarding of marks defeats the potential of these tests in facilitating student learning.

## Case study

### Error free calculations

Skill development in pharmaceutical calculations is challenging; there are basic concepts and definitions and the solving of relatively simple calculations, all of which need to be mastered prior to solving calculation-focused case studies. In this case, simple calculations questions are defined as those which require only a single step to solve, whereas calculation-focused case study questions are word problems that require multiple steps to solve.

It is also important to note that Australian students' mathematics performance has declined in absolute terms over the past decade (Turner

& Tout, 2014), with particular difficulties noted in students' ability to grapple with ill-formulated questions that require transformation of the problem into a form amenable to mathematical treatment.

This case study describes a second year unit I coordinated that includes as one of its learning outcomes "*demonstrate extended skills of pharmaceutical calculations*". In this unit, which has been organised in its current format for the past two years, learning opportunities are provided online through our university's LMS (in this case Moodle). In this unit, there are multiple small pieces of assessment within semester; there is also a final invigilated timed unseen examination.

One of the within semester assessments focuses on pharmaceutical calculations; this is an online quiz which has a unique set of questions for each student, extracted from a large number of questions in an online question bank. Students are required to obtain 100% in this quiz in order to pass the unit. Students have multiple opportunities to achieve 100% in this test. On each occasion when the student takes the test, the student will see a different set of questions. The online test is timed. In the past two years, 94 students have completed the unit, and only one student has not been successful in obtaining 100% after multiple attempts.

Assessment of pharmaceutical calculations proficiency also occurs through the inclusion of two calculation-focused case study questions in the unseen invigilated timed examination paper. The two questions included in the examination paper are identical to those that students would be familiar with from the online quiz. The questions which are included in the paper are those which, through analytics of the quiz questions, are in the category of being higher order "troublesome"; however, after multiple attempts students are able to obtain the correct answer. Through a simple review of the examination papers I was able to identify that, out of 94 students, only 43% were successful in answering both questions correctly and 29% were not able to answer either question correctly. There are two questions that this case study raises that need to be explored.

1. why was there such a significant difference between student outcomes as demonstrated through the online test and the invigilated unseen test?; and

2. how we can possibly assure learning outcome achievement through assessment?

In order to explore the first question, I have evaluated the design of the quiz assessments and the underpinning learning opportunities and resources against principles of good teaching, assessment and feedback practice (Rohrer & Pashler, 2010; Nicol & Draper, 2009; Gibbs & Simpson, 2004-05; Nicol & Macfarlane-Dick, 2006). To explore the second question I have, first, further examined the implications of the 50% pass mark and, second, iterative curriculum design.

## Evaluation against principles of effective learning opportunities, assessment and feedback

In this unit, there was no formal instruction in pharmaceutical calculations; students were encouraged to engage in student-to-student and student-to-staff discussions through a discussion link set up on the LMS. There was also a range of resources presented to the students at the commencement of the semester. Analytics were used to identify those questions which presented difficulties for the students; these questions were used as the focus of additional resources provided to the students through the LMS during the semester. We know that quizzing is a tool to help students remember (Roediger & Karpicke, 2006); a practice quiz and the assessment quiz provided multiple opportunities for self-testing.

It has also been shown that learning is more durable when study time is distributed over a longer rather than a shorter period (Rohrer & Pashler, 2010) and effective assessment tasks capture sufficient study time and distribute student effort over time (Nicol & Draper, 2009). Lastly, interweaving different types of practice problems also improves learning (Rohrer & Pashler, 2010).

The practice and assessment quizzes both presented a range of problems – simple and calculation-focused case studies. However, analysis of the use of the practice quiz and the assessment quiz revealed that, once students had achieved 100%, they did not access the quiz format again, even though they knew that there would be calculations questions in the final examination. The assessment quiz had a due date approximately two thirds of the way through the study period, but some students did not commence work on the resources, practice quiz or indeed assessment quiz until just before the due date. This pattern of student effort distribution is not an isolated phenomenon and has been reported by others (Jordan, 2011).

In this case study, learning opportunities through assessment align with recognised good practice. It has also been suggested that teachers use "little and often" assessment to encourage student pacing of work (Gibbs & Simpson, 2004-05). Analysis of student behaviour around engaging with the learning opportunities, even though not my intent, suggests that this may be a useful approach for inclusion in future iterations of the unit. Good feedback practice should help:

+ clarify what good performance is;

+ facilitate the development of self-assessment and reflection; and

+ deliver high quality information to students about their learning.

Good feedback practice also helps students self-correct, encourages teacher-student and student-to-student dialogue around learning and provides opportunities to act on feedback (Nicol & Draper, 2009).

In this case study, feedback was in the form of the correct answer. The marks for each quiz were also provided. How does the feedback provided to students in the quiz assessments compare to what is recognised as good practice? Some students engaged in student-to-student or student-to-staff discussion, although the majority didn't. Students were not provided with a detailed analysis of their answers. Thus, developing a process to introduce systematic feedback in these quizzes deserves attention in future iterations.

In this case study, some areas for enhancement have been identified with respect to the learning opportunities provided to students – improving feedback and the distribution of study time on calculations. The student interaction with the LMS was highly variable, which meant that the overall design of this part of the unit did not achieve its intent.

The issue remains that, in spite of students achieving 100% in the test quiz, the learning underpinning this was by no means uniform, as evidenced by students' achievement in the end-of-semester examination. Validity and reliability of assessment are frequently discussed in the literature. The validity of an assessment is the extent to which it measures what it was designed to measure, without contamination from other characteristics. The assessments could be considered as valid but the online non-invigilated short form tests in this case study had poor reliability – the mark achieved by many students in the test quiz was a poor reflection of the students' pharmaceutical calculations knowledge and skills as evidenced in the final examination.

## Further considerations around assessment criteria

The assessment criteria for pharmaceutical calculations in this case study, in both the online test and the final examination, were very simple. The answer was either correct (full marks) or incorrect (zero marks). The decision to employ these criteria was based on the serious patient consequences of calculation errors. Providing scaffolding for the learning of pharmaceutical calculations through assessment criteria wasn't considered in the initial unit design.

Pharmacists are required to accept responsibility for the accuracy of their calculations and so should be able to check that the answers obtained are indeed reasonable. Reflecting on the central role of assessment in curriculum in this case study presents an example of assessment which did not develop students' capacity to make judgements about their own work, required for promotion of self-regulation and students' development towards becoming effective practitioners (Boud, 2010).

There are examples of work in assessment in which categories of decision quality – "I am guessing", "I am rather uncertain", "I am rather sure" and "I am very sure" – are included in online selected response question sets, on the basis that confidence in decision quality may lead to an action or not, which in turn may be beneficial or harmful. This very much aligns with the decisions that need to be made regarding pharmaceutical dosing (Kampmeyer *et al*, 2015). The aim is to encourage reflection and appropriate levels of confidence. No examples could be located in published literature in which the confidence in decision quality has been incorporated into constructed response online quizzes.

## The student response

Online evaluations, conducted by a central university unit at the end of each teaching period, give students the opportunity to provide anonymous feedback. These comments were obtained from the central university unit and evaluated. A number of comments received about this unit indicated that students had a poor understanding of the nature and function of assessment. These included the following representative comment:

+ *"The one thing I would like to criticise about this unit, is that there was too much assessment, given the amount of work required as well as the due dates of each assessment item"* and *"Too many assessments worth very small percentages.....It was hardly worth doing the amount of work required."*

The role of assessment as a learning opportunity was clearly not apparent to some students. As regards the resources that were provided through the LMS, there were two differing points of view, again shown through representative comments.

+ *"All material provided up front allowing for self-directed study to be planned."*

+ *"Students need to be given worked solutions to the calculation problems...It would be helpful if the lecturer showed the students how to solve some of the calculation problems."*

The missing elements, identified through student feedback, in the design of learning opportunities and assessment are the teacher's explanation around the point of the quiz assessment and a rationale for the self-directed nature of the work. The work of Kirschner *et al.* (2006:75), although widely debated, provides useful direction for enhancing the scaffolding in this unit regarding *"approaches that place a strong emphasis on guidance of the student learning process"* and *"reduction of guidance when learners have sufficiently high prior knowledge to provide 'internal' guidance"*. The unit described in this case study is located in the second year of the programme; an argument for guidance of the student learning process can be made.

There is also the consideration that in this case the *"assessment is a hurdle to be negotiated, a game to be played, at the expense of learning"* (Gibbs, 2006: 25). A student could pass the unit by passing *only* the online test, without engaging in deep learning to be able to demonstrate calculations proficiency in the final end-of-semester invigilated examination.

# Assuring achievement of learning outcomes

The second question that this case study raises is how we can possibly assure learning outcome achievement? First we need to consider the role of the invigilated timed end of semester examination which includes two calculation-focused case study questions calculations. Students are able to pass this examination and thus potentially complete the unit without achieving all learning outcomes, such as the learning outcome under consideration in this chapter, "*demonstrate extended skills of pharmaceutical calculations*". Learning outcomes are specified at a minimum acceptable level. In a unit such as that presented in this chapter, the achievement of some learning outcomes and failure to attain others means that, in practice, the students should fail the unit and "*technically this represents a confusion between a grading system and the use of a threshold learning outcome system.*" (Moon N.D. webpage). A student's achievements in some sections of an examination paper may compensate for poor performance in other sections, such as the calculations section, and thus students may "numerically" pass the unit. To date, Australian universities have not tackled this issue.

Second, we need to consider how learning outcomes map to the programme. Pharmaceutical calculation skills underlie a number of the learning outcomes for pharmacy graduates. Regular reinforcement of these skills throughout the programme of study in this case study is being undertaken. This approach is consistent with evidence from studies of medical students showing development of their calculations skills over four years (Harries & Botha, 2013). This approach also aligns with high level curriculum design work around graduate attributes, which has suggested an iterative cycle of engagement in the development of the attributes (Lawson, 2013; Hager, this volume). In this context, the teaching team members of this programme are focusing on the development of reliable high quality integrated assessments which students need to pass prior to graduation, so that students are able to demonstrate achievement of *all* learning outcomes. Thus, even though students may pass the second year unit discussed in this chapter, they will not be able to pass the integrated assessments of the final year of the programme unless they are able to demonstrate *all* learning outcomes.

# Conclusion

Success in an online short form test may be used by both students and staff to assure achievement of learning outcomes. However, I have presented data that demonstrates that it cannot be assumed that students have the ability to undertake error-free calculations simply based on online short form test results. When students are presented with identical questions to those utilised in the online test in an invigilated examination, achievement of learning outcomes can no longer be demonstrated by a significant proportion of students.

Evaluation against principles of effective learning, assessment and feedback indicated some areas for improvement in this unit (Nicol & Draper, 2009), particularly the distribution of study time and improvement in feedback practice. The case study illustrates the issue around reliability of assessment. The assessment design was easily executed but potential benefits of the approach were not necessarily realised. Comments from students point to a need for greater scaffolding of student learning. Most importantly, the case study indicates shortcomings in the use of simplistic online constructed response questions of this type, i.e. correct or incorrect, with respect to assuring learning outcomes, which is of critical concern when learning outcomes are non-negotiable.

# About the Author

Ieva Stupans is Professor of Pharmacy at the University of New England. She can be contacted at this email: ieva.stupans@une.edu.au

# Bibliography

Azzopardi, L. M.; A. Serracino-Inglott & M. Zarb-Adami (2007). Writing examination and assessment papers. In M. C. Stuart (Ed.) *The Complete Guide to Medical Writing*, London: Pharmaceutical Press, pp. 217-232.

Bennett, R. E. (2011). Formative assessment: a critical review. *Assessment in Education: Principles, Policy & Practice*, Vol. 18, No. 1, pp. 5-25.

Boud, D. (2010). Assessment 2020: Seven propositions for assessment reform in higher education. Online Resource: http://www.uts.edu.au/

research-and-teaching/teaching-and-learning/assessment-futures/overview [Accessed 13 January, 2015].

Chickering, A. W. & Z. F. Gamson (1987). Seven principles for good practice in undergraduate education. *AAHE bulletin*, Vol 3., No. 7.

Cross, K. P. (1999). Learning Is about Making Connections. The Cross Papers Number 3.

Crossley, J.; G. Humphris & B. Jolly (2002). Assessing health professionals. *Medical Education*, Vol. 36, pp. 800-804.

Eisenkraemer, R. E.; A. Jaeger & L. M. Stein (2013). A Systematic Review of the Testing Effect in Learning. *Paidéia (Ribeirão Preto)*, Vol. 23, No. 56, pp. 397-406.

Gibbs, G. & C. Simpson (2004-05). Conditions under which Assessment Supports Students' Learning. *Learning and Teaching in Higher Education*, Vol. 1, No. 1, pp. 3-31.

Gibbs, G. (2006). How assessment frames student learning. In C. Bryan & K. Clegg (Ed.) *Innovative assessment in higher education*, Oxon: Routledge pp. 23- 36.

Harries, C. & J. Botha (2013). Assessing medical students' competence in calculating drug doses: original research. *Pythagoras*, Vol. 34, No. 2, pp. 1-9.

Institute for Safe Medication Practices. Online Resource: https://www.ismp.org/NAN/default.asp [Accessed 13 January, 2015].

Jordan, S. (2011). Using interactive computer-based assessment to support beginning distance learners of science. *Open Learning*, Vol. 26, No. 2, pp. 147-164.

Kampmeyer, D.; J. Matthes & S. Herzig (2015). Lucky guess or knowledge: a cross-sectional study using the Bland and Altman analysis to compare confidence-based testing of pharmacological knowledge in 3rd and 5th year medical students. *Advances in Health Sciences Education*, Vol. 20, No. 2, pp. 431-440.

Kastner, M., & B. Stangla (2011). Multiple Choice and Constructed Response Tests: Do Test Format and Scoring Matter? *Procedia-Social and Behavioral Sciences*, Vol. 12, pp. 263-273.

Kirschner, P. A.; J. Sweller & R. E. Clark (2006). Why Minimal Guidance During Instruction Does Not Work: An Analysis of the Failure of Constructivist, Discovery, Problem-Based, Experiential, and Inquiry-Based Teaching. *Educational Psychologist*, Vol. 41, No. 2, pp. 75-86.

Lawson, R. (2013). Principles for Designing a Curriculum to Develop and Assure Student Learning Outcomes. *IICE-2013*, pp. 43.

Lawson, R. (N.D.). Assuring Learning, Online Resource: http://www.assuringlearning.com/curriculum-design-fellowship-background [Accessed 13 January, 2015].

Markle, R.; M. Brenneman; T. Jackson; J. Burrus & S. Robbins (2013). Synthesizing frameworks of higher education student learning outcomes: Research Report No. RR-13-22). Princeton, NJ: Educational Testing Service.

Moon, J. (N.D.) Linking levels, learning outcomes and assessment criteria. Online resource: http://www.josemnazevedo.uac.pt/proreitoria/docs/040701-02Linking_Levels_plus_ass_crit-Moon.pdf [Accessed 31 May, 2015].

Mueller, J. (2005). The authentic assessment toolbox: Enhancing student learning through online faculty development. *Journal of Online Learning and Teaching*, Vol. 1, No. 1.

Newton, D. W.; M. Boyle & C. A. Catizone (2008). The NAPLEX: evolution, purpose, scope, and educational implications. *American Journal of Pharmaceutical Education*, Vol. 72, No. 2.

Nicol, D. & S. Draper (2009). A blueprint for transformational organisational change in higher education: REAP as a case study. *Transforming higher education through technology enhanced learning.*

Nicol, D. & D. Macfarlane-Dick (2006). Formative assessment and self-regulated learning: A model and seven principles of good feedback practice. *Studies in Higher Education*, Vol. 31, No. 2, pp. 199-218.

Postareff, L.; V. Virtanen; N. Katajavuori & S. Lindblom-Ylänne (2012). Academics' conceptions of assessment and their assessment practices. *Studies in Educational Evaluation*, Vol. 38, No. 3-4, pp. 84-92.

Roediger, H. L. & J. D. Karpicke (2006). The power of testing memory: Basic research and implications for educational practice. *Perspectives on Psychological Science*, Vol. 1, No 3 , pp. 181-210.

Rohrer, D. & H. Pashler (2010). Recent research on human learning challenges conventional instructional strategies. *Educational Researcher*, Vo.. 39, No. 5, pp. 406-412.

Spady, W. G. (1994). *Outcome-Based Education: Critical Issues and Answers.*: American Association of School Administrators, 1801 North Moore Street, Arlington, VA 22209.

Stewart, D.; P. Panus; N. Hagemeier; J. Thigpen & L. Brooks (2014). Pharmacy Student Self-Testing as a Predictor of Examination Performance. *American Journal of Pharmaceutical Education*, Vol. 78, No. 2.

Stupans, I.; S. McAllister; R. Clifford; J. Hughes; I. Krass; G. March & J. Woulfe (2014). Nationwide collaborative development of learning outcomes and exemplar standards for Australian pharmacy programmes. *International Journal of Pharmacy Practice.* First published online.

Tao, J., & Z. Li (2012). A Case Study on Computerized Take-Home Testing: Benefits and Pitfalls. *International Journal of Technology in Teaching & Learning,* Vol. 8, No. 1, pp. 33-43.

Turner, R. & D. Tout (2014). Does it all add up? What's the story with mathematical literacy and numeracy? Where to next? Online resource: http://works.bepress.com/dave_tout/45 [Accessed 25 May, 2015].

Wellman, G. S. (2005). Comparing learning style to performance in on-line teaching: Impact of proctored v. un-proctored testing. *Journal of Interactive Online Learning,* Vol. 4, No. 1, pp. 20-39.

# More Than a Mirage: The Role of Assessment Design in International Accreditation

Nicholas Cifuentes-Goodbody and Andreas Karatsolis

| Assessment Agency | Student-driven | | Teacher-driven | * |
| Assessment Outcomes | Flexible | | Fixed | * |
| Assessment Focus | Process | | Outcome | * |
| Assessment Context | Transferrable | * | Specific | |

## Introduction

This chapter shows the important role that assessment must play in accreditation. Our goal is to reveal the unique character that assessment and accreditation take on in the context of the Arabian Gulf, in what we have termed "home-grown" institutions of higher education (IHEs). To this end, we use the case study of the Translation and Interpreting Institute (TII) in Doha, Qatar, and the accreditation of its Master in Translation Studies (MATS) by the University of Geneva during 2013 and 2014. This is important as the states of the Arabian Gulf are now dotted with new Institutions of Higher Education (IHEs), pristine campuses that carry the names of top universities from the United States and Europe. Given that these gleaming buildings often occupy spaces that were desert only a few decades ago, it is easy to fall under the assumption that they somehow appeared out of thin air. In fact, one reporter for *The Telegraph* went so far as to describe Qatar's Education City as a sort of mirage: *"Instead of shimmering pools of water that vanish on closer inspection, huge structures rise from the bone-dry landscape*" (Ahuja, 2012). What descriptions like this fail to recognize, however, is that the seemingly sudden emergence of places like Education City in Doha is grounded in both the history of higher education in the Arab world over the last half-century and in the larger global trends in higher education of the last fifteen years. The appearance of these institutions raises important questions about the role of assessment and programme design in the context of transnational higher education and accreditation. Reading this chapter, you will gain the following insights as we discuss the accreditation of TII and the role that assessment played in that process:

1. we explain the context out of which such "home-grown" IHEs have emerged. For that reason, we provide a brief history of higher education in the Middle East, showing the unique circumstances under which home-grown institutions have developed in the Arabian Gulf and the subsequent importance that these institutions must place on accreditation by international agencies;

2. we also provide some background on how student learning has come to occupy a central place within the accreditation process generally;

3. we show how the faculty of TII used accreditation to reconcile the realities of their classrooms with the outcomes that were built into the original programme proposal; and finally

4. we discuss the outcomes of the accreditation process at TII, paying special attention to the improvement in the programme's curriculum and its assessment of student learning.

At first glance, our chapter may seem like an outlier in this anthology. Geographically, while the majority of the chapters come from scholars based in countries such as Canada and Denmark, only two contributors (Hunter & ourselves) are based in the Arabian Gulf, in countries that have not been associated with higher education in the modern era. Academically, while the other authors have written compellingly about assessment (from building online portfolios [Hager, in this volume] to taking students' personal growth [Pauna & Branch, in this volume] into account), we focus on curriculum design and accreditation. However, one of the goals for our text is to speak to both of these centre points from a sort of periphery in order to open up a wider dialogue on the nature of higher education. On the one hand, we want to show that the assessment practices put forward by our colleagues in this volume are most effective when applied within a larger curricular and accreditation framework that encourages a "culture of assessment". We feel that learning and higher education are global in nature, and that any discussion of their core principles and values must take into account the geographical, cultural, and economic diversity in which they operate. In doing this, the key lesson from our chapter is that the assessment of learning is an essential component of institutional culture, programme quality assurance, and achieving accreditation. This connection is especially important for new, local institutions to consider as they use international accreditation and strive to become global universities.

## The Emergence of Home-grown IHEs in the Arabian Gulf

In order to understand the emergence of a home-grown IHE such as TII – and thus put into context both its desire to seek international accreditation and the centrality of assessment in that process – it is necessary to give a brief overview of higher education in the Middle East and North Africa (MENA) over the last several decades.

Following World War II, universities became a central focus of governments in the region, when ruling parties tied their own legitimacy to the creation of economic growth and social welfare. In this context, large public institutions emerged to not only educate students but to create middle-class employment for the public and train future party elites (Buckner, 2011). Beginning in the early 2000s, MENA governments began to introduce a series of reforms in response to a demographic youth bulge in the region and pressure to liberalize their economies (El Hassan, 2012). In the case of the Arabian Gulf, leaders opted for a model of "*imported internationalization*" (Buckner, 2011), in which universities (primarily from the United States) established partnerships or opened satellite campuses in Bahrain, Kuwait, Oman, Qatar, Saudi Arabia, and the United Arab Emirates (C-BERT 2015).

It is important to remember that the new, "imported" IHEs in the countries of the Arabian Gulf reflect the same overall trend of internationalization that has become prevalent in higher education over the last fifteen years (Altbach *et al.*, 2009:7-8). However, it is also important to recognize that some of the goals driving internationalization in the Gulf are unique to the region. Places like Education City in Qatar form part of high-profile, government projects that aim to cultivate a knowledge economy in countries that have traditionally depended on resource wealth. Some scholars posit that the rhetoric of the countries of the Group of Eight (G8) has driven these initiatives more than local concerns (Donn & Al Manthri, 2010); others point out that the exact mechanism through which transnational institutions will produce local knowledge is still unclear (Okruhlik, 2014). Nonetheless, the guiding philosophy behind these efforts is straightforward: the most effective way to create a world-class educational system is to directly import the most prestigious universities from other parts of the world.

In addition to government initiatives to internationalize higher education, there are two global trends that are shaping the emergence of a new kind of IHE in the Gulf region:

- universities are turning less to government institutions for their certification and more to peer institutions or parastatal accreditation agencies (Altbach *et. al.*, 2009; Lynch, 2015);

- these same accreditation agencies have increasingly become transnational and commercial ventures (Altbach & Knight, 2007).

If the two extremes of higher education in the MENA region are the large public institutions of the mid-twentieth century and the imported branch campuses of the early twenty-first, it is our assertion that the global trends outlined above have led to the appearance of a third category of IHE in the Arabian Gulf. Neither a large, state-sponsored school nor a European or North American satellite, these are home-grown institutions whose mission is to address national needs with a curriculum based on international standards. Striving to combine local understanding with global excellence, these schools enjoy the support that comes with having a royal founder or namesake, but they also seek international accreditation in order to garner the legitimacy needed to fulfil their missions.

Such is the case for the institution that is the focus of this chapter, the Translation and Interpreting Institute at Hamad bin Khalifa University. The institute forms part of the same Education City that serves as home to American university satellite campuses. However, unlike those satellites, it is not directly associated with another foreign-based institution. Instead, TII was established in 2011 by the Qatar Foundation with the mission of building translation and language capacity in the State of Qatar.

Following the pattern of many educational projects in the Gulf, TII's mission came out of a government initiative *"to meet labour market needs"* (GSDP, 2011:138; also see Stasz, 2007) by increasing post-secondary educational opportunities. TII planned to open several Master's programmes in successive academic years, and to have each of those programmes externally accredited by the time their first classes graduated. In 2012, the institute opened its Master in Translation Studies (MATS) with six students. In 2013, it applied to the University of Geneva's Faculté de traduction et d'interprétation (Faculty of Translation and Interpreting) for accreditation of the programme. Thus, the postgraduate programme found itself with a mission to meet local market needs while also demonstrating that it satisfied international standards for graduate education in Translation Studies.

## The Role of Student Learning and Assessment in Programme Accreditation

The previous section described the social and historical context in which IHEs emerged in the Middle East and traced the creation of home-grown IHEs in the Arabian Gulf to a complex set of global affordances. In this section, we will provide a similar outline of the history of quality assessment and accreditation, especially in the United States, and then proceed to sketch the theoretical framework within which the accreditation of the MATS programme took place.

The question of the value of IHEs to society is not a recent one. As early as the end of the sixteenth century, John Case was writing in defence of the Elizabethan universities, saying that they constituted *"the soul of the world"* (Shattock, 1991:58). In the United States, initial attempts to assess IHE's contribution to society began at the end of the nineteenth century. These efforts were based on admission standards, and the accreditation process was driven for many decades by regional agencies that engaged in numerical analysis of various indicators to determine if those standards had been met (Alstete, 2004). It was only in the 1980s that the emphasis began to shift to large-scale self-studies that provided coordinated assessments and introduced the model of periodic evaluations. Within that model, the evaluation of student learning outcomes was introduced and eventually placed at the centre, pushing aside externally imposed and largely arbitrary standards (Alstete, 2004).

The focus on student learning outcomes (SLOs) coincided with the publication of theoretical work by Vygotsky (1978; 1986), and Cronbach and Snow (1977), who introduced concepts such as the learning environment, skill levels, and the importance of social factors and complex individual interactions in learning. Very soon thereafter, and with the help of the assessment evidence some institutions had newly acquired as part of accreditation efforts, general principles about good practices in higher education began to emerge.

In most cases, these general principles included recommendations such as increased peer interactions, instructor feedback, conceptual instruction, and even explicitness and clarity (e.g. Chickering & Gamson, 1987). More recently, these recommendations have been elaborated upon and expanded, most notably after the explosion of pedagogically-driven research from disciplinary fields that has produced work by authors, like Ambrose et. al. (2010), who have synthesized and identified patterns or principles of learning-in-action. It comes as no surprise, therefore, that the focus of the accreditation process has become the extent to which an institution applies or promotes these patterns in achieving desirable SLOs. Institutional effectiveness was – and still is – largely determined by the alignment between institutional mission, curriculum development, and student achievement of learning outcomes (Keeling et. al., 2008).

Given the socio-historical tradition we have just described, one would expect that all of the above would apply only to US institutions. However, as discussed in the previous section, the US has managed to exert its influence globally, claiming a position of power in what constitutes scientific knowledge and research (Alstete, 2004). Therefore, this reframing of the evaluation process has implications for institutions beyond the US, including those in the MENA region.

Before explaining in detail the role of assessment in the accreditation process for the particular case of TII, it is important to describe the theoretical framework within which the accreditation process was designed and successfully completed. It is also important to pay special attention to the issues that arose between the original, explicit curriculum for the MATS and the taught, implicit curriculum being enacted by faculty.

The explicit curriculum was originally designed by an external expert committee based in a UK institution. At the heart of the new MA was a list of programme outcomes and a set of course-unit descriptions, which included learning objectives deemed appropriate for an MA curriculum based on the state-of-the-art in translation theory and practice. However, very soon after the programme started, it became clear that the individual course-unit objectives were neither aligned to each other nor to the programme outcomes in general. This, coupled with the prior knowledge and experience of the first student cohort, led to the conclusion that the implicit and explicit curricula needed to be better aligned. The first consideration framing the MATS accreditation came from the need to negotiate the multiple curricula and especially to understand if there were gaps between the official (or explicit), the taught (or implicit), and the learned curriculum (Cuban, 1993).

Generally speaking, it is important to promote a culture where educators are given the agency to question the assumptions behind the existing curriculum and imagine its transformation. This agency can be possible within a conceptual framework where the faculty's pedagogical beliefs and subject knowledge are at the centre of determining what students are expected to learn. It is equally important, however, that this framework interacts with the administration and the accreditation body's expectations. Traditional approaches have focused on a limited set of system components that interact in the curriculum development and revision process. For example, Schwab (1973) described only five curriculum "commonplaces" (learners, teachers, context, subject matter, and curriculum making) in his system. However, more recent attempts, such as Entwistle & Peterson's (2004), have captured a more complex set of relationships within a comprehensive activity system, which can include a curriculum specialist who can guide the accreditation process (see Figure 1). One key contribution of this chapter will be to show how curriculum revision can be included in this complex system.

*Figure 1: Learning as a Complex Activity System.*

The second framing consideration came from the very nature of the MATS programme as a professional graduate degree. The faculty, staff, and administration had to begin to build a professional learning community by reflecting on student outcomes originating in course-work, internship experiences and other, non-degree instruction such as information literacy and leadership. Such an approach enacted some of the "Big Ideas" that DuFour (2004) discussed in relation to professional learning communities, namely the "culture of collaboration" and the "focus on results." At its heart, the approach was one of creating a coherent learning organization, engaging all stakeholders, from students to staff, administration and prospective employers in a culture of continuous improvement.

However, the learning organization was not profession-based (limited to the craft or profession of translation and interpretation) but extended into the academic practice of theorizing and researching the discipline of Translation Studies. Within such a framework, several opportunities were designed to support groups and individuals, who could be called "legitimate peripheral participants," mainly through their mutual engagement (Wenger, 1998). For example, an informational lunch meeting was held for all faculty and staff in which the self-study committee presented their timetable and solicited the assistance of all the units or individuals who could contribute to the document they were producing. Thus, the creation of ties within the community, which helped to establish norms and a curricular direction, became one of the core frameworks of engagement.

Finally, given the unique constraints of this effort, issues of responding to local context as well as questions of organizational power and influence became very prominent. It is well known that transparency is one of the primary measures of assessment rigor because it allows for an articulation of the overall purpose of the assessment, the values it is based on, and the methodological perspective driving it (Keeling *et. al.*, 2008). In addition, transparency allows for the intended use of the assessment to be made clear from the beginning of the process. The tension, of course, between transparency and organizational control can possibly be resolved through a thoughtful model of the assessment cycle that places student learning at the centre, as we will discuss in the next section.

## Curriculum Mapping and Outcomes-Based Learning in the MATS Accreditation

Before we discuss in detail the activities that were designed and implemented to foster a culture of assessment within TII, we have to provide an overview of the assessment principles in which they were framed. Following Brennan's (2000) descriptions of methods for institutional quality assessment, we identified a number of critical parameters for TII's quality assurance method:

+ being systematic and incorporating "feedback loops" in the form of departmental peer reviews and self-assessments. This approach matches the principle of the American Society of Higher Education (ASHE) about the assessment of student learning as ongoing and systematic instead of episodic and opportunistic;

+ using a variety of assessments for different purposes instead of only one type of measure. Thinking of this approach in relation to student learning, we can refer to ASHE's principle that assessment is most effective when it reflects an understanding of learning as multidimensional, integrated, and revealed in performance over time;

+ promoting positive change instead of accountability in institute-wide monitoring through surveys of students, faculty, and staff. Again, we know that for student learning, assessment improvement is more likely when it is part of a larger context that promotes change.

In order to begin enacting the above principles, TII engaged in a number of activities to help foster the development of a learning organization and support the alignment towards the overall improvement of student learning, starting with a curriculum mapping process. At the outset, the goal of this process was to describe the taught curriculum, but it also yielded paths to revising it with an eye towards the implicit curriculum. Generally speaking, previous curriculum mapping efforts from different disciplines (Veltri *et al.*, 2011; Zelenitsky *et al.*, 2014) have shown that such an activity is useful as an evidence-based approach to continuous quality improvement. However, one additional goal in the case of TII was to engage the larger community (including students, staff, and the administration) towards a more nuanced understanding of the most appropriate curriculum, without disregarding the local context.

The faculty-driven committee in charge of the accreditation effort, which had been formed to execute a self-study with the support of an external curriculum specialist, was tasked with mapping programme outcomes to learning objectives met through course modules or other opportunities in the curriculum. This effort required the analysis of all faculty syllabi in order to identify the specific module goals, their level of delivery and their methods of assessment. It also meant including all the goals students met through required internship activities, language-learning courses, and other workshops offered within the larger context of Education City.

As part of this process, faculty found an opportunity to step outside their individual classes by holding working sessions and interacting with internship proctors, librarians, language teachers, and all the staff that supported TII's programmatic goals related to leadership or professionalism. This level of collaboration with the common goal of tackling the curriculum alignment activity for the purposes of the self-study served one more purpose: it created a shared understanding of what constitutes knowledge for the program and allowed for the implementation of what Applebee (1996) would have called *"knowledge-in-action"*, especially as it relates to the multiple stakeholders and the values each brings to support curricular decisions.

Extending Applebee's metaphor about knowledge-in-action being the result of an ongoing conversation in which students engaged about things that matter, we can imagine such a conversation at the level of institutional stakeholders, who are interested in identifying and supporting knowledge-in-action as it translates to the larger institutional reflection on the road to the self-study. The first step in this conversation at TII was a town-hall style meeting, in which the committee in charge of accreditation gathered all the members of TII to explain the accreditation process. They reviewed:

+ the criteria of the self-evaluation report in detail, explaining how students, faculty, and staff would contribute to its writing, and

+ the timeline for the report's creation, showing when and how each party would make its contribution.

These steps proved invaluable in creating a sense of community from the outset of the accreditation effort and making clear that all members of TII were stakeholders in the process.

In addition, the faculty engaged in mapping the curriculum by collecting formative assessment data from their courses in order to provide evidence of sequencing and alignment. According to the International Centre for Student Success and Institutional Accountability (ICSSIA), mapping learning is the first area of competency that educators must consider in order to understand student outcomes (Keeling *et. al.* 2008). Developing this topography, both inside and outside the classroom, reveals the intentional alignment of student outcomes to the institutional mission and goals. However, creating this mapping can be conceptually and logistically challenging because the tools to establish connections across courses and identify gaps and/or overlaps are simply not adequate.

To their credit, the faculty involved in this effort showed remarkable persistence in overcoming the challenges of documenting learning outcomes and mapping them in relation to programmatic goals which had not necessarily been aligned in the first place. Moreover, since this effort was "across-the-board", all faculty engaged in conversations on the curriculum not only between themselves and the committee, but also with the students. Several focus groups with the students were analysed for patterns of engagement with the learning outcomes of individual courses and the curriculum as a whole, and became the basis for revisions in course instruction and assessment. Thanks to this multi-faceted approach, the completed mapping showed a clear need for the customization of learning goals to match student needs and market trends in the local professional context.

Underlying this entire process was a series of workshops led by an external expert in assessment, in which faculty were introduced to curriculum mapping as a process for collecting and recording curriculum-related data that identifies core skills and content taught, processes employed, and assessments used for each subject area in order to improve communication and instruction in all areas of the curriculum.

In addition, curriculum mapping was presented as a system that thematically aligns curriculum and instruction, which gave faculty the opportunity to begin identifying the components of the system already in place and imagine the ones necessary to make the system more coherent. Figure 2 shows a snapshot from one such workshop, in which the participants began to identify the relationship between specific course learning objectives and programmatic outcomes. During this effort, they were introduced to the common distinction between four levels of coverage of learning objectives (namely, Introductory, Emphasized, Reinforced, and Applied), which they then used to describe the relationships between courses in terms of meeting programme objectives.

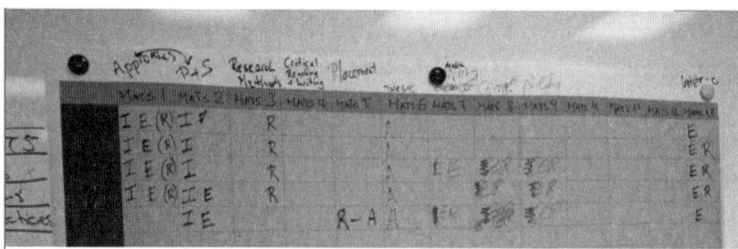

*Figure 2: Identifying coverage in MATS courses during a workshop.*

This process became the basis for a subsequent exercise aimed at rethinking the curriculum and the relationship between required and elective courses at the level of aligning course objectives to programme outcomes. In this phase, the faculty were able to articulate relationships between courses they had been assigned to teach but had not had much input on their position and role in the curriculum.

At first, explicit descriptions of the connections between courses were easier to be made, but then, by identifying gaps and overlaps, the opportunity to revise existing courses and imagine new ones became clear. As Figure 3 shows, using the previous nomenclature of levels of coverage for course learning outcomes, the required and elective courses from the four semesters of the MATS programme were mapped in relation to each other. Figure 3 has captured the opening stages of this process, as the faculty were beginning to establish connections across courses in terms of programme outcomes.

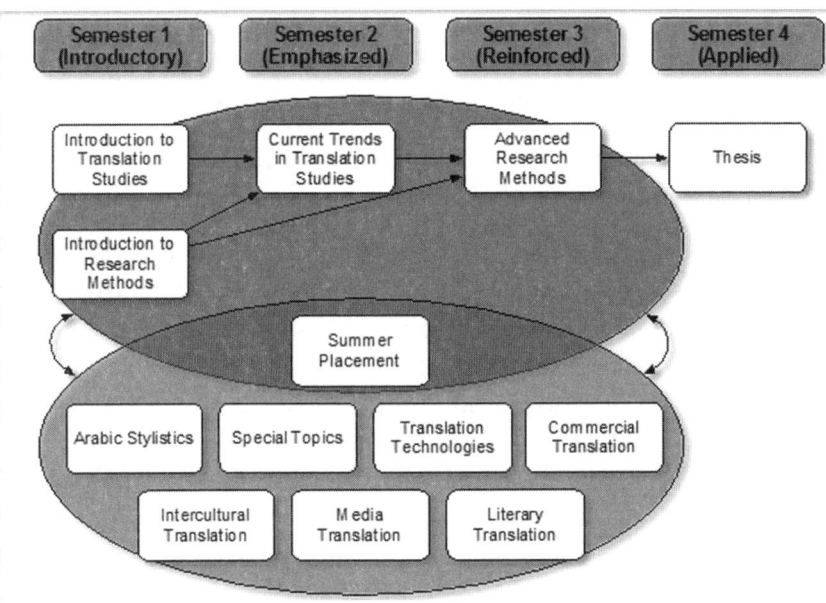

*Figure 3: Initial efforts to map relationships between modules in the MATS.*

Overall, the first part of the process allowed learning objectives and programme outcomes to begin to take form, and therefore it became easier to manipulate and revise, as Huet *et al.* (2009) have suggested in their work. This way, it was much easier not only to describe the curriculum in meaningful detail for the purpose of the self-study, but also to propose concrete plans for its revision, which were communicated to the administration. Returning to the point made in the second section about relationships of power and organizational control, the faculty were able to re-position themselves in relation to the administration through their thoughtful analysis and recommendations on the overall curriculum.

A component of this first part was also the introduction of the faculty and validation committee members to the framework of "backward course design" in order to begin placing emphasis on assessment-driven instruction. Through this model, faculty were able to:

+ reflect on how to design tests, homework, and practice activities that were better aligned with desired outcomes;

+ design and structure instructional activities that better supported student learning and met performance objectives; and

+ explain and justify clearly to the administration and students the purposes and goals of instructional and assessment activities.

The second assessment activity relates to the way the outcomes-based culture of assessment was designed to be sustained beyond the self-study and accreditation process. During the workshops that the faculty had attended on the curriculum mapping process, the concepts of IHEs as learning organizations had been introduced, following Strange and Banning's (2001) review work on ways to create effective campus learning environments. Particular emphasis was placed on strategies to help design the last step in the process, namely designing for campus assessment and action through a series of recurring assessment efforts, beginning with capturing the students' prior habits of mind and knowledge as they entered the programme, and continuing with analyses of their performance in required courses, as well as self-assessments in relation to specific course outcomes.

Given that many members of the faculty served on the validation committee, beginning with an assessment-powered model in their own courses helped significantly in promoting the discussions of what baseline data on student learning should be collected or what kinds of qualitative data from students would be useful to help understand their level of engagement with the programme and attainment of programme outcomes. The combination of these two core assessment approaches and their corresponding strategies led to significant outcomes, which we will discuss in the next section.

## Outcomes: Local Needs, Global Standards

Even in advance of the on-site visit by the University of Geneva, the accreditation process yielded many significant results for the MATS programme, both in reshaping the curriculum and in changing how professors assessed student learning. First and foremost, it allowed for the reconciliation of implicit and explicit curricula. Initially, this was a question of curriculum alignment. It entailed the creation of learning outcomes for each module, taking into account students' abilities and prior knowledge while also contributing to the fulfilment of programme outcomes. It required that professors examine how the outcomes for their modules related to those of their colleagues, which in turn revealed how programme objectives could be fulfilled incrementally across several course units.

This process also made clear that one of the MATS's strengths was the fact that course modules fell into two distinct but complementary groups. The first focused on research methods and theory, while the second gave students hands-on practice in the many areas of professional translation. This core realization led to the creation of a curriculum map that made explicit this difference by grouping modules into what were dubbed "Critical Core" and "Specialization and Practice". This map proved so useful that, even though it had been designed exclusively for the self-evaluation report, it was included in the next edition of the student handbook and was even presented in the following year's orientation so that incoming students could better visualize the overall progression of the programme (see draft in Figure 3 and final version in Figure 4).

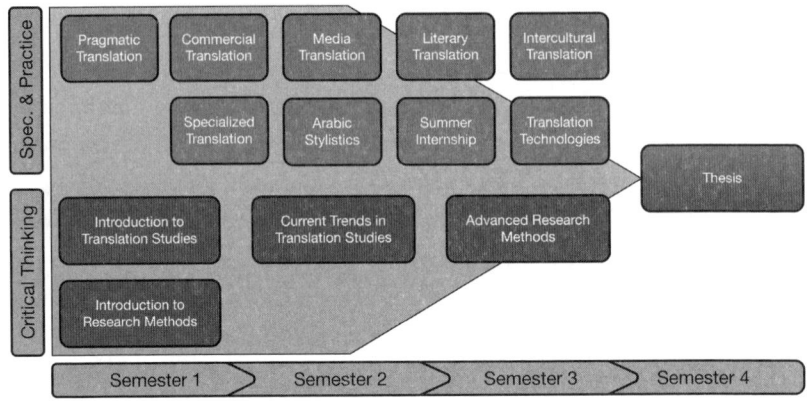

*Figure 4: MATS Curriculum Map.*

In addition to the creation of a curriculum map, the reconciliation of the original curriculum with the realities of the classroom brought about a new model for student assessment. Once faculty stepped outside their own courses and realized that programme objectives could be fulfilled incrementally across several course-units and semesters, they stopped evaluating students based on one or two high-stakes summative assignments and began to employ multiple and diverse assessments (both high- and low-stakes) that each targeted a smaller range of course learning outcomes. This is similar to the process that Tobler describes in this volume. For example, whereas the first-semester class "Introduction to Research Methods" originally determined final grades based on two essays alone, the revised version included ten short formative assignments, and two portfolios that documented the research, writing, revision, and reflection on a project assigned in another Critical Core class. This allowed for further collaboration between professors in achieving learning outcomes, and it even improved student success in the programme overall.

| Original Grade Components | | Revised Grade Components | |
|---|---|---|---|
| Component | % of Grade | Component | % of Grade |
| 1500-word essay #1 | 50% | class participation | 10% |
| 1500-word essay #2 | 50% | formative assignments (10) | 25% |
| | | portfolio #1 | 20% |
| | | technology project | 15% |
| | | portfolio #2 | 30% |

*Table 1: Student Assessments in "Introduction to Research Methods".*

Another important outcome of accreditation was that it allowed TII to institute a "culture of assessment" within the MATS course. This term refers to the same use of diverse assessments (aligned with specific course outcomes) as discussed above, but it also alludes to the creation of systems and channels through which the programme could be evaluated and improved. More specifically, the accreditation process:

+ became a way for professors and administrators to reflect systematically on the current state of the course, identify gaps and areas in need of improvement, and put forward a plan for development;

+ motivated the establishment of regular professional development workshops in the areas of module design and curriculum alignment, which has allowed faculty (both old and new) to continue to improve the programme as a whole beyond the immediate pressures of the initial accreditation; and

+ created channels at TII through which students, faculty, and administrators could express their concerns about the programme to each other (measures such as course-unit evaluations, student focus groups, faculty surveys, and committee) and then use this information to adjust aspects of the programme.

Furthermore, the fact that all of these processes needed to be documented continually for the purposes of the programme's re-accreditation in coming years means that the institute had to commit to "closing the loop" in the evaluation of the MATS – that is, folding the information gathered from all parties into the improvement of the programme.

With all of these changes already in place by the time the University of Geneva conducted its on-site visit of the MATS, their evaluation of the programme focused primarily on how the MATS curriculum should relate to the demands of the professional world. While evaluators acknowledged the complementary nature of the "Critical Core" and "Specialization and Practice" courses, they deemed that students needed even more hands-on practice in the work of translation, and that the demands of the local market should help shape the nature of that practice. To this end, they recommended that the existing module "Special Topics in Translation" become a requirement for graduation and that the faculty create a new required module called "Pragmatic Translation". For both modules, the content would be determined by the demands of the local market, i.e. the types of translation that clients in Qatar required.

## Conclusion

In May of 2015, the University of Geneva awarded the MATS its "Faculty of Translation and Interpreting Quality Label". While Geneva and TII agreed that such a new programme would require another round of evaluation to better assess more long-term criteria (such as job placement and relationship with alumni), the success of this first step gave the institute the firm footing it needed to better undertake the challenges implicit in its ambitious growth plan. In the fall of 2014, the institute opened a second MA course in Audiovisual Translation (MAAT), and the faculty grew from three full-time members to eight – all of whom come from different countries and have differing conceptions of teaching and student assessment. Thus, the first challenge was bringing new professors into this "culture of assessment". The fact that TII had already put in place a series of professional development workshops for faculty made this task relatively easy. The second was squaring the implicit and explicit curricula of the MAAT programme. Again, the systems put in place during the MATS accreditation aided in this process. Adding to this was the fact that the University of Geneva agreed to evaluate the MAAT programme for accreditation, which provided the external motivation for faculty and administrators to move forward with these changes.

The continuing challenge of TII's postgraduate programmes is finding ways of improving its ability to assess students and ensure they fulfil the outcomes expected of a master's degree recipient. While faculty and administrators have invested much effort in soliciting qualitative feedback on the shape of TII's courses and the effectiveness of its assessment of students, they continue to look for more empirical ways of measuring students' progress in their courses and the extent to which student learning matches programme outcomes. An effort like this requires that faculty continue to work closely with each other, that they come to a mutual understanding of the relationship between translation theory and practice as it relates to pedagogy, and that they encourage students to engage in higher-level cognitive thinking while also initiating them into the professional world of translation – and all of this within the short time span of a two-year degree. In short, the challenge for TII and its postgraduate programmes is to stay focused on its local mission and its demanding growth plan while also meeting international standards, thus showing accreditors and faculty from around the world that that the home-grown institutions of the Arabian Gulf are anything but a "mirage".

## About the Authors

Nicholas Cifuentes-Goodbody is an Assistant Professor and Program Coordinator at the Translation and Interpreting Institute of Hamad bin Khalifa University. He also chairs the committee that oversaw the accreditation of the MATS program by the University of Geneva. He can be contacted at this email: ngoodbody@qf.org.qa

Andreas Karatsolis is the Associate Director or Writing, Rhetoric and Professional Communication at Massachusetts Institute of Technology, and previously the Associate Director of the Eberly Center for Teaching Excellence at Carnegie Mellon University Qatar. He can be contacted at this email: karatsol@mit.edu

# Bibliography

Ahuja, A. (2012). A new golden age rises under the desert sun. *The Telegraph*. Online Resource: http://www.telegraph.co.uk/news/science/9266426/A-new-golden-age-rises-under-the-desert-sun.html [Accessed 14 May 2015].

Alstete, J. W. (2004). *Accreditation matters: Achieving academic recognition and renewal*. San Francisco: Jossey-Bass.

Altbach, P. G. & J. Knight (2007). The internationalization of higher education: Motivations and realities. *Journal of Studies in International Education*, Vol. 11, No. 3-4, pp. 290–305.

Altbach, P. G.; L. Reisberg & L. E. Rumbley (2009). *Trends in global higher education: Tracking an academic revolution*. Paris: UNESCO.

Ambrose, S. A.; M. W. Bridges; M. DiPietro; M. C. Lovett & M. K. Norman (Eds.). (2010). *How learning works: Seven research-based principles for smart teaching*. San Francisco: Jossey-Bass.

Applebee, A. N. (1996). *Curriculum as conversation: Transforming traditions of teaching and learning*. Chicago: The University of Chicago Press.

Brennan, J. (2000). *Managing quality in higher education: An international perspective on institutional assessment and change*. Buckingham: Open University Press.

Buckner, E. (2011). The role of higher education in the Arab state and society: Historical legacies and recent reform patterns. *Comparative & International Higher Education*, Vol. 3, No. 1, pp. 21–26.

Chickering, A. W. & Z. F. Gamson (1987). Seven principles for good practice in undergraduate education. *AAHE Bulletin*, Vol. 3, pp. 2–6.

Cross-Border Education Research Team. (2015). C-BERT branch campus listings [data originally collected by Kevin Kinser and Jason E. Lane]. Online Resource: http://www.globalhighered.org/branchcampuses.php [Accessed on 18 March 2015].

Cronbach, L. & R. Snow (1977). *Aptitudes and instructional methods: A handbook for research on interactions*. New York: Irvington.

Cuban, L. (1993). *How teachers taught: Constancy and change in American classrooms, 1890-1990*. New York: Teachers College Press.

Donn, G. & Y. Al Manthri (2010). *Globalisation and higher education in the Arab Gulf states*. Didcot, Oxford: Symposium Books.

DuFour, R. (2004). *Whatever it takes: How professional learning communities respond when kids don't learn*. Bloomington: National Educational Service.

El Hassan, K. (2012). Quality assurance in higher education in 20 MENA economies. *Higher Education Management and Policy*, Vol. 24, No. 2, pp. 73–84.

Entwistle, N. & R. E. Peterson (2004). Learning Styles and Approaches to Studying. In C. D. Spielberger (Ed.), *Encyclopedia of Applied Psychology*. Boston: Academic Press, pp. 537–542.

General Secretariat for Development Planning [GSDP] (2011). *Qatar national development strategy 2011-2016*. Doha: General Secretariat for Development Planning.

Huet, I.; J. Oliveira; N. Costa & J. Estima de Oliveira (2009). The effectiveness of curriculum maps of alignment in higher education. In C. Nygaard; C. Holtham & N. Courtney (Eds.) *Improving students' learning outcomes*, Copenhagen: Copenhagen Business School Press, pp. 275–287.

Keeling, R. P. P.; A. F. Wall; R. Underhile & G. J. Dungy (2008) *Assessment reconsidered: Institutional effectiveness for student success*. Washington, DC: National Association of Student Personnel Administrators.

Lynch, S (2015). A growing number of Arab universities seek international accreditation. *Al Fanar Media*. Online Resource: http://www.al-fanarmedia.org/2015/03/a-growing-number-of-arab-universities-seek-international-accreditation/ [Accessed 2 June 2015].

Okruhlik, G. (2015). Missing linkages: The ironies and ambiguities of trans-national education in a globalized world. Presented at the Liberal Arts International Conference, Doha, Qatar.

Schwab, J. J. (1973). The Practical 3: Translation into Curriculum. *The School Review*, Vol. 81, No., pp. 501–522.

Shattock, M. (1991). The evaluation of the university's contribution to society. In U. Dahllof (Ed.), *Dimensions of Evaluation: Report of the Imhe Study Group on Evaluation in Higher Education*, London: Jessica Kingsley, pp. 57–85.

Stasz, C.; E. Eide & F. Martorell (2007). *Post-secondary education in Qatar: Employer demand, student choice, and options for policy*. Santa Monica, CA: RAND-Qatar Policy Institute.

Strange, C. C. & J. H. Banning (2001). *Education by design: Creating campus learning environments that work*. San Francisco, CA: Jossey-Bass.

Veltri, N. F.; H. W. Webb; A. G. Matveev & E. G. Zapatero (2011). Curriculum mapping as a tool for continuous improvement of I.S. curriculum. *Journal of Information Systems Education*, Vol. 22, No. 1, p. 31.

Vygotskij, L. S. (1981). *Mind in society: The development of higher psychological processes*. Cambridge, MA: Harvard University Press.

Vygotsky, L. S. (1986). *Thought and Language.* Cambridge, MA: The MIT Press.

Wenger, E. (1998). *Communities of practice: Learning, meaning, and identity.* Cambridge: Cambridge University Press.

Zelenitsky, S.; L. Vercaigne; N. M. Davies; C. Davis; R. Renaud & C. Kristjanson (2014). Using curriculum mapping to engage faculty members in the analysis of a pharmacy programme. *American Journal of Pharmaceutical Education*, Vol. 78, No. 7, pp. 1–9.

Chapter 13

# Deconstructing Constructive Alignment: How to Make Relational Knowledge and Dialectical Assessment in Higher Education

Jens Smed Rasmussen and Grethe Heldbjerg

| Assessment Agency | Student-driven | x | Teacher-driven | x |
|---|---|---|---|---|
| Assessment Outcomes | Fixed | | Flexible | x |
| Assessment Focus | Process | x | Outcome | x |
| Assessment Context | Specific | | Transferrable | x |

## Introduction

External pressures on Higher Education Institutions (HEIs) to improve quality in education (Pettersen, 2015; ter Bogt & Scapens, 2012) have led to the development of a managerial logic of modularisation and standardisation. This has led to the widely use of the notion of constructive alignment and its SOLO Taxonomy (Biggs, 1995, 1996) in relation to teaching and assessment. We argue that constructive alignment has infiltrated teaching and assessment practices to such a degree that planning teaching and assessment using the SOLO Taxonomy has somewhat become a substitute for logics of learning. Ironically, it seems like the managerial logic of modularisation and standardisation has become a threat to the very ideas inherent in the notion of constructive alignment itself (Biggs, 1995, 1996). The same has happened with the notion of learning orientated assessment (LOA) (Carless, 2007), which has as its aim to enhance student learning through assessment.

We argue that teachers and academics responsible for assessment of modules and programmes will benefit from substituting their managerial logic of standardisation and modularisation with a new logic of learning. This is indeed the case in modules and programmes, where students are doing independent research into social settings of practice. Focusing on such a learning context is relevant due to the dialectic nature of doing research and making theory of practice (Bourdieu, 1977) and the dialectic nature of learning from research experiences (Kolb, 1984), meaning that the learner will constantly be faced with contradictions which can only be overcome by making new understandings. It is therefore obvious that, due to the involved dialectics, rigid standardisations and codifications of learning and educational quality can come to contradict the need to produce knowledge in an evolving research-based learning process.

Contradiction enters into the process when students experience research difficulties in dealing with dualities between theoretical perspectives and between objectivist and subjectivist knowledge stances, or difficulties in learning from experiences gained from social settings of practice, between for example 'assimilation by theory' and 'accommodation to social settings by adaptation'.

In philosophy of science, dialectics is defined to mean: "*The process of thesis, antithesis and synthesis, that is, relationships and situations where people constantly reinterpret and give different meaning [on assessment] value. This is also the process where the knowledge-creator gives scientific meaning to his/her interactive diagnosis.*" (Arbnor & Bjerke, 2009:419-420). Thus, in doing research into social settings of practice, trying to deal with the contradictory dualism between objectivist and subjectivists knowledge stances, Bourdieu's (1977) theory of practice suggests to the student researcher that he first make a break with theoretical understandings of the practice under study and then make a break with rules presented to him by the practice under study. Thus, aiming for a situated theory of the practice, such a theory will neither be a pure subjectivist or objectivist theory but a synthesis. Likewise, according to Kolb (1984), apprehension and comprehension of a practise situation is dialectically constituted between 'concrete' or 'theoretical' understandings. Transformation of this contradictory experience into learning means solving a dialectic between thinking internally with theory or trying to externalise the experience in an effort to converge knowledge to the external situation, eventually in an experiment (Kolb, 1984), which is to form a synthesis.

We therefore propose that assessment in such a dialectic research-based learning context demands the use of advanced combinations of multiple perspectives on assessments in an effort to enhance learning and to fully assess actual learning and educational outcome, but also to communicate and convey educational outcomes to stakeholders. A LOA practice (Carless, 2007) must therefore be enabled to assess and enhance learning in particular kinds of research-based learning. An interpretative case study of an assessment practice done in this chapter therefore concludes by offering a dialectical assessment perspective constructed to serve the purpose of LOA besides remedying the threat from colonizing managerial logics.

From years of teaching, we have observed that quality of learning becomes visible and partly gets constructed through 'assessment practices in use' (James, 2014) and the Humboldtian university tradition has been our 'expressed theory' on assessment. Therefore, we place value on dialogues among peers to assess learning and quality of learning outcome.

Positioning ourselves like Peters & Bartholomew (this volume) in the current 'dialogic turn' in contemporary research literature on assessment as seen by McDonnell and Curtis (2014:933), we are puzzled by the current process of 'managerial instrumentation logic' spreading from a business world into Higher Education Institutions (HEI). This leads to creation of multiple logics inside the institutions on the quality of educational outcome (Pettersen, 2015). In the Humboldtian university tradition, quality of learning is determined in discourses between academic teachers and students but according to the case study done by Pettersen (2015), quality standards are now determined in discourses between academic teachers and professional university management. We are therefore interested in the role for assessment and the historical situatedness in the institutionalisation of HEIs, like Cifuentes-Goodbody & Karatsolis (this volume).

'Counting' educational outcomes to be aggregated into statements of 'educational results' from the individual HEI is one possible managerial consequence from the managerial discourse impacting on future assessment practice. But such 'counting' poses a danger on creativity and innovation in HEI and research (ter Bogt & Scapens, 2012). Assessment issues and issues of performance management can easily transform into a dysfunctional judgemental form opposed to a developmental form (Pettersen, 2015; ter Bogt & Scapens, 2012). Thus, according to ter Bogt and Scapens (2012), when the subjectivity involved in judgement was made peripheral and distant from the local interaction, this produced situations of anxiety and stress among researchers in UK and Netherlands. Emotional discomfort was also observed in democratic dialogical assessment practices, according to McDonnell and Curtis (2014). But in their experiment with dialogical assessment, students and teachers became enabled by the democratic dialogue to create development, enhance student's self-confidence and enhance their courage to learn advanced topics. This interest in dialogical and peer assessment is shared with Peters & Bartholomew (this volume) along with an interest in student agency in peer assessment to foster critical reflectivity in student learning, which we share with Fleischmann (this volume). These observations of learning enhancement by assessment contrast sharply with those effects reported by ter Bogt and Scapens (2012), from research assessment done according to standards enacted in a discourse distant from those whom the assessment of research performance concerned.

The research question for the case study presented in this chapter is therefore: *How can students and teachers, in a context of increasing managerial discourses on standardisation and management of educational outcome quality, made external to the situated research-based learning process in context, continue to enhance learning and educational quality by applying a dialectical assessment practice?*

Reading this chapter you should gain the following insights:

1. theoretical insights into the current case of assessment in research based learning processes of students doing research in HEIs under external institutional pressure for standardisation. In the first sections we apply an interpretative case study approach, giving centre stage to conceptualising and theorising on the current assessment situation from a critical theoretical perspective, resulting in a deconstruction of the notion of constructive alignment (Biggs, 1995, 1996).

2. theoretical insights into different perspectives on assessment integrated into a theory of learning orientated dialectical assessment. This is described in the next sections. The notion is constructed to encompass the dialectics of social construction and the evaluation criteria of historical situatedness (Arbnor & Bjerke, 2009; Guba & Lincoln, 1994). 'Insights from multiple perspectives on assessment' – a notion borrowed from James (2014) – is then integrated into the developed notion of dialectic assessment by integrating five different perspectives in an effort to make dialectic assessment able to be LOA (Carless, 2007) while also able to assess more learning outcomes.

3. initial practical insights on how to eventually use the constructed concept of learning orientated dialectic assessment. From dialogues and conversations with students and examiners, the case study is empirically based on observations from our own assessment practice, thus grounding the resulting vignettes (Heldbjerg & van Liempd, forthcoming) in real experiences stemming from learning processes consisting of student research. Learning orientated dialectic assessment, emphasizing the dialogical assessment perspective, is thus demonstrated by example through vignettes.

# Theoretical Issues in Assessment for Research Based Learning Dialectics

Different perspectives on assessment point to different aspects of learning enhancing effects from practising formative and summative assessment in higher education. Theoretical deduced evidence of enhanced learning from applying a dialectic perspective on assessment is therefore discussed and analysed in this section from a perspective of critical theory, arguing that there is a case for dialectic assessment. This is followed by an immanent critique of the notion of constructive alignment and the corresponding and widespread use of the SOLO Taxonomy, resulting in deconstructing this notion. The need for theoretical enhancements by constructing a learning orientated dialectic assessment perspective, integrating multiple perspectives on assessment, follows from this section.

## Critically Analysing aspects of Assessment

Recently, James (2014) identified three perspectives commonly used to investigate assessment practices; the *technical*, the *humanistic* and the *interactionist perspective* on assessment of learning, while pointing at a recently developed *learning cultural perspective* aiming to improve on the other perspectives. According to James (2014:156), applying only the notion of constructive alignment, teachers risk being left with no 'real "*opportunity for classical rational action*"' due to growing centralised specification of learning and constraints put on the teacher's real possibilities to align teaching and learning, together with a too heavy reliance on codification. In contrast, the proposition argued in this chapter is to combine a dialogical perspective on assessment with other perspectives and thus enable both practitioners and assessment researchers to understand and apply learning orientated assessment in dialectic learning processes involving student research. Apart from descriptive understandings, we also aim for normative indications for learning enhancement from assessment practice – especially in regard to student research into social settings of areas of practice. As recent research testifies on effects of enhanced learning from using dialogue in assessment (McDonnell & Curtis, 2014; Peters & Bartholomew, in this volume), a dialogical perspective is therefore used analytically in the following.

A 'dialogical turn' in the current assessment literature was observed by McDonnell and Curtis (2014). This turn might in fact represent a response from educational research to the recent 'managerial turn' on assessment in HEI. Educational researchers might in fact be pointing to results of enhanced learning experienced during attempts to reinstitute dialogical assessment practices. According to Habermas (1981: Ch VIII, 2), areas of activity which basically function by social integration, communicative actions and discourses of consensus are easily colonised when mediated by 'a legislation process'. Pedagogics in education represents such an area of activity.

In the case of Norwegian and Swedish Universities, Pettersen (2015) found that the external pressure for standardisation translates into a discourse between academic teachers and professional university management. It is further argued that, to be able to teach, the academic teachers need to make the multiple logics from a business world valid in relation to academic values (ibid). Whether this fully removed the dialogue on quality of learning outcomes from teaching and assessment practices was not researched by Pettersen (2015). Yet, a technical reasoning can overrule competing forms of reasoning as the technical reasoning will be seen as an instrumental reasoning (Alvesson & Deetz, 2000). Reasoning thus becomes focused on control through the development of mean-ends chains, which is opposite to the practical reasoning or interest: "... *practical interest: 'a constitutive interest in the preservation and expansion of the inter subjectivity of possible action-oriented mutual understandings."* (Alvesson & Deetz, 2000:86; Op.cit. Habermas 1971:310). Thus, if a systems world of technical reasoning dominates the life world, turning it into systemic, instrumental rules or procedures, an uncomplimentary imbalance is created between those two forms of reasoning (Alvesson & Deetz, 2000).

We do however have reasons to propose that academic teachers in HEI might also be involved to remedy such tendencies of colonisation, eventually by attempts to reinstitute communicative actions and consensus discourses into teaching and assessment in higher education. According to Burawoy *et al.* (1991), these effects of system mediating that evoke attempts to resist the dysfunctional and distorting effects are more observable in micro sociologic processes than in macro. Such resistance might also resemble a steering mechanism (Laughlin, 1987) from the life world onto the system. Studying summative and formative assessment practices empirically in micro at the level of each class, module, department or university, might thus reveal renewed modalities of system and life world institutionalisations (Burawoy *et al.*, 1991) to encompass communicative relations and consensus discourses in the learning milieu among teachers and students. In a context of increasing managerial discourse on quality of learning and mediation by rules and regulations, deliberate attempts to apply dialogical assessment in pedagogical practices would thus, in theory (Burawoy *et al.*, 1991; Habermas, 1981), actually resemble an attempt to innovate learning enhancing assessment. Thus we argue a proposition on normative innovation of assessment; that resistance among academic teachers and students to actually reinstitute communicative actions in assessment in HEI, when technical reasoning threatens to take over, is a rational innovation process.

Assessment is considered to be one of the stronger forces impacting on learning outcome quality in higher education. Recent experiences from our own assessment practice during exams pointed us towards an interesting observation of enhanced leaning outcomes among students. In our immediate reflections, this could be ascribed to processes of dialogue in teaching especially related to formative assessment during the learning process and partly to summative assessment for marking during exam.

Some postgraduate master students having followed an internship module even showed an advanced interest in dialogue during exam to see changes made in future curriculum in their programme of study regarding their metacognitive competences. Another but similar instance saw a postgraduate master student writing transcripts of his conversations with his supervisor during supervision into his final master thesis. He wanted to show how the formative assessment dialogue advanced his research and learning. Considering these observations done in relation to student research into areas of social settings of practices, and looking backwards to the Humboldtian tradition of determining quality of learning and educational outcome by discourses between teachers and students, we are forced to look into this phenomenon of highly valued assessment practice. Thus, referring to critical social theory (Bourdieu, 1977; Habermas, 1981), and old institutional economics (Burns & Scapens, 2000), we must empirically expect dialogical assessment to be considered valuable in practice along with complimentary perspectives on assessment.

Relating the above reflections to our role as academics teaching students to research to produce good and valid situated theory, meaning that theory becomes dependent on both theory in general and the particular social context of study, we are warned by Tinker (1991) to be aware that teachers have a mediating role in learning orientated assessment. This is similar to an accountant who recognises the need to exercise practical reflexivity towards accounting standards as they are socially constructed by nature. This makes the accountant an interested part in their construction. *"Practical reflexivity"* in accounting (Tinker, 1991:301) and, here we add, in assessment of teaching, aspires unfortunately *"to negate the negation"*; for instance, when we say power is absent in a given situation after we talk about 'power over', 'power to' and 'power with' related to the very situation in question. Standards and criteria for learning are therefore to be understood as dialectics and not as positive rules of truth. A reflective teacher thus becomes involved in their de- and reconstruction. In research-based teaching and assessment, this position can become a matter of mediating between the different kinds of dialectic interplay between an objectivistic stance and a subjectivist stance in student research. In teaching, where experiential learning is involved in the research process, assessment can become a matter of mediating in the experiential learning process as well as mediating between this process and epistemic positions, theories and methods of the subject matter concerned.

## The Dialectics of Constructive Alignment

Provoked by the notion that educational outcome considerations and not psychometrics or politics should guide assessment in higher education, Biggs (1995) was inclined to forward his notion of constructive alignment. He intended to fit assessment into a constructivist stance of knowledge, at least concerning the way students learn (Biggs, 1996). He related the notion of constructive alignment to a paradigmatic change in higher education. He wanted to normatively substitute 'assessment of learning' on objectives aligned to the instructional design of learning processes for 'assessment by the numbers' as conceived inside a predominantly statistical trait theorem of stable dimensions for measuring learning outcome (Biggs, 1995). Summative and formative assessment was thus revolutionised in theory and aimed to enhance learning, not least by positive repercussions from instructional aligned learning outcomes which could be described in the SOLO taxonomy. The taxonomy was considered to be comprehensibly applicable. However, implementing 'constructive alignment' might not be easy due to resistance at the system level of the institution of HEI, according to Biggs (1996).

Seen from a constructivist perspective alone, Biggs (1996) might be right in his observation that the university system is resisting the constructive design and alignment. However, from a dialectical perspective, there is reason to argue that the notion of constructive alignment is actually dialectically constituted. On the one hand, constructivists designing and aligning learning should produce enhanced communicative relations to construct knowledge and criteria for assessment of learning. On the other hand, administrative logics can rise or be imported to take over from the communicative relations during construction of the alignment and employment of the SOLO taxonomy. We thus want to argue, from an immanent critique, that there is reason to propose that the concept of constructive alignment is dialectically constituted. The learning enhancing potential, which is the purpose of using constructive alignment, is actually at risk of being negated by negations of its own dialectic. Two reasons can be forwarded, substantiating this proposition.

First reason: In the literature on assessment research, constructive alignment is now beginning to be compared more with a technical perspective on assessment than an interactionist, humanist or cultural perspective (James, 2014).

Second reason: Considering the SOLO taxonomy from theory of cognitive learning, psychology and instructive design, the concept of constructive alignment is undoubtedly a learning enabling concept. This is true when comparing the concept with its counterpart of trait theory and psychometrics in assessment practices. In this theoretical understanding of the concept along with the SOLO taxonomy, discourses about accountability, creation of communicative relations among academics and among teachers and students should be expected to happen when applying constructive alignment and the Taxonomy. This is also the very idea of constructivist learning theory. These discourses would then in principle enable and guide formative assessment and feedback to enhance production of constructivist knowledge in the learning process. Negative repercussions on the learning process by summative assessment, applying criteria from psychometrics and a monolithic objectivist knowledge stance, is thus avoided. The highest categories of the SOLO taxonomy are also suitable to describe advanced learning from doing research. However, when constructive alignment is applied as planning of the learning process and the SOLO taxonomy is applied as a measurement scale, dialectics from *pedagogics of planning* risk being invoked. This was empirically studied by Oakes *et al.* (1998:285) in a field of cultural institutions consisting of museums doing research and educational tasks, where government reforms mandated the institutions to make business planning and corresponding performance measurements. Using Bourdieu's notion of how pedagogics place positive value on the things 'named' in a process and thus exclude other things, Oakes *et al.* (1998) studied how pedagogics of business planning in these cultural institutions became dominated by the field of government and turned into 'a field in cultural transformation'. This empirically rich case study showed how pedagogics of planning changed allocations of capital among positions in the field of cultural institutions. It also showed how the language of planning created symbolic violence on habitus in the field and *"deplace[d] other forms of expression"* (Oakes *et al.*, 1998:284-285) and *"destruct[ed] their instruments of expression"* (Oakes *et al.*, 1998:261).

Rationalisation of assessment practices in HEI to constructively align assessment by applying strong curriculum planning, informed by the notion of constructive alignment and the SOLO Taxonomy in an effort to codify and standardise learning and levelling performance, risk negating in the planning process that quality of learning that acts subtly as a controlling pedagogic power.

Constructive alignment and the SOLO Taxonomy is not just a neutral technical instrument. In subsequent case studies of the reforming of the cultural institutions, the researchers also found a mechanism related to rationalisation of the institutions by performance measurements created in parallel with the business planning, where the logics of administration takes over from rationalisations informed by a conception of enlightened dialogue of quality in cultural institutions (Townley *et al.*, 1999). But some attempts to reinstitute a new dialogue of what accountability should concern for the cultural institutions was also found in a subsequent study (Townley *et al.*, 2003). Thus, in the field of cultural institutions, changing from fields of *specialized production* to fields of *large scale production* by the pedagogics of planning (Oakes *et al.*, 1998), and the rationalisation leading to administrative logics taking over the process (Townley *et al.*, 2003), some resistance (Burawoy *et al.*, 1991) was consequently invoked by academics in the cultural research and education institutions. But whether this resistance resulted in a new institutionalisation – a new modality of system and life world – with practical and technical reasoning complementing each other, is not known. Academic teachers in HEI who read this and reflect upon their own experience from implementing 'constructive alignments' and 'descriptions of learning goals' in the SOLO taxonomy – in contexts of external pressures on HEI transforming higher education into a field of large scale education – might have noticed the forces of 'the pedagogics of planning' and 'the administrative logics'.

What James (2014) saw as teachers' restricted opportunities for rational action related to the notion of constructive alignment might very well be explained by the technicalities inherent in the notion of constructive alignment and the SOLO Taxonomy.

Thus, deconstructing the notion of constructive alignment by theoretical deductions and using case studies with empirical findings from fields similar to HEIs gives reason to conclude:

1. that dialogue between students and teachers might be used to avoid that pedagogics of planning and the administrative logics take power and control over quality of learning to eventually exclude learning from student research;

2. that an epistemology of dialectics can be proposed to construct a theory of assessment to guide both students and teachers in their continued effort to reflexively produce and adjust a framework of assessment to assess learning and educational outcome quality from research-based learning processes into social settings of practice.

## A Dialectical Perspective on Assessment: Theory as Method – Method as Theory

In this section, a dialectic perspective on assessment is developed in a twofold and interactive way. Referring to Bourdieu (1977) and his concept of *theory-as-method*, knowledge interest becomes an interest in methodology on how conditions for knowledge creation develop due to developments in knowledge; and then *method-as-theory* might dialectically be seen as the other side of this coin through which we see and interpret the world. But to avoid committing intellectual fallacy, the researcher has to break first with rules and theory presented to him by the practices under study, and next with his general theory in use concerning the practices (Bourdieu, 1977). It is therefore impossible for the researcher to make these breaks without acting, aiming to make an empirical observation to 'break by'. But similarly, acting is in vain without applying theoretical knowledge positions to 'break from'.

In a dialectical research perspective, theory and method thus become conceptual ways of viewing and acquiring knowledge on assessment, at least epistemologically seen, as language is the means of acknowledgement. Theory constitutes and becomes method, and method constitutes and becomes theory, when brought together through the dialectics of hermeneutics. This is the epistemological perspective on how we generate knowledge, taking the view of a critical research perspective. Before doing this in Table 1 below, two central concepts of understanding must be put forward.

*Dialectics* means: *"The process of thesis, antithesis and synthesis, that is, relationships and situations where people constantly reinterpret and give different meaning [on assessment] value. This is also the process where the knowledge-creator gives scientific meaning to his/her interactive diagnosis"* (Arbnor & Bjerke, 2009:419-420) on assessment and how assessment of learning in higher education has to be done.

*Diagnosis* means: *"A way to interactively interpret and understand actors in situations of everyday life [of doing assessment] through deeper insight and broadened perspectives"* (Arbnor & Bjerke, 2009:419). Diagnosis is made through interactive communication on assessment, striving to interpret and understand the concepts and meanings which are at stake among students and teachers.

When it comes to an evaluation of critical research carried out through a dialectical perspective, we have to abandon the traditional criteria of validity and reliability. Guba and Lincoln (1994) offer four sets of evaluation criteria, two of which we will concentrate on here. The critical-theoretical set puts weight on the criteria of *Historical Situatedness*, and the social constructivist set puts weight on the criteria of *Authenticity*. As the two sets of criteria might be seen as overlapping, and the criteria of *Authenticity*, among others, are specifically pointing towards *"...critique and transformation; restitution and emancipation."* (Guba & Lincoln, 1994:112). We adapt the integration of these two sets of criteria into the critical-theoretical perspective of *Historical Situatedness* (Heldbjerg & van Liempd, forthcoming).

| The Concepts of Social Construction of Reality through Hermeneutics | The Criteria of Historical Situatedness |
|---|---|
| 1. Intentionality | *Historical Situatedness*: the perspective that inquiry is guided by awareness of time and space, drawing attention to the institutional antecedents of the situation being studied. As such the history of cultural-, economic-, political-, and social conditions, among others, are taken into account. |
| 2. Subjectification | |
| 3. Externalisation | *Ontological Authenticity*: given the historical embeddedness in time and space, stating and making basic assumptions; i.e., values and beliefs, transparent, enlarges and strengthens personal constructions; i.e., |
| 4. Institutionalisation | |
| 5. Legitimisation | *Eroding Ignorance and Misapprehensions*: By strengthening the *educative authenticity*, leading to improved understanding of the constructions of others, and thereby being able to evaluate to which extent an inquiry leads to actions, eroding of ignorance and misapprehensions, and then is: |
| 6. Objectification | |
| 7. Internalisation | *Providing Stimulus to Action*: Focusing, drawing attention to *catalytic authenticity*, stimulating to action; i.e., *Transformation of Existing Structure*: Empowerment of *tactical authenticity*, leading to action. |

*Table 1: The Dialectics of Social Constructions as Embedded in Historical Situatedness. Source: Arbnor & Bjerke (1997:182); Heldbjerg & van Liempd (2015); Guba & Lincoln (1994:112-114).*

## Intentionality

Intentionality is seen as: "*The dimension, process and structure behind intention that gives a meaning to experience [of assessment]; ...*"(Arbnor & Bjerke, 2009:422). Different forms of assessment are already in existence as structures which are more or less embedded and taken for granted at the HEIs. They have a history; i.e., they are constituted at a given time in a given situation. Due to the partakers taking action by using them, they are acknowledged differently by the partakers during the process; i.e., they are interpreted and comprehended in various ways, thereby attached to various ranges of meanings. Then, as meanings are subjectively constituted, they motivate to various intentions when they are more or less iteratively transformed and used by partakers in different situations of assessment.

The worldview attached to intentionality might be *consensus* oriented, as expressed by the metatheoretical view of Social Constructivism, or conflict oriented, as expressed by the metatheoretical view of Critical Theory. As Alvesson and Deetz (2000:9) wrote: *"Critical social research is thus oriented towards challenging rather than confirming that what is established, disrupting rather than reproducing cultural traditions and conventions, opening up and showing tensions in language use rather than continuing its domination, encouraging productive dissension rather than taking surface consensus as a point of departure."* The intention of doing critical social research on such a phenomenon as assessment of learning *"… is thereby to contribute to emancipation, for example, to encourage rethinking and the emotional as well as cognitive working through of ideas and identities which are repressive."* (Alvesson & Deetz, 2000:9).

## Subjectification

As humans are seen as a subjective reality in doing assessment, subjectification is seen as: *"The process of consciousness by which we create and constitute ourselves as intentional subjects"* (Arbnor & Bjerke, 2009:426). In other words: with reference to intentionality, human beings constitute their subjective meanings of life; i.e., their worldview, and thereby their way of acknowledging their view of assessment, which might be more or less tacit. This then concerns the dialectical processes of habitual reflexivity in our minds (Bourdieu 1977), by which we create and decide, among other things, what the field of assessment of learning is all about for us and our own intentions as subjects, when we enact our diagnosis.

## Externalisation

As society is a result of human activity, externalisation on assessment is seen as: *"The process by which we make our subjectivity available to others*" (Arbnor & Bjerke, 2009:420); i.e., how we express our different and various interpretations and meanings on assessment of learning as intentions, when we are talking to other students, teachers and possible stakeholders on the types, forms and possibilities in doing assessment. By explicating to others their preferences of meaning forefighting some assessment perspectives and criteria, more points of view are brought at stake. Following Martin (2002), some might be in harmony, some in conflict, and others again might be blurred or fragmented. Here it is important to erode misapprehensions and ignorance, in order to achieve mutual understanding, not necessarily in the meaning of total consensus.

## Institutionalisation

During iterative, dialectic processes of externalisation, interpretation and intentionality, institutions of assessment are constructed. Then, institutionalisation is defined as: "*The process of establishing values, norms, routines, etc. as institutions in the socially constructed reality*" (Arbnor & Bjerke, 2009:422). This happens if, over time, certain forms of supervision and assessment become a rule or routine from which it is no longer appropriate, or well seen, to express deviant attitudes and meanings, neither by students nor by potential supervisors. On the contrary, this does not need to happen or be wanted: Institutionalisation might be processual; i.e., securing the ongoing interaction on how to learn and do assessment in a way which always provides stimulus to action. By drawing attention to the partakers' catalytic and educative authenticity which are always at stake or in focus, this becomes the dialectic way of how evaluation has to be done, thereby legitimating the dialectics as a process. Cultural framing by using the dialectics as a process is here the routine; i.e, you always have to strive for openness, understanding and actions leading to transformation of structures which are not supporting and enhancing students' learning during their research processes, thereby empowering their acknowledgeability and academic skills.

## Legitimisation

Legitimisation of institutionalised assessment is seen as: "*The process of justification of institutions in socially constructed reality; ...*"(Arbnor &

Bjerke, 2009:422). This can be done *linguistically, proverbally* and *theoretically* (Arbnor & Bjerke, 1997:182; 2009:422) and happens when we are told: "You can see how well our new system of assessment is working. The marks have been 0.5 points higher on average since we implemented the new assessment system!" or "It is evident, the figures speak for themselves!" As (James, 2014) states: *"Regulations, systems and institutional practices for assessment will usually be shaped and justified with reference to some arguments from a technical perspective: [... among others cross-referring...] to module or programme objectives or learning outcomes."*(James, 2014:158). Here, it is important to point to the difference to the students between *legitimisation* and *legalisation*: where the first one is a given society's (organisation, group) justification of institutionalised social constructions, the latter one concerns the law; i.e., what is put on the Statute Book by the Parliament/rulers of a given nation state.

## Objectification

As society is also to be perceived as an objective reality, objectification of assessment means: *"The process by which an externalised human thought and/or act might attain the characteristics of a socially constructed objectivity"*(Arbnor & Bjerke, 2009:423). Following Alvesson and Deetz (2000:9) and James (2014:158), this is when the technical perspective on assessment of learning as an instrument is almost taken for granted and becomes an end in itself. If not challenged, it confirms a surface consensus, encompassing self-suppression, leading to structural dominance, power and control. In other words, students and supervisors are becoming disempowered in following what they acknowledge as their own true interests of assessment.

## Internalisation

As humans are also a societal result, internalisation, here of assessment criteria, is defined as: *"The process by which we take over the world in which others already live ..."*(Arbnor & Bjerke, 2009:422). This points to the already dominant objectified assessment forms which newcomers to HEIs meet. To be 'good' students and, later on, supervisors, they might to a certain degree strive to 'learn how to pull the ropes' at the HEI.

Even if they are challenging the system of assessment, they have to abide by it as individuals or they will fail. Sticking to it without reflection, the way of doing assessment becomes internalised and proverbially seen as 'the way we do things around here!' Reflections (subjectification) and discussions (externalisation) among colleagues challenges the existing assessment practices and constitutes new processes of reflections though active dialoguing. Due to this way of acknowledging and interpreting dialectics, a discourse on assessment of learning is also inspired by James's (2014:158-161) perspective of *learning cultures*.

The evaluation criteria of Historical Situatedness have to be seen as an interwoven, or embedded, part of the dialectical process. They are regarded as an integrated, critical perspective throughout the dialectics in the social construction of various social realities and the changing or transformation of these. In other words, construction and deconstruction can take place during the same processes of dialectics. We point to the importance of this for example, regarding the perspective of *learning cultures*. Interpreting James (2014), culture is historically situated, and so are the technical, the humanist and the interactionist perspectives. These three different learning perspectives are then to be seen as encompassed subcultures of the same historically situated culture of a given society, or HEI. Following Martin (2002) on cultural perspectives, the learning perspectives are also to be seen as both diverging from and complementing and blurring one another, at the same time, in such cultural spaces as the HEIs, both when looking at HEIs as singulars at the micro level and as a unity at the macro level.

## Multiple Perspectives on Assessment

The initial construct for the present case study was deduced in part from an early analysis of our data (Silverman, 2013). Thus, observations from our teaching resulted in an analytical effort to combine five perspectives on assessment to explain the observed learning enhancement. During efforts to synthesise our analysis, the notion of LOA (Carless, 2007) became important along with the critical dialectic perspective on assessment, which has been constructed above.

Using LOA involves primarily a way of thinking to make learning part of the assessment tasks according to Carless (2007), who noted two different conceptions of this among colleagues:

1. Those who conceived this as a matter of planned formative assessment, placing heavy workloads on lectures. So called instrumental students *"may also interpret some types of formative assessment as extra work for no marks"* (refering to Yorke 2003 in Carless, 2007:58).

2. Those who interpreted it from a more constructivist orientation and found learning oriented assessment to be just a fundamental part of good teaching. In essence, the challenge in LOA is to stimulate intended learning by assessment tasks.

Student assignments involving independent research can be considered such a learning task, capable of priming deep learning when students move towards the advanced learning goals. According to Biggs (1995), these goals would also fit into the highest category of learning on the SOLO taxonomy. A second element in LOA concerns student's involvement in assessment to enhance understanding of the learning goals and engage actively with criteria. According to Carless (2007), the third element is feedback. This concept was later developed into a concept of sustainable feedback by Carless *et al.* (2011). Trust, which seems to be an issue related to academic staff, is a prerequisite for implementing LOA, according to Carless (2009). In reality however, and counter to the creation of trust, a culture of accountability in HEIs seems to produce incitements to make arbitrary and non-professional choices regarding learning and assessment of learning among teachers in contemporary milieus of HEI (Carless, 2009).

*Interaction* between students and between students and teachers to form socialisation processes was found by Rust *et al.* (2003) to be necessary in an effort to *"improve students' learning by developing their understanding of assessment criteria and processes"*. There was a need to make tacit knowledge more explicit in developing students' competences of self-assessment. Teachers can actively design and sustain the learning milieu and thus establish *"conditions in which students can operate with agency"*(Boud & Molloy, 2012), thus repositioning the demands of the teacher in feedback. Interaction between teachers and students can thus be designed to foster student agency related to formative assessment by feedback: *"from an act of teachers to an act of students"* and further on through interactions between the two parties; from *"monologue to dialogue"* and into feedback, which almost always implicates peers (Boud & Molloy, 2012:710). From the *interactionist perspective* we thus see how assessment is viewed as a matter of designing peer dialogue and how interaction is necessary to transfer tacit knowledge.

A *humanistic perspective* on assessment is widespread according to James (2014). Studies on questioning practices in HEI are typically carried out from a humanistic perspective, pointing to arbitrary questioning during exams, etc., where the assessment task actually demands a completely opposite form of questioning. Often there are no answers as to why this happens. In contrast, Webster (2005) conducted a study of the technologies of power in use during exams in design studios in the education of architects. The study showed how students were forced by power to reproduce staff-centred constructions of architectural habitus. This study made it evident that both the dialogue during an exam and dialogical assessments can be considered safeguards against these forms of power and dysfunctional repercussions on student's motivation to learn and develop.

The *learning cultural perspective* forwarded by James aims at turning Bourdieu's theory-as-method notion useful, making it possible, first of all, to study assessment practices as relational, and furthermore to look for the relational knowledge generation (James, 2014). This perspective has been elaborated in the above section where it is part of the dialectic perspective on assessment.

From a *dialogical assessment perspective,* McDonnell and Curtis (2014) reported how, related to peer assessment, students are not equally prepared, and how peer assessment processes can turn emotional. Peer review of student research is a central element in the interpreted case, and the external discourse on standards of learning outcome thus contributes to the dialectics. In this present study, the dialogical assessment perspective is essentially a dialectic perspective.

By using each of these four perspectives as dimensions in the study of assessment practices, and applying a *dialogical perspective* as the fifth dimension, the cases are constructed and interpreted along these dimensions as shown in the following subsection.

## Generating Data for Constructing and Using Vignettes

Vignettes can be defined and used in different ways with various intentions. The following definition is not value laden until it is brought into use by interpreting it into a given metatheoretical and methodological perspective.

*"A vignette can take the form of a scenario or a story; i.e., a short description, or a snapshot, of one or more persons in a social situation, portraying an everyday event. The portrait can be written text, or consist of images, short movies, and other forms of stimuli. The stimuli/content of the vignette may stem from materials, such as diaries, field notes, audio- and/or video records, computer animations, cartoons, and more."* (Heldbjerg & van Liempd, forthcoming).

Using vignettes corresponds methodologically with interviewing, making it necessary to clarify the kind of data we get: *"[Interviews] provide uncertain but often interesting clues for the understanding of social reality and ideas, beliefs, values and other aspects of 'subjectivities'. [...] As Mills (1940) noted, we cannot really investigate motives but we can study vocabularies of motives."* (Alvesson & Deetz, 2000:74-75). It is then necessary to consider the existence and variety of: *"...social norms for talk, scripts for discourses available, the relative autonomy of discourses in relationship to other phenomena (beliefs, social reality out there), anticipations of the intentions and uses of the interview material, and mutual identity constructions and interactive dynamics in the researcher-interviewee interaction..."* (Alvesson & Deetz, 2000:75). These considerations must be made to avoid the fallacy of taking it for granted that language and habitus is homogeneous among all actors in HEI. Furthermore, this urges us to put (more) weight onto observation during the interviews, in order to grip both the spoken and unspoken language among the partaking actors.

The intention of using vignettes is to show scenarios or situations, which students have experienced beforehand and through dialogues, activating their reflections in the form of subjectifications. The dialogues are initiated by posing initial questions in relation to each vignette to achieve mutual understanding. Through externalisation and reflexivity, insights are thus made into phenomena of learning. A group dialogue with vignettes may have partaking actors in the numbers of two to four students and one to two researchers. Constituting *heterogeneous* groups might be ideal to maximise differences between reflections and interactions throughout dialogue but, in reality, too much heterogeneity can be a threat to the relationships of trust and confidence that are necessary to get values and norms internalised and externalised. Constituting groups that are too *homogeneous* can result in no challenging of objectified and internalised perceptions and conceptions during the dialogues, i.e., the partakers confirm each other in their attitudes and opinions, and then almost no new interpretations and transformations/transformative actions take place (Heldbjerg, et. al. 2009).

The procedure of carrying out group dialogues with vignettes builds on the construction of First Generation Vignettes, which are presented in the following tables. The way this has been done is described above through our dialectical deducted theory as method.

At the end of each dialogue session, we find it of relevance to present the vignettes in their entirety, as they are seen in the tables below, especially Table 3, in order to let the students have the possibility to reflect and summarise. Depending on the students' level, it might be a choice to present the whole of Table 3 for supplemental interpretations and meanings or, for the time being, only former levels of experience. It may also be interesting to listen to students' common reflections on their future studies by presenting to them the vignettes on future projects and thesis. Repeating the practice of dialoguing through vignettes can lead to the constitution of Second Generation Vignettes, and then further generations of vignettes, until a meaningful saturation for all partakers – i.e., Gestalten/Post-understanding – is reached. Eventually, this might also lead to changing, or new, vignettes and research questions, as the field of learning oriented assessment is always to be seen as in flux.

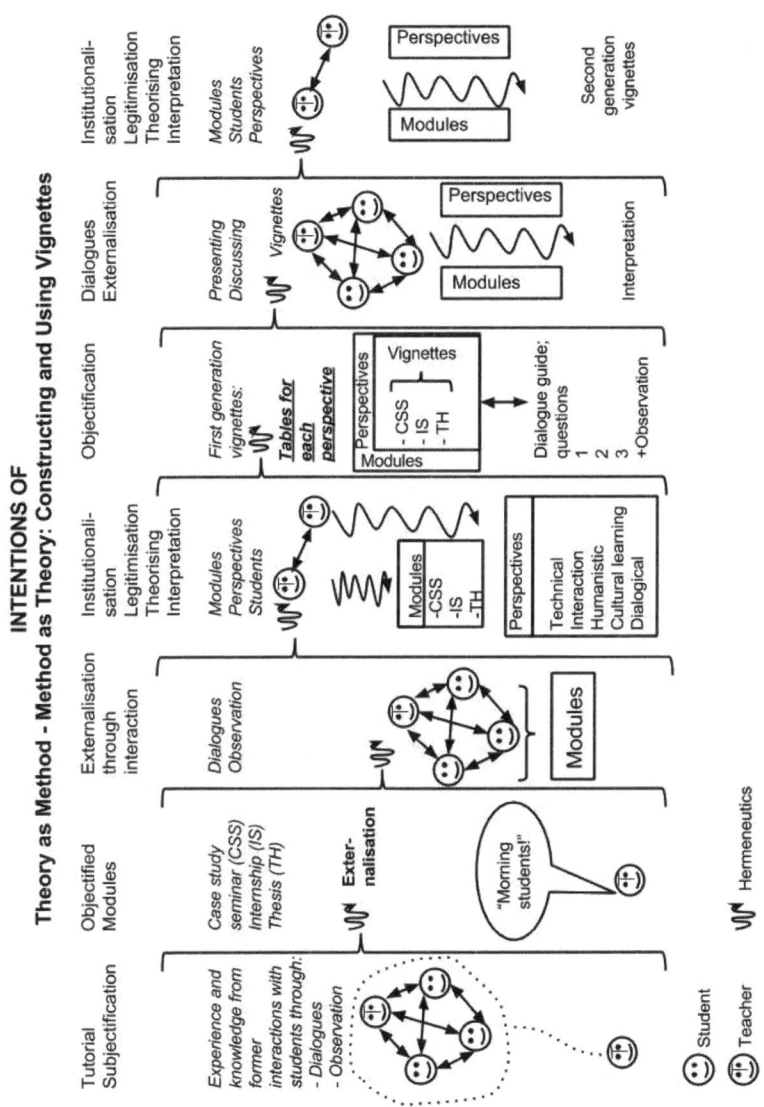

*Figure 1: Own compilation with reference to Table 1. Theory as Method – Method as Theory: Constructing and Using Vignettes.*

In the following tables we present three settings of dialectical experience, learning and assessment, involving student research. Table 2 concerns three settings or modules of student research.

| Three settings of dialectic experience, learning and assessment involving student research | |
| --- | --- |
| Case study research and seminars | Peer review of case study reports in two seminars during the learning process and once for seminars applied for exam and marking by the teacher. These three seminars are uniformly implemented on each occasion. |
| Research based internship | Dialogue and reflection seminars between peers and teachers arranged three to four times during an internship over one semester designed as assessment for learning from working with a portfolio of assignments. The final oral exam is based on dialogue among examiners and student to elicit learning from the portfolio. |
| Supervision of thesis work | Collective supervision aimed for peer review in dialogue to make assessment for learning along individual supervision. Thesis work is finally marked upon oral exam and assessment of the written thesis. |
| **Major thrust on assessment for learning** | |
| Case study research and seminars | Peer review in writing and dialogue to create common understanding between students and teachers on criteria for research into the subject area and the field together with and understanding of academic virtues. |
| Research based internship | Constructive alignment is designed to be flexible but the initial dialogue seminar applies a workshop utilizing Kolb's theory about experiential learning (Kolb, 1984). Kolb's theory and the activity create dialogues among teachers and students initiated by students' need to understand what they experience during their internship stay, and how to construct criteria for their own learning to be assessed in dialogue for their final exam and marking. |
| Supervision of thesis work | Constructive alignment has to be in a productive state of flux. It would spoil the learning if assessments were allowed to backwash on students' autonomous research. Autonomously selecting collective supervision with the possibility to receive and give peer review assessment as an elective |

*Table 2: Settings of student research and assessment.*

In Table 3 the five perspectives of assessment are compared to the three settings, and in Table 4 they are compared with the main findings. The content of the three tables in total are to be seen as our First Generation Vignettes, especially focusing on those of Table 3.

**The Technical Perspective: Description/Definition**

Curriculum is planned and learning is described for the modules in question. The constructive alignment of teaching and learning are only described in open terms to be interpreted in the process, except for the main learning activities such as doing case study research, writing a master thesis, and some mandatory readings, etc.

Level of learning performance is described using the SOLO Taxonomy in open descriptions of learning into categorical descriptions, while substance in these categories is not detailed.

| | |
|---|---|
| Case study research and seminars | Constructive alignment is designed for teaching of the subjects and arranging two collective seminars. Case study is however autonomously chosen by students but under supervision. Students can choose between some different theory positions but they must account for their choices, which is part of the research-based learning objectives. This leaves room for emergent constructive alignment of learning. |
| Research based internship | Constructive alignment is made flexible and open for dialogue. |
| Supervision of thesis work | Research methodology, method and subjects are discussed via dialogues – eventually via collective dialogues. |

**The Interactionist Perspective**

Assessment is primarily viewed as a matter of designing possibilities for peer dialogue and supporting interaction between students and between students and teachers to secure transfer of tacit knowledge.

| | |
|---|---|
| Case study research and seminars | Assessment is done by teacher in supervising groups of students, regarding their interaction with social settings in practice under study.

Peer review assessments are interactive. |

| | |
|---|---|
| Research based internship | Assessment is done based on students' performance while interacting with host organisation and with peer students and teachers during seminars. |
| | Student agency is designed as an important part of the learning milieu. Students interact with many stakeholders when working on their portfolio of assignments. Students act as knowledge agents producing cases – the lecturer acts as facilitator. |
| Supervision of thesis work | Interactivity on assessment for collective learning is offered as a deliberate possibility by teacher. Individual tutoring is then still a possibility, especially for the writing of the final thesis. Often, individual tutoring goes along with collective tutoring, especially in the phases of finishing and finalising the thesis. Students continue this interaction on their own and most often in interaction with organisations. |

**Humanistic Perspective**

A view on assessment to avoid arbitrary assessments, symbolic violence, colonisation of the life world and disempowerment.

| | |
|---|---|
| Case study research and seminars | Undergraduate students make their own stance in research and subject area – mainly as result of the dialogic dimension. |
| | Undergraduate students put value to academic freedom – mainly as a result of the cultural learning dimension. |
| | Some students refer to assessment of the learning and educational outcome from this course in student organs and point towards how the research-based learning from this course in principle could benefit other courses and their constructive alignment. |
| Research based internship | Self-assessment and the ability to be proactive in making the curriculum visible and participate in the construction of the curriculum. |
| | Dialogic assessment during oral exam makes many qualitative learning outcomes visible for teacher and student. |
| | Students' assessment of learning outcome urges students to demand changes in curriculum of their main study program (Ms. Art. Design Management) and Ms. Sc. (Buss. Econ.). |

| Supervision of thesis work | Cases show students' actions as a result of reflections, leading them to propose agendas during the process of supervision. After the first group meeting, some students arrange pre-meetings, on the same day as the next meeting. Here, they discuss the individually proposed agendas, preparing a new agenda in common and eliminating questions they can solve among themselves, and present the solutions. This means focused and emergent agendas from students followed by questions and dialogues, and alternative proposals to discuss and reflect upon throughout the phases of supervision and tutoring. |
| --- | --- |
| | One case showed how a student deliberately acted and reflected to strengthen transparency and argumentation. He included a transcript from recording the process of supervision into his master thesis as an appendix. This was to show how the special assessment for learning during the dialogic assessment had enhanced his understanding of his research project substantially. As one example, he wanted to show his recognition of different paradigmatic perspectives. |

## The Cultural Learning Perspective

Learning cultures are to be seen as discourses among members of both a single culture and across cultures, constituting, reconstituting, challenging, and (maybe) transforming the interpretations, meanings and relations of the existing cultural values, routines, norms and institutions. Culture is Historically Situated and encompasses both Field and Habitus in reflecting upon the interactions and relationships between individual identity and societal claims (Guba & Lincoln, 1994; James, 2014; Martin, 2002; Wallace & Wolf, 1998).

| Case study research and seminars | Students meet three times during one semester module for seminars on their independent case study research to assess their research and learning. Students' habitus becomes invoked in different forms of even extraordinary discourses and different forms of capitals are identified, drawn upon, utilised and enhanced when recognised in the acculturation. Formative peer assessment takes place among peers in different encounters – also outside the formal assessment arrangements – during the one semester module, when groups of students enter the field of management practices to do academic research in the field. |
| --- | --- |

| | |
|---|---|
| Research based internship | Individually, students learn about their Habitus and dispositions as they enter into the Field of social settings of management practices and business administration. Collective assessment and self-assessment during their work with their portfolios. |
| Supervision of thesis work | Individually, students become more reflexive, learning about their own Habitus and dispositions as they enter into the Field of collective assessment, and acknowledge self-assessment through the work on their projects and thesis in the Field of one or more organisations.<br><br>Exams are evaluated by 'marks', and short feedback/verbal evaluation. |

**The Dialogical Perspective**

Dialogues among peers – reasoned argumentation for validity of truth, rightness and expressivity.

| | |
|---|---|
| Case study research and seminars | Peer review in writing and oral dialogues between peers informs and creates the basis for assessment, which eventually is done for the final marking by the teacher in the last seminar meeting at the end of the semester. Formative assessment is carried out twice during the semester in a similar dialogical process of written peer review and intermediate seminar meetings to serve as feedback aimed for learning.<br><br>Students learn to practice the reasoned academic dialogue and are assessed and graded upon their ability to master this process besides being marked for their written case studies. |
| Research based internship | Dialogue is the major assessment for learning along with self-assessment.<br><br>Students are expected to explain in a reasoned argument what they have learned from working with their portfolios. |
| Supervision of thesis work | Dialogues between peers are an important assessment for learning along with self-assessment supported by supervision and tutoring, both individually and in groups.<br><br>Exams = 'defence' ~ presentation and dialogue, evaluated by 'marks' and a verbal feedback and evaluation. |

*Table 3: Five Perspectives on Assessment Compared Along with Three Learning Settings.*

The final Table 4 depicts major findings on enhanced learning associated with the dialectic perspective on assessment as shown in the first generation vignettes.

| Main findings | |
| --- | --- |
| Case study research and seminars | Undergraduate students make their own stance in research and subject area – mainly as result of the dialogic dimension. |
| | Undergraduate students place value on academic freedom – mainly as a result of the cultural learning dimension. |
| | Some students refer to the assessment of the learning and educational outcome from this course in student organs and they highlight how research based learning from this course in principle could benefit other courses and their constructive alignment. |
| Research based internship | Self-assessment and the ability to partake very actively in making curriculum visible and take part in construction of curriculum. |
| | Dialogic assessment during oral exam makes many qualitative learning outcomes visible for teacher and student. |
| | Students' assessment of learning outcomes urges students to demand changes in curriculum of their main program of study (Ms. Art. (Design Management) and Ms. Sc. (Buss. Econ.). |
| Supervision of thesis work | Cases show students' actions on behalf of reflections, leading them to forward agendas during the process of supervision. After the first group meeting, some students arrange pre-meetings, on the same day as the next meeting. Here, they discuss the individually forwarded agendas, preparing a new agenda in common and eliminating those questions they can solve among themselves and present as solutions. This means focused, and alternating agendas from students, followed by questions/dialogues, and alternative proposals to discuss and reflect upon, throughout the phases of supervision/tutoring. |
| | One case shows how a student acts and reflects deliberately to strengthen transparency and argumentation. He included a transcript from taping the process of supervision into his master thesis as an appendix to show how the special assessment for learning during the dialogic assessment had enhanced the understanding of his research project substantially, by his acknowledgements on paradigmatic perspectives among others. |

*Table 4: Main Findings.*

Finally, a few dialectical deductions from the interaction with the students have to be brought into perspective. It is important to be aware of the difference from one cultural setting of supervision, etc., to another; what works for some students – and supervisors – does not necessarily work for others. And, what has been working for students in one academic setting and culture, does not necessarily work for the same students in another academic setting and culture; this goes for tutors, too!

One of the answers to this is to remember the consequences of thinking and acting in a critical dialectical way when concerning the issues of assessment: it is always evolving, in flux. We have to view assessment of learning and teaching as a process of running transformation. Our Second Generation Vignettes are not a final outcome. More generations of vignettes might develop into new practices of dialectic assessment of interactive learning; i.e., creating both new research questions and new experiences turned into knowledge, interpreted and transformed into new vignettes, which in turn include new feedback from students; i.e., using the research questions as a template or disposition, forwarding/leading to further/new acknowledgement. The dialectics of learning assessment is ongoing, as evidenced by the partakers' acknowledgements, since interpretations of their experiences are not fixed, but in flux!

## Concluding Remarks

Dialogical assessment enhances learning in the context of students' research into social settings of practices. A dialectic perspective on assessment as proposed in this chapter, based upon a deconstruction of the notion of constructive alignment and the case of practising LOA in dialogue with students, is thus a tentative answer to the research question, offering a dialectic perspective to remedy the consequences of managerial logics colonising assessment in research-based learning processes. Thus, the tentative reconstruction of constructive alignment, by synthesising a dialectical perspective with LOA and other perspectives on assessment done in this chapter, needs more research. We have only offered first generation vignettes, and the conclusion is heavily based on theory alone, whereas the proposed perspective actually calls for understandings produced through further empirical studies of assessment in practice. However, in our observation, students did support and challenge each other in dialogues on issues and proposals brought into the dialogue forum and framed and promoted by peer students or the supervisor. Supervisors mediated the dialogue and guided the students to act communicatively and refrain from being personal. Succeeding in these academic dialogues, students will strengthen their self-confidence and be aware of how to act communicatively when invited. Or, they will invite themselves to possibilities of doing research in social settings of practice, while preserving the capability to act critically by applying own values and norms, and relying upon their own knowledgeability and experiences.

Some further evidence for enhanced learning effects from the dialectical assessment relying on Historical Situatedness and Learning Cultures, are those students who return for dialectical tutoring again.

## About the authors

Jens Smed Rasmussen is Assistant Professor at University of Southern Denmark, Faculty of Social Science and Business. He can be contacted at this email: jsr@sam.sdu.dk

Grethe Heldbjerg is Associate Professor at University of Southern Denmark, Faculty of Social Science and Business. She can be contacted at this email: gh@sam.sdu.dk

## Bibliography

Alvesson, M. & S. Deetz (2000). *Doing Critical Management Research*. London: SAGE Publications.

Arbnor, I. & B. Bjerke (1997). *Methodology for Creating Business Knowledge*. London: SAGE Publications.

Arbnor, I., & B. Bjerke (2009). *Methodology for Creating Business Knowledge* (3rd ed.). London: SAGE Publications.

Biggs, J. (1995). Assessing for learning: Some dimensions underlying new approached to educational asessment. *Alberta Journal of Educational Research*, Vol. 41, No. 1, pp. 1-18.

Biggs, J. (1996). Enhancing teaching through constructive alignment. *Higher Education*, Vol. 32, No. 3, pp. 347.

Boud, D. & E. Molloy (2012). Rethinking models of feedback for learning: the challenge of design. *Assessment & Evaluation in Higher Education*, Vol. 38, No. 6, pp. 698-712.

Bourdieu, P. (1977). *Outline of a theory of practice*. Cambridge: Cambridge University Press.

Burawoy, M.; A. Burton; A. A. Ferguson; K. J. Fox; J. Gamson; N. Gartrell; L. Hurst; C. Kurzman; L. Salzinger; J. Schiffman & S. Ui (1991). *Etnograpy Unbound – Power and Resistance in the Mordern Metropolis*, Berkely: University of California Press.

Burns, J. & R. W. Scapens (2000). Conceptualizing management accounting change: an institutional framework. *Management Accounting Research*, Vol. 11, No. 1, pp. 3-25.

Carless, D. (2007). Learning-oriented assessment: conceptual bases and practical implications. *Innovations in Education & Teaching International*, Vol. 44, No. 1, pp. 57-66.

Carless, D. (2009). Trust, distrust and their impact on assessment reform. *Assessment & Evaluation in Higher Education*, Vol. 34, No. 1, pp. 79-89.

Carless, D.; D. Salter; M. Yang & J. Lam (2011). Developing sustainable feedback practices. *Studies in Higher Education*, Vol. 36, No. 4, pp. 395-407.

Guba, E. & Y. S. Lincoln (1994). Competing Paradigms in Qualitative Research. In K. D. Norman, & Y. S. Lincoln (Eds.), *Handbook of Qualitative Research*, London: SAGE Publications, pp. 105-117.

Habermas, J. (1981). *Teorien om den kommunikative handlen* (J. Cederstrøm, Trans.): Aalborg Universitetsforlag 1996.

Heldbjerg G.; H. Damgaard-Hansen; L. Schmidt Hansen & A. Kråkenes. (2009) Kulturfoståelse og forandring. Frederiksberg: Samfundslitteratur.

Heldbjerg, G. & D. van Liempd (forthcoming). A Critical Theoretical Approach on Studying Power Relations Through Vignettes. In P. Freytag & L. Young (Eds.), *Methods and Methodology*.

James, D. (2014). Investigating the curriculum through assessment practice in higher education: the value of a 'learning cultures' approach. *Higher Education*, Vol. 67, No. 2, pp. 155-169.

Kolb, D. A. (1984). *Experiential learning: Experience as the source of learning and development*. Englewood Cliffs: N.J. Prentice-Hall.

Laughlin, R. (1987). Accounting Systems in Organisational Contexts: A Case for Critical Theory. *Accounting Organisations and Society*, Vol. 12, No. 5, pp. 479-502.

Martin, J. (2002). *Organisational Culture. Mapping the Terrain.* London: SAGE Publications.

McDonnell, J. & W. Curtis (2014). Making space for democracy through assessment and feedback in higher education: thoughts from an action research project in education studies. *Assessment & Evaluation in Higher Education*, Vol. 39, No. 8, pp. 932-948.

Oakes, L. S.; B. Townley & D. J. Cooper (1998). Business Planning as Pedagogy: Language and Control in a Changing Institutional Field. *Administrative Science Quarterly*, Vol. 43, No. 2, pp. 257-293.

Pettersen, I. J. (2015). From Metrics to Knowledge? Quality Assessment in Higher Education. *Financial Accountability & Management*, Vol. 31, No. 1, pp. 23-40.

Rust, C.; M. Price & B. O'Donovan (2003). Improving Students' Learning by Developing their Understanding of Assessment Criteria and Processes. *Assessment & Evaluation in Higher Education*, Vol. 28, No. 2, pp. 147-164.

Silverman, D. (2013). *Doing Qualitative Research* (4th ed.). London: Sage.

ter Bogt, H. J. & R. W. Scapens (2012). Performance Management in Universities: Effects of the Transition to More Quantitative Measurement Systems. *European Accounting Review*, Vol. 21, No. 3, 451-497.

Tinker, T. (1991). The Accountant as Partisan. *Accounting Organizations and Society*, Vol. 16, No. 3, pp.

Townley, B.; D. J. Cooper & L. Oakes (1999). Performance measures and the dialectic of rationalization. *Paper ved EIASM Manufacturing Accounting Research Conference, Kolding, Denmark.*

Townley, B.; D. J. Cooper & L. Oakes (2003). Performance Measures and the Rationalization of Organizations. *Organization Studies*, Vol. 24, No. 7, pp. 1045-1071.

Wallace, R. & A. Wolf (1998). *Contemporary Sociological Theory. Expanding the Classical Tradition.* Upper Sadle River, N.J.: Prentice Hall.

Webster, H. (2005). The Architectural Review: A study of ritual, acculturation and reproduction in architectural education. *Arts and Humanities in Higher Education*, Vol. 4, No. 3, pp. 265-282.